THE ROW HOUSE IN WASHINGTON, DC

THE ROW HOUSE IN WASHINGTON, DC A HISTORY

ALISON K. HOAGLAND

University of Virginia Press
Charlottesville and London

University of Virginia Press

Printed in the United States of America on acid-free paper

First published 2023
First paperback edition published 2025
ISBN 978-0-8139-5447-9 (paper)

9 8 7 6 5 4 3 2 1

The Library of Congress has cataloged the hardcover edition as follows:

Names: Hoagland, Alison K., author.
Title: The row house in Washington, DC : a history / Alison K. Hoagland.
Description: Charlottesville : University of Virginia Press, 2023. | Includes bibliographical references and index.
Identifiers: LCCN 2022035688 (print) | LCCN 2022035689 (ebook) | ISBN 9780813949451 (hardcover) | ISBN 9780813949468 (ebook)
Subjects: LCSH: Row houses—Washington (D.C.)—History. | Architecture, Domestic—Washington (D.C.)—History. | Architecture and society—Washington (D.C.)—History.
Classification: LCC NA7238.W3 H63 2023 (print) | LCC NA7238.W3 (ebook) | DDC 728/.31209753—dc23/eng/20220824
LC record available at https://lccn.loc.gov/2022035688
LC ebook record available at https://lccn.loc.gov/2022035689

Publication of this volume was assisted by a grant from Furthermore: a program of the J. M. Kaplan Fund.

Cover art: Mary McLeod Bethune Council House National Historic Site, 1318 Vermont Avenue NW, Washington, DC. (Jack E. Boucher, photographer, Library of Congress, Prints and Photographs Division, HABS DC, WASH, 589—34 [CT])

CONTENTS

ACKNOWLEDGMENTS

I moved into my first row house in Washington, DC, in 1977, and I feel that I've been studying them ever since. I would like to thank all the friends who shared my row houses and theirs, whether for a dinner, a summer, or several years, enriching my experience of the building type. Living on Capitol Hill and walking the neighborhood extensively has undoubtedly framed my understanding of row houses, and I'm sure this would be a slightly different book if I had inhabited another neighborhood.

Gaining access to private homes is always tricky, but Washington's custom of open houses promoted by real estate agents enabled me to see dozens of row houses. My thanks to all those agents, who did not know what I was doing there but were hospitable nonetheless. To spend enough time in a house in order to measure it or study it closely cannot be done on the sly, however, and necessitates homeowners whose generosity outweighs their natural reluctance. I am very grateful to all who let me and my team spend hours measuring, studying, and photographing their home: Deb Hurtt, Bronwyn Irwin, Jodie Larkin, Janet Rankin, Leila Smith, Niko Smith, and Blake Vining. And thanks too to those who showed me their houses or who arranged for me to meet a neighbor who would share their house: Brian Biles and Diane Rowland, Betty Bird and Jeff Domber, Jerry Block, Diana and Mike Enzi, Anthony Howard, Leslie Hulse, Robert and Susan Meehan, Betsy McDaniel, Jim Smailes, Lex Rieffel, Peter Wolff, and especially Charles Robertson. For measuring and drawing the row houses, I am indebted to Robert Arzola, Catherine Lavoie, Ruben Melendez, Onairis Perez, and especially Mark Schara.

As Google reminds us, we stand on the shoulders of giants. One such giant in this field is Nancy Schwartz, who passed away during the preparation of this book. Nancy started me on the course of researching Washington buildings, and row houses in particular, when we volunteered for Don't Tear It Down's Downtown Survey, back in 1979. I am sorry that she is not here to see this long-gestating product. But she was far from the only helpful historian I encountered in my years of researching DC architecture and in writing this book. My sincere thanks to scholars of various fields: Sally Berk, Betty Bird, Catherine Bishir, Johanna Bockman, Bill Bonstra, Phylicia Bowman, Mara Cherkasky, Jeff Cohen, Al Cox, John DeFerrari, Andrew Dolkart, Charlie Duff, John Edwards, Mark Edwards, Matt Gilmore, David Haresign, Deb Hurtt, Richard Longstreth, Carol MacLennan, Melissa McLoud, Brendan Meyer, John Sandor, Sarah Shoenfeld, Kim Williams, and especially Al Chambers. With some of these colleagues, there has been a dialogue stretching across the years; for others, a quick question; but all have been generous.

Research is dependent not only on wise colleagues but also on various repositories that have carefully guarded the information that I needed. My thanks to the staffs at the following places, who were able to retrieve the documents or point me in the right direction: at the Library of Congress, the Prints and Photographs Division, Geography and Map Division, and Main Reading Room; the DC History Center; the DC Public Library; Special Collections at the George Washington University Library; and the National Archives and Records Administration, both downtown and College Park facilities. My gratitude too to Furthermore, which provided a grant for the publication of this book.

While it's not ideal to finish a book in the midst of a pandemic, in a broader way the timing was good. Since I began working on row houses, many sources have been put online, some of which are mentioned in the Note on Sources, at the end of this book. Special thanks to Brian Kraft, who was able to provide some quantification for my hypotheses. Also online in recent years is the full text of Washington newspapers, including the *National Intelligencer,* the *Evening Star,* and the *Washington Post,* as well as deed records and survey plats. My thanks to the archivists and bureaucrats who made these resources so accessible.

Documents tell only a part of the story, though. My greatest thanks are due to all those who built, inhabited, and preserved the rich collection of Washington's row houses. This city is a better place for your efforts.

ABBREVIATIONS

Floor Plans

B	Bedroom
Ba	Bathroom
DA	Dining Area
DR	Dining Room
K	Kitchen
LR	Living Room
P	Parlor

CHRONOLOGY

1790 George Washington signs the Residence Act authorizing development of a capital city

1791 Peter C. L'Enfant produces a plan for the new city; George Washington issues first building regulations

1800 Federal government moves to the District of Columbia

1822 City Council issues building regulations, ratifying and supplementing Washington's

1846 Congress retrocedes portion of District to Virginia

1871 City Council permits bay windows to project onto public space; Congress establishes territorial government

1872 Board of Public Works issues first comprehensive building regulations

1874 Congress establishes temporary commissioner government

1878 Organic Act makes commissioner form of government permanent

1881 Commissioners issue first plumbing regulations

1892 Commissioners effectively ban new alley dwellings

1894 Commissioners limit height of buildings in residential areas

1905 Regulations require larger open court, affecting viability of back buildings on row houses

1907 Regulations require bathtubs in new houses

1909 Regulations permit skylights to ventilate bathrooms, allowing interior placement

1914 Alley Dwelling Act is first attempt to eliminate existing alley dwellings

1920 Congress creates Zoning Commission, which establishes zoning code

1926 Supreme Court upholds housing discrimination through restrictive covenants

1934 Congress creates Alley Dwelling Authority with mandate to clear slum areas

1937 Federal Housing Administration fails to insure mortgages in Black neighborhoods

1945 Redevelopment Act creates agency to acquire slum areas and redistribute the land

1948 Supreme Court ends housing discrimination through restrictive covenants

1950 Old Georgetown Act creates first historic district

1956 Redevelopment of Southwest Washington begins; regulations permit interior kitchens with mechanical ventilation

1957 Regulations permit interior bathrooms with mechanical ventilation

1974 Home Rule Act goes into effect and residents elect first mayor in more than a century

1978 D.C. Historic Landmark and Historic District Protection Act prevents demolition or alteration of designated buildings without review

THE ROW HOUSE IN WASHINGTON, DC

Introduction

Washington, DC, the nation's capital, is known for its celebration of the monumental. Large-scale predominantly classical structures that house the federal government dominate the cityscape; statues and monuments that commemorate people and events in the history of the nation mark primary spaces in stone and bronze. This is by intention. George Washington, Thomas Jefferson, and Peter L'Enfant designed a capital city that would glorify its nation's government.[1] But they also designed a city for row houses.

This book examines the most ubiquitous but largely overlooked architecture of the capital, the city's row houses (see fig. 1). A study of the more modest dwellings of the middle and working classes, it celebrates the city's other side. In fact, the city and its architecture cannot be understood without considering its row houses and the people who live in them. The contrast of their presence in the nation's capital, alongside its monuments, underscores the importance of the residential architecture built for regular people, the human infrastructure of the nation. Neither the housing for the elites, who owned freestanding houses or perhaps a custom-designed row house, nor for the poorest, who occupied shanties or small flats, speculative row houses accommodated the government clerks, tradesmen, and artisans of the middle class. They used row houses as homes, but also as sources of income and as statements of attainment. How they lived in these houses—in nuclear families or with boarders, as homeowners or renters, with long tenancy or short stays—is explored in this book.

Floor plans tell a large part of the story of row houses. Their peculiar constraints—being bounded on both sides so that front and back present the only opportunities for light and air—become readily apparent in the plans, which tend to be similar within a given time period. Accordingly, six typical plans, described in chapter 1, form the framework for the discussion of row houses. The plans' evolution draws not only on stylistic influences, but also on concerns for light and air, responses to changing regulations, builder-developers' capabilities, introduction of utilities and new technologies, and

Figure 1. Row houses, 202–24 Eleventh Street SE. Bay windows and lively rooflines characterize Washington's row houses of the late nineteenth century. (Photograph by the author, 2021)

a number of other elements. These factors, which differ from city to city, produce a vernacular architecture, in the sense that the row houses are *of the place.* Rather than derive from the place in terms of row houses' building materials or their occupants' cultural traditions, this book argues that the combination of building regulations and other factors produced distinctive row houses, seen in the evolution of the plan.[2] In the late nineteenth century, this distinctive row house had back buildings, or rear ells, and front bay windows that projected onto public space, consequences of both the city plan and building regulations. In the early twentieth century, the row house made an abrupt shift to flat fronts with porches and no L-plan extension in the rear, due once again, in part, to building regulations. In addition to reflecting regulatory constraints, by delineating spatial relationships plans also suggest how houses were used. Halls, stairways, separate bedrooms, and kitchen locations help determine the privacy of family members, how guests might be received, who is undertaking the domestic tasks, and how boarders and extended family members might be accommodated.

Broadly defined, row houses date back to ancient Rome and are found in densely occupied cities throughout the world. Early versions of them appeared in the United States in the seventeenth century and, though they came to define the housing stock of Baltimore and Philadelphia, they populate many other cities in the Middle Atlantic and Northeast as well. In Washington, row houses have been the most common building type in the city.[3] Although small in scale, through their numbers they dominate many neighborhoods.

Washington makes a particularly good place to examine this middling range of housing.[4] With its origin as a planned city and its unique position as the bastion of the federal government, Washington is undeniably different from any other American city. Factors such as the city's plan and regulations, the time in which much residential development occurred, and its convoluted political history, which both hampered and encouraged row-house development, affected the appearance of this housing stock. But Washington is also in many ways a typical mid-Atlantic city, both southern and northern, both Black and white, thriving in the late nineteenth century and expanding in the twentieth. And like many cities in northeastern America, Washington's streets are lined with row houses, the housing for the broad middle class.

The existence and appearance of row houses in the late nineteenth and early twentieth centuries resulted in part from modern industrial capitalism and related societal changes. As the growth of industry fostered the rise of big business, scientific understanding, technological change, and mass production, housing itself became an industry that embraced these trends.[5] Builders and developers constructed multiple houses as investments marketed to unknown buyers. Advances in health and science led to new standards for sanitation and ventilation, mandated by government regulations on buildings. And technological gains resulted in new understandings of comfort, so that the row house expressed modernity in its use as well as its mass production.

As the city burgeoned, the middle class grew. In Washington the expansion of the federal bureaucracy and the numerous clerks required to staff it contributed to the city's growth and, in turn, to the need for tradesmen, artisans, teachers, salesmen, and others, who also joined the middle class. The housing most appropriate for that growing middle class, being an affordable family dwelling, was the row house. Work took place not only in shops and government offices but also within the row house, as domestic labor shifted from servants to housewives, aided by utilities and new technology.

Increased racial segregation in row houses in the early twentieth century illustrated the pervasive racism that has haunted the city. The African American population of Washington has always been significant, constituting roughly between a quarter and a third of the population until 1960, when it became a majority, then declined to a slight minority in the twenty-first century. The architecture of row houses did not differ according to the race of their occupants, and the racial composition of many row-house residents changed while the architecture stayed the same.[6] But row houses were the form of housing that was most contested as racial segregation in housing, which was always pervasive, took on distinct patterns in the twentieth century. Once limited to the shoddiest dwellings but located throughout the city, African Americans and in particular their rising middle class acquired more substantial row houses, but increasingly white developers and residents limited their options geographically, through deed restrictions and other forms of institutional racism.

A row house, for the purpose of this book, is a house abutted on both sides by adjacent dwellings, regardless of whether a house was built simultaneously with its neighbors as part of a coherent row, or whether its neighbors were added later. The party walls on the sides produce a distinctive plan, one that differentiates row houses from all other housing types, and the plan is the focus of this book. Speculative rows, in which three or more dwellings were built according to identical or similar plans at the same time by a single developer, receive particular attention. The term "row house" rarely appeared before 1910. Instead, a row house might be referred to as an "inside house," meaning that it was in the midst of a row, or as a "corner house" if it was on the end of a row, such as in this 1889 ad: "We can sell inside houses for $3,800 and $3,900; corner houses about $4,600." Architect E. C. Gardner, who wrote about Washington houses in a series of articles in the 1880s, referred to a row house as "a house in a block," referring to a block of houses, not a city block full of houses.[7] (Because of the potential for confusion, city blocks are referred to as "squares," the legal term, in this book.) After 1910, usage of "row house" became more common, so that the daily newspaper the *Evening Star* had 46 mentions of "row house" in the 1910s, 983 in the 1920s, and 1,881 in the 1930s.

More specifically, this study concentrates on the row houses built for the city's middle and lower classes, those built en masse for the market. Building them speculatively as commodities to be marketed and sold, developers preferred a dwelling that would sell—not too innovative, but meeting all the basic requirements. These row houses illustrate their developers' understanding of the marketplace. And row houses are particularly well suited to speculation, as they are relatively inexpensive, built to identical plans, arranged to save on land costs, and benefiting from economies of scale.[8] Rows of multiple dwellings, constructed at the same time and authorized by a single building permit, are the subject of this book.

Rather than forming a linear chronology, the chapters in this book are organized around topics, but within each chapter the arrangement is generally chronological. The first chapter introduces the six plans that serve as an orienting premise. While exceptions to these plans abound, their ubiquity argues for their consideration as representative examples that enable an understanding of the evolution, use, and purpose of various row-house designs. Specific houses illustrate these plans, while the historical forces that explain them are explored in subsequent chapters.

Chapter 2 provides an overview of the history of the city, interwoven with a discussion of the city plans, regulations, and zoning codes that affected the row house. Not a state, but more than a city, Washington lacked an elected municipal government for a full century, from 1874 to 1974, but regulations instituted by appointed officials and congressional acts contributed to the distinctive appearance of its row houses. Regulations also determined where row houses could be located.

Having established the basic plan and historical parameters of the row house, the book addresses other aspects of the house, outside and inside, in chapters 3 and 4. A discussion of the row house's front facade in chapter 3 explains the importance of architectural style, particularly during times when the row house fell out of fashion. Beginning in the 1920s, when the row house became associated with cheap construction and lower-class dwellers, developers promoted fashions such as the Old English and the Colonial Revival in order to enhance the row house's reputation. Chapter 4 ventures inside the house, where regulations guided efforts to employ light and air to achieve health and comfort, which ultimately differentiated Washington's row houses from those in other cities. The provision of water and sewer service, gas, and electricity affected the plan and also indicated changing expectations for convenience and comfort.

The next two chapters turn to people who were involved with row houses. Chapter 5 looks at builder-developers responsible for much of the speculative row-house construction in the city. Their approach to speculative building, evolving from small rows built by poorly capitalized builders to the enormous undertakings of well-financed developers known as operative builders, changed the appearance of Washington over time, as long rows of repetitive designs characterized the expanding city. Marketing row houses in a competitive atmosphere meant advertising the neighborhood as much as the house, and developers found it profitable to promote racially segregated neighborhoods. To reassure some buyers, developers attached deed restrictions, ultimately creating a segregated city.

Chapter 6 examines the occupants of row houses, both owners and renters. To delve deeper than city-wide statistics, the chapter looks at four representative squares, or city blocks, through time, in order to link specific occupants to specific buildings. By identifying these buildings with the typ-

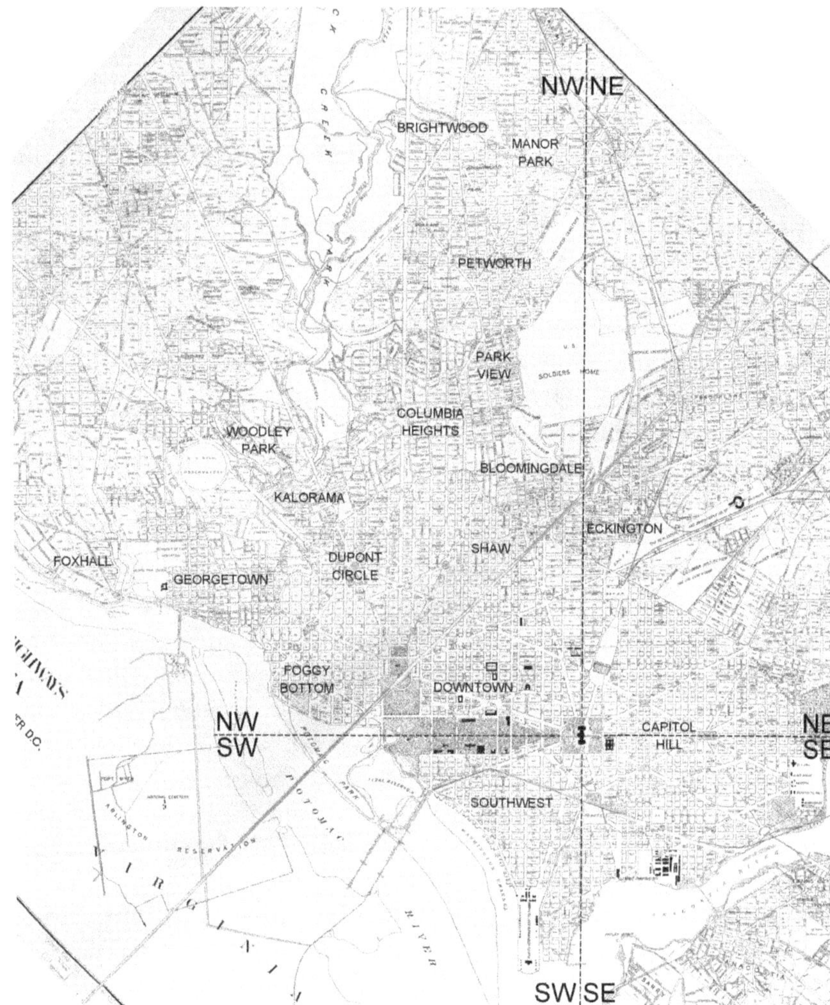

Figure 2. Map of central Washington, DC, showing some of the neighborhoods discussed in this book. (Overlaid on detail of "Map of the Permanent System of Highways, District of Columbia," DC Office of the Engineer Commissioner, 1914, Library of Congress, Geography and Map Division, annotations by Mark Schara)

ical plans introduced in the first chapter, the size and arrangement of the row house are connected to the families inhabiting them and to some understanding of how they lived. Through this close study, the life cycle of a house becomes apparent, as it moves from new and well equipped to a decline as amenities and spatial arrangements become outdated, to reinvestment and resurgence, often resulting in racial change. In this way, the row house proves its adaptability, as nuclear and extended families, boarders and lodgers, and homeowners and renters occupy the house at different times.

Arguing that urban vernacular architecture requires a new approach, this book on Washington has ramifications for other cities and other building types. While the plan of the row house is unusual in that the building is constrained on two sides, the focus on the plan in the first chapter reveals the changes experienced by this modest building type. Each city's history and governance, especially in the area of building regulations, will yield different buildings, as shown in the second chapter. While architectural style and domestic technologies are in some ways universal across the country, chapters 3 and 4 point to the ways in which these can prompt distinct variations from city to city. Chapter 5 argues that builders and the building industry, though constrained by numerous factors, were far more important than architects in determining the form of speculatively built houses, as well as who got to live where. And finally, the story of occupants in the sixth chapter shows the ebb and flow of people as well as how the dwelling functioned.

Despite the ubiquity of row houses in nineteenth- and twentieth-century Washington, fewer row houses are built in Washington today. Luxury apartments and condominiums designed for mobile, unencumbered young adults portend shifting demographics in the midst of an overall growth in population. Although row houses meet many requirements of "smart," or environmentally sustainable, growth, only a third of the city's residential land is zoned for them. Row houses use land efficiently, packing units densely together. Because of their shared walls, row houses are also energy efficient. And with individual entrances and yards, and no strangers occupying units above or below, they approximate the independence and privacy of a freestanding home. Pressures on existing row houses are intense as inner-city real estate becomes increasingly valuable. For instance, a common rehabilitation of row houses in the northwest neighborhood of Park View takes a two-story row house and converts it into two condominium units by digging out the basement to create one unit on the first and basement levels, and then adding to the roof so that the second unit has the second and new third floor. Where row houses are protected by historic-district designation and visible additions are discouraged, homeowners convert basements to rental units and add onto the back of the house for additional space.[9] Given the pressures on, and possibilities of, row houses, they are overdue for an examination.

The history of Washington's row houses intersects with many aspects of the city's governance and development, making them an ideal vehicle for understanding the past. Delving into one of the most intimate aspects of people's lives and placing it in the context of larger historical forces, this book shows row houses to be both personal and public. Modest dwellings that are easily overlooked among the capital's grand architecture, row houses reveal the broad sweep of American history intersecting with a tiny slice of life—the home—right in the nation's capital.

1

Six Plans

A few floor plans characterized Washington's speculative row houses. Why the range was so limited, and what these plans tell us about this place and its people at specific times in the past, are explored in the rest of this book. To start, though, discussions of each of these plans ground them in the specific even as they represent the general. Each of these plans was, of course, adapted and changed as they were employed, so there was a wide variety within a basic plan. Common variations are discussed, but their broad similarities enable the identification of these six typical plans.

Two-Room Plan

"Started 1796 . . . Completed 1966," blared the ad for a house in Wheat Row in Southwest Washington.[1] It is also a loose slogan for the two-room plan, which started to be used for row houses in Washington in the 1790s—even earlier in Georgetown—and endured for more than a century. The two-room plan is oriented one room behind the other, so that the narrow end faces the street. It can be grander, with a side hall and three or more stories, or more modest, with no hall and just two stories. Row houses with this plan appeared in the 1790s, dominated as gable-roofed dwellings for the next half century, persisted as small, flat-roofed alley dwellings until their construction was banned in 1892, and then revived through preservation efforts in the 1950s and 1960s. A grand row house from the 1790s is the starting point.

Most likely started in 1794 and completed by 1796, Wheat Row was an ensemble of four brick row houses constructed by three early real estate investors: James Greenleaf, John Nicholson, and Robert Morris. When a newspaper asked in 1926, "Where is the oldest building in Washington?" Wheat Row was one of the two contenders for the title.[2] Because of this distinction, the Historic American Buildings Survey, funded by the Works Progress Administration, documented the row in 1937. And also because of this distinction, it was one of a handful of buildings saved when most of Southwest Washington was razed for urban redevelopment in the 1950s and 1960s. Architect Chloethiel Woodard Smith oversaw the restoration of the buildings and incorporated them into her new development called Harbour Square.

At Wheat Row, located at 1315–21 Fourth Street SW, architect Joseph Clark designed four three-story row houses gathered under a hipped roof and crowned by a central pediment (see fig. 3). The plan of each of the four units is a two-room, side-hall plan, with kitchen and dining room in the basement, two parlors on the first floor, and bedrooms on the second and third (see fig. 4). The dimensions are a generous 26 by 35 feet, notably wide for a row house. Areaways front and back permit direct entry into the basement. The side hall contains the stairway, as well as a foyer on the first floor and a small bedroom on the third floor. A fireplace heats each room. Despite these embellishments, the basic plan is set: two rooms per floor, each directly illuminated by windows.

A more modest example of the two-room plan is the house at 22 D Street SE, documented in 1937 and demolished shortly after. Built in about 1820, this wood-frame house had two rooms, with fireplaces on the partition wall (see figs. 5 and 6). At 14 feet wide, the house was too narrow for a side hall, so entry was directly into the front room. The winder stairs were in the corner of the back room. These narrower houses—and the 16-foot width was about where the demarcation was made between those with halls and those without—faced a challenge as to where to put the stairway. Winder stairs, tucked next to the chimney; transverse stairs, separating the two main rooms; or longitudinal stairs along the wall opposite the fireplaces were also common solutions. The goal was to place it in such a way that it did not consume too much valuable floor space.

The placement of the kitchen is a critical factor in the analysis of plans, and both of these examples put the kitchen in the basement. The families occupying houses in Wheat Row undoubtedly had free or enslaved servants prepare and serve the meals, whereas a family occupying the small house on D Street probably did not. There, the housewife would have prepared and served the meals in the back room. Detached kitchens in the yard, very common in rural areas, especially in the South, were also an option, although there are very few survivals in Washington.[3]

In the early nineteenth century, a row house with a two-room plan was usually covered by a gable roof, clad in either wood shingles or slate. Because row houses could not shed water to the sides, the ridge of the roof was parallel to the street and directed water to the front and back. The gable roof worked particularly well in a two-room plan, because each slope of the roof essentially covered one room, or one half the plan.

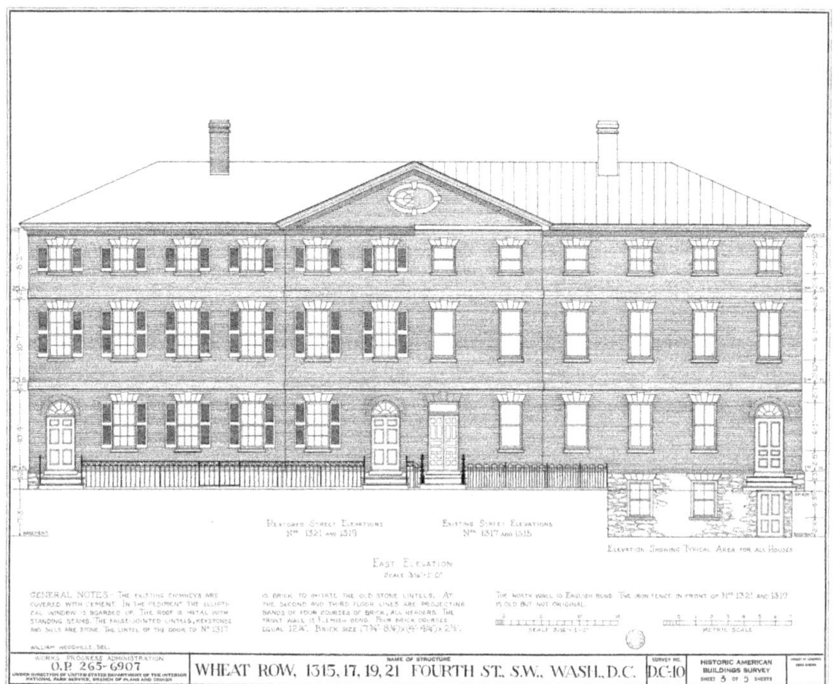

Figure 3. Wheat Row, 1315–21 Fourth Street SW. The row, designed by Joseph Clark in the 1790s, consisted of four row houses united by a cohesive facade. (William Woodville, delineator, 1936, Library of Congress, Prints and Photographs Division, HABS)

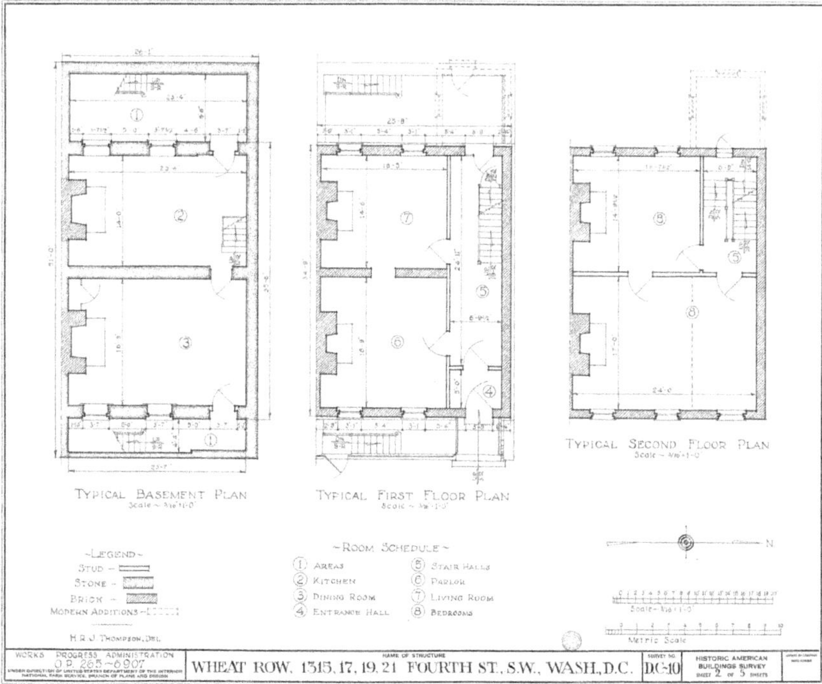

Figure 4. Wheat Row, typical plans. The houses had two-room plans with generous side halls and additional below-grade areas in the front and rear. The kitchen and dining room were in the basement. (H. R. J. Thompson, delineator, 1936, Library of Congress, Prints and Photographs Division, HABS)

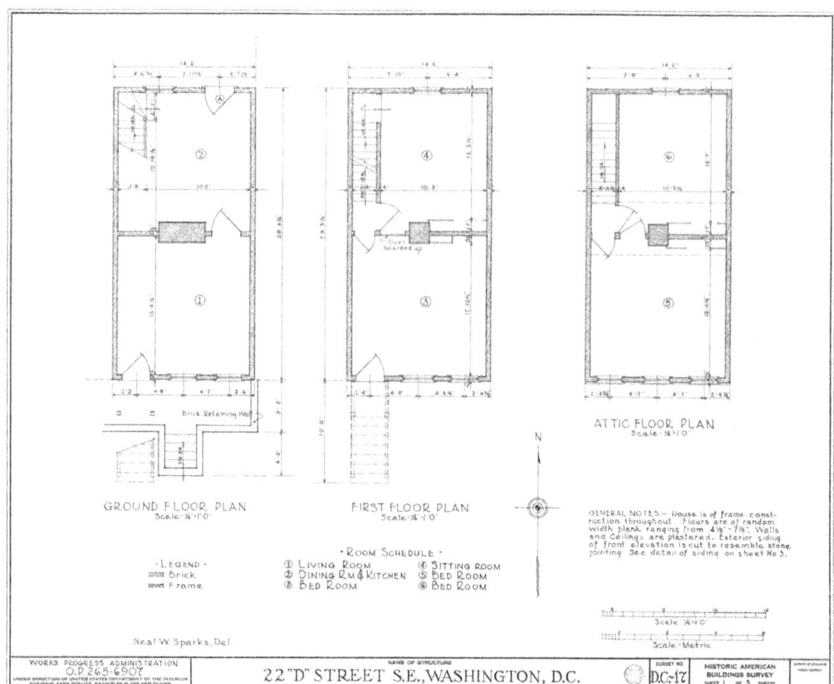

Figure 5. Row house, 22 D Street SE, plans. Built in about 1820, the house had a two-room plan without the side hall. The exterior stairs were added later, when the street grade was raised. (Neal W. Sparks, delineator, 1937, Library of Congress, Prints and Photographs Division, HABS)

Figure 6. Row house, 22 D Street SE, elevations. Homeowners added a door at the second level when the street grade was raised; the restored elevation shows the original appearance. The three-bay facade with a side-gable roof was typical for row houses in this period. The wood siding cut to resemble stone was an elegant enhancement for a modest house. (Neal W. Sparks, delineator, 1937, Library of Congress, Prints and Photographs Division, HABS)

The two-room plan continued to be a popular choice during the first half of the nineteenth century. Smaller, flat-roofed versions of the plan, intended for lower-class occupants, were built until the end of the nineteenth century, especially in alleys. Alley dwellings were viewed as the worst housing in Washington, poorly equipped, crowded, unsanitary, and by the early twentieth century occupied by a largely African American population. Until prohibited by law, alley dwellings might be as narrow as 9 feet wide.[4]

L-Shaped Plan

In 1874, Clarinda Henkle bought the house at 1538 Ninth Street NW (see fig. 7). One in a row of nine identical dwellings recently built by developers Joshua Whitney and Brainard H. Warner, the house was three stories tall with Italianate detailing. Clarinda, who was unmarried, kept house for her widowed brother, Saul Henkle, a prominent lawyer and former Ohio state legislator. Saul's son, Edward, lived with them, as well as a live-in servant, Mary Brisco,

Figure 7. Woodson House, 1538 Ninth Street NW. One of a row of nine dwellings built in 1874, this three-story row house was the home and office of noted African American historian Carter G. Woodson in the twentieth century. (Photograph by the author, 2021)

a twenty-nine-year-old African American. By 1889, Saul had remarried and moved out, Edward had married and moved to Philadelphia, and Clarinda advertised the house to rent—furnished, six rooms, $50 a month. But the house had ten rooms, plus a basement, and Clarinda continued to live in the house for several more years. The house became an investment property for subsequent owners until noted African American historian Carter G. Woodson acquired it in 1922, making it his home and office until his death in 1950.[5]

The house has a two-room-deep, side-hall plan with an extension on the rear known as a back building, creating the L-shaped plan (see fig. 8). This back building is narrower than the main block, creating a light court that is nearly 6 feet wide. Unusual for a side-hall plan, the stairs are placed not in the side hall but at the juncture of the back building and main block. The curving stairway is lit by a window onto the court. Behind the stairway is a room that may have served as a kitchen, or more likely as a dining room, with the kitchen below it in the basement. The rearmost room on the plan was part of a two-story addition that Clarinda Henkle had built in 1880, and the kitchen was probably moved there at that time.[6] The bathroom was on the second

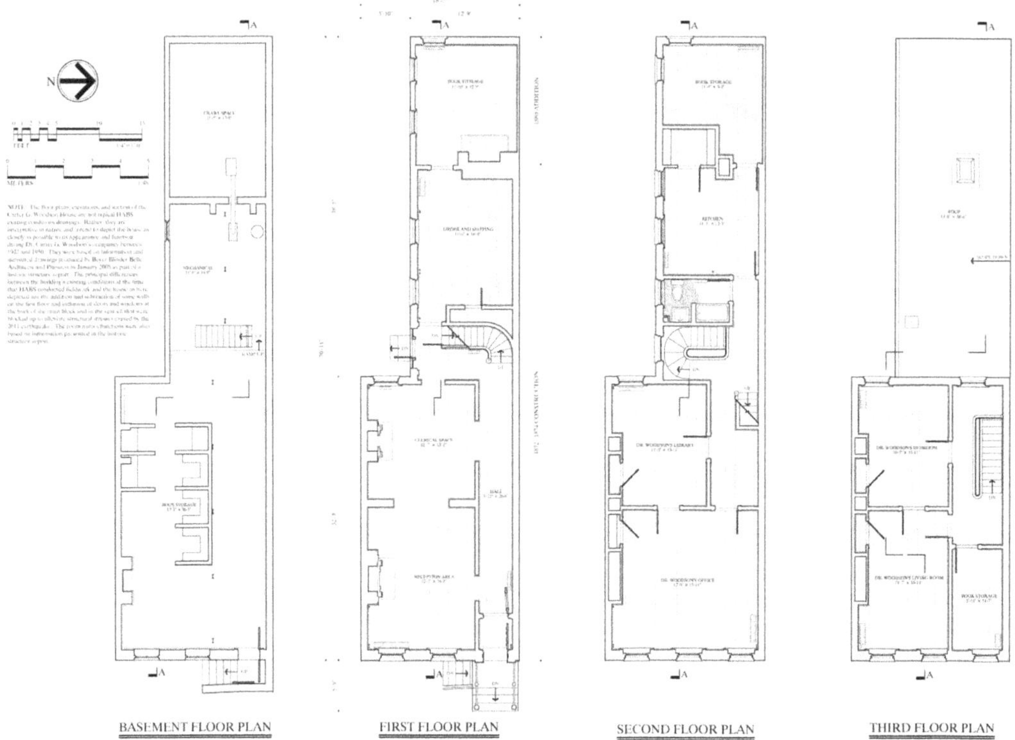

Figure 8. Woodson House, plans. The L-shaped plan had two rooms in the main block of the house, and a rear wing, known as a back building, that contained one room; the rear-most room was added later. In a slightly unusual arrangement, the stairway was not in the side hall, but at the beginning of the back building. (Beyer Blinder Belle, delineator, 2012–13, Library of Congress, Prints and Photographs Division, HABS)

floor, in the back building. The house had several genteel touches: marble lintels and entrance stairs, slate fireplace surrounds with faux-marble mantels, central heating, and a bathroom.

The L-plan was a common solution to extending a row house. Simply adding a third room to a two-room plan renders the middle room dark and airless, so the narrower extension allowed for a window in the middle room. Rooms in the back building were also lit by windows that faced onto the court. The narrower back building provided capacity for expansion, as seen here, and row houses could extend 50 feet or more and contain as many as five rooms on a floor. In this plan, the dining room could be located as the second room, instead of a back parlor, or as the first room in the back building, as it is here.

In the 1850s, flat roofs, which were not strictly flat but sloped gently away from the street, replaced gable roofs as the preferred roofing form. A technological change aided this shift: wood shingles and slate require a fairly steep slope to shed water effectively, but the introduction of cheaper metals enhanced the feasibility of flat roofs. Tin-plated iron roofs, which were cheaper, lighter, and more easily maintained than other metal roofs, proved ideal for gradual slopes; the material became widely available after the Civil War. In Clarinda Henkle's house, the Italianate bracketed cornice hides the junction of wall and roof, providing a suitable finish to the facade.

The L-shaped plan often accompanied a significant change to the front of the building, the bay window. First permitted in 1871 by the building regulations, which are discussed in the next chapter, bay windows characterized Washington's larger row houses in the 1880s and 1890s, providing a rhythm to the street facades and a touch of gentility to the speculative house (see fig. 1). One row near Dupont Circle illustrates the possibilities of this form on a small yet ambitious scale.

The seven row houses constructed at 1520–32 T Street NW in 1891–92 were planned as an investment and probably never even seen by their original owners, whose story reads like a soap opera (see fig. 9). The property had been owned by Joshua Peirce, along with a considerable amount of land in what is now Rock Creek Park, then passed to his nephew, Joshua Peirce Klingle. O. C. Green, an employee of the Washington Loan and Trust Company, commissioned the row houses for him just before Klingle's death in 1892, and they passed to his daughter, Susan Juliet Gay Beatrice Klingle. Six years earlier, Beatrice had eloped with Edward Darling, a composer of comic opera, and they had had two children, Nancy and Charles. When Edward died at the age of thirty-one after a lingering illness, Beatrice's mother-in-law accused her of conspiring with his doctor to slowly poison her husband. A year later, in 1894, the widowed Beatrice Darling married her late husband's doctor. At her death just one year after that, the property passed to her two young children. In

Figure 9. Row house, 1524 T Street NW. This house was one of a row of seven built in 1891. Although modest in size, being just 17 feet wide and two stories tall, each of them had an elaborate bay window. (Justin Scalera, photographer, 2018, Library of Congress, Prints and Photographs Division, HABS)

trust for the children, the bank rented the house to a series of tenants, such as Jared G. Smith, a botanist at the Department of Agriculture, who lived there with his wife, Grace, their young son, and Emma Harris, their African American cook. The Smiths moved into the house in 1900 and stayed for only two or three years. In 1919, after both Nancy and Charles Darling had reached the age of majority, they sold the houses. After several decades of having been rented to white clerks and other government employees, the houses were purchased by African Americans, reflecting larger changes in the neighborhood. John H. Thomas, a chauffeur, and his wife, Susie, acquired the house at 1524. After John Thomas's death in the 1930s, his widow took in boarders and continued to live there until about 1970.[7]

The builder and probable designer of these houses was Thomas J. King. A prominent builder and secretary of the Builders' Exchange at the time, King also identified as an architect.[8] The houses he designed here were bay-fronted with L-shaped plans. Just 17 feet wide, the plan included a side hall,

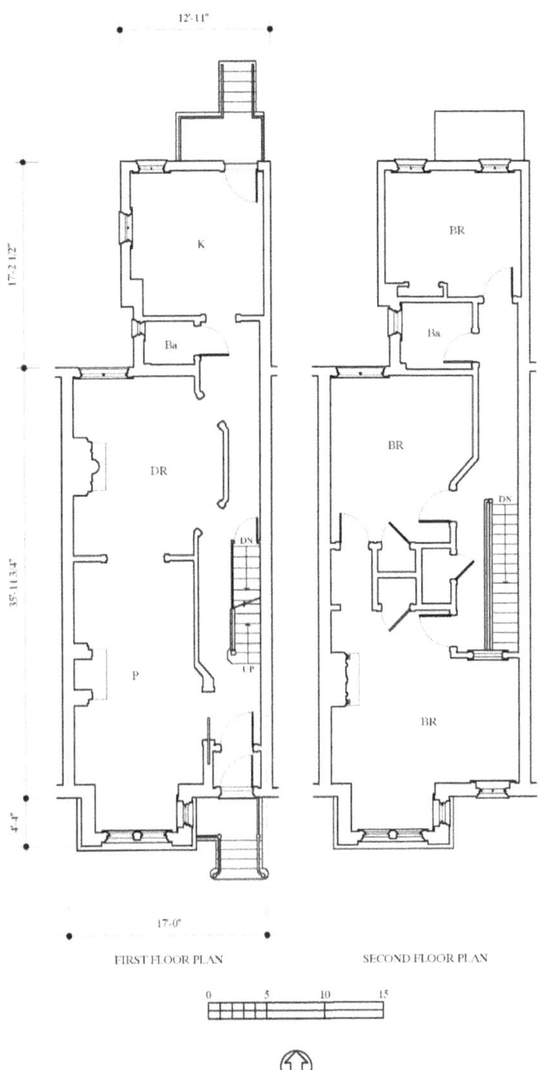

Figure 10. Row house, 1524 T Street NW, plans. The plan shows a parlor, a dining room, and in the back building a kitchen, with three corresponding bedrooms on the second floor. Between the kitchen and the dining room was a bathroom with sink and toilet and, above it on the second floor, a full bathroom. These are conjectural original plans; in 1940, owner Susie Thomas added a room to the rear of this house. (Emelyn R. Najera, Taurean J. Merriweather, and Robert R. Arzola, delineators, 2018, Library of Congress, Prints and Photographs Division, HABS, redrawn by Onairis Perez, Ruben Melendez, and Mark Schara)

with a slight widening to accommodate the stairway (see fig. 10). A parlor in the front had the use of the bay window, while the dining room behind had a large window into the court. A small bathroom and the kitchen were in the back building. The second floor had three bedrooms with closets and a bathroom with three fixtures—sink, toilet, and tub. In the basement were provisions for laundry and the storage of coal.

While multistory bay windows were very popular beginning in the 1880s, they were not universal. For row houses narrower than about 16 feet, marketed to the working class, builders usually dispensed with the bay window. About half of the speculative row houses built in the 1880s fell into this category of narrow houses, but in the 1890s, only a third. For the narrower houses, side halls were also dispensed with. As New York architect William B. Tuthill wrote about "city residences" in 1890, the side-hall plan "may be used on a lot as narrow as 15 feet, but the dimensions of the rooms become too diminutive and the proportions too generally poor to give satisfaction." As with the two-room plan, the stairway could be in a variety of places and arrangements in a narrow house.[9]

Even with a back building, a late nineteenth-century row house often had the kitchen in the basement. Sometimes the dining room was located there too, in the front of the house, which made the basement kitchen slightly less inconvenient. Mostly, though, the basement kitchen was dark, damp, and inconvenient for the servants who worked there, despite the presence of a dumbwaiter, which enabled the food to be hoisted to the dining room. Many years later, James A. Gannon recalled his childhood home of the 1890s, which had a bay window and a back building: "The rear room [on the first floor] was for dining . . . a dumb waiter in the corner transported food from the basement kitchen. . . . The back stairs led to the basement. The kitchen was large and the stove was heated by wood. A shelf was lined with spices. Adjoining the kitchen was the cellar in which a wash tub was present. There were shelves loaded with preserves, a ham or two suspended from the rafters, and the barrels containing apples and potatoes and perhaps cider along the walls." A less fond reminiscence comes from Mary Church Terrell, who swore off basement kitchens after living in a house with one: "No more basements for me, running up and down the steps to answer the doorbell when I was busy in the kitchen and there was no one to help me!"[10]

Despite the persistence of basement kitchens, the promise of the back building was that it could elevate the kitchen into a place that was convenient and well lit. Attention focused mostly on the front of the house, though, with the location of the kitchen rarely mentioned in real estate ads. The common terminology for the bay-fronted houses was "bay-window brick," as in this real estate ad from 1894: "For Rent: No. 1413 17th St., N.W., bay-window brick, 11 rooms and bath; newly papered and decorated; all mod. imps.; location very desirable, being fashionable, etc.; rent $50 a month." Or, for only $31.50 a month, "2009 Portner Place; comparatively new bay-window brick, containing 6 rooms, bath and cellar; newly papered and painted; all mod. conveniences."[11] In the late nineteenth century, the addition of the bay window to the L-shaped plan was enough of a selling point for it to be called out in advertisements.

Three-Room Plan

In 1902 Frederick Albert Ruff, a machinist at the Navy Yard, bought the row house at 2310 First Street NW, in the newly developing Bloomingdale neighborhood (see fig. 11). He and his wife, Bernice Gertrude Ruff, never had children, but they did house three female relatives, a cousin and two sisters who worked at the Bureau of Printing and Engraving and as a teacher in the public schools. Gertrude Ruff kept house for these people, and after her husband died in 1923, she also housed two nieces, also grown single women, one of whom was a cataloguer at the Library of Congress and the other a stenographer at the Department of Agriculture. The single-family row house accommodated a family, to be sure; but it was one made up of four or five adults.[12]

The row house that accommodated the extended Ruff family was part of an ambitious development built by the young firm of Middaugh and Shannon, whose career is explored in chapter 5. The plan of the row house had three main rooms on the first floor, plus a kitchen in the back building (see fig. 12). The three-room plan illustrates the difficulty of lengthening the row house,

Figure 11. Row houses, 2300 block of First Street NW. Middaugh and Shannon developed this block of row houses in Bloomingdale, designed by Joseph Bohn Jr., in 1902. Frederick and Gertrude Ruff bought the house at 2310, the tallest one in this photograph. (Photograph by the author, 2022)

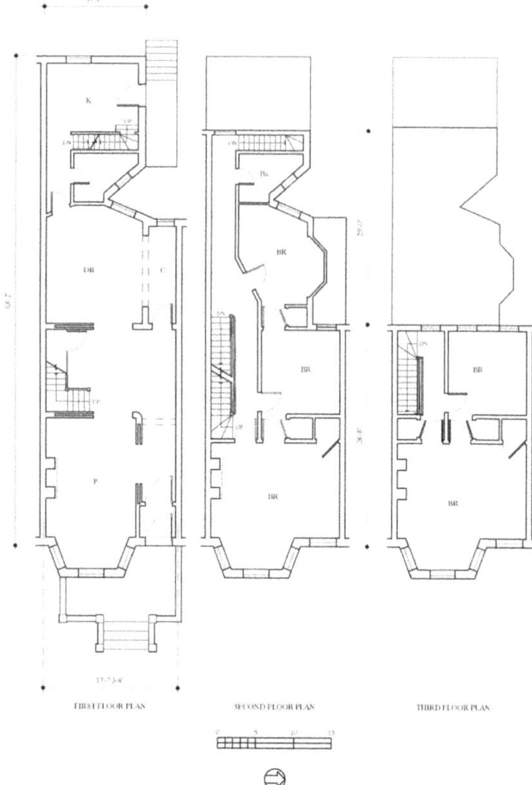

Figure 12. Row house, 2310 First Street NW, plans. The three-room plan included a reception hall between the parlor and dining room. Joseph Bohn's plan incorporated a notch designed to let more light into the dining room, as well as a glass-roofed conservatory (C) at one end of the dining room, intended to flood the dining room and reception hall with light. (Ruben Melendez, Onairis Perez, and Mark Schara, delineators, 2019, Library of Congress, Prints and Photographs Division, HABS)

because it leaves the middle room without a window. Accordingly, the middle room was devoted to the stair hall and reception—not spaces where people would loiter. The parlor in the front was an elegant bay-windowed space; the entrance hall beside it could be a little narrower than in other plans, because it did not have to accommodate the stairway. Behind the reception hall was the dining room, which took light from the rear court. The back building housed the kitchen; many three-room plan houses dispensed with the back building and placed the kitchen in the basement (see fig. 112).

The drawback of the three-room plan—that the middle room had little natural light—is also shown in this plan through attempts to ameliorate it. Wide openings with sliding doors between the dining room, reception hall, parlor, and entrance hall shared light among these spaces. Another strategy was to place angled windows in the dining room and pantry, in order to bring more light into the dining room. This innovation can be credited to the MIT-trained architect B. Stanley Simmons, whom Middaugh and Shannon hired to designed the west side of the 2200 block of First Street NW, in 1899.[13]

The next innovation, apparent on the houses on the 2300 block of First Street, belonged to architect Joseph Bohn Jr., whom Middaugh and Shannon hired to designed the houses in 1902. Bohn's houses were similar to Simmons's, with Roman brick fronts and alternating shapes of two-story bay windows on three-story buildings. Bohn's houses were a little narrower, though, 18 feet wide compared to Simmons's 20 feet. More significantly, he added a glass-roofed "conservatory," or greenhouse, to the dining room along the party wall, which in theory would bring natural light through the conservatory roof to spill into the dining room and the reception hall. This would make the dining room "well lighted and cheerful at all times," according to the newspaper. Middaugh and Shannon advertised, "For the first time, we introduce these features in a city house which we have originated and protected by copyright," although there is no record of any copyright. Besides the conservatory, "with glass roof and ends, opening from reception hall by French beveled glass door and from dining room by archway," the ad mentioned the brownstone porch running across the front of the house and "perfect ventilation by wide doors between all rooms on every floor." A laudatory history called this plan "an arrangement originated and copyrighted by the firm, for the perfect lighting of the dining room. This arrangement stands as one of the greatest achievements of modern architecture in the problem of home building on an inside lot [i.e., a row house], completely overcoming the usual difficulty of the dark dining room, when built between party walls, and presenting one of the prettiest interior effects ever obtained on a city lot."[14]

Whether the addition of the glass-roofed conservatory was successful in illuminating the dark dining room and even darker reception hall is uncertain. All of the conservatories in this row have been roofed over. Mary F. Rainey, who owned the house across the street at 2313 First Street NW, similarly designed by Bohn, complained about the building's defects in 1903: "There is a skylight in the dining room which should be protected in case of a heavy storm or other accidents might break the outer glass of said skylight, there is nothing to prevent it falling thru and breaking the inner glass, thereby endangering the life or lives of any person or persons who may happen to be in the room at the time. Three of said glasses have already fallen causing me considerable expense, inconvenience and damage, it has been leaking ever since the house was built."[15]

Creative attempts at improvement aside, the three-room plan met with some modest success. Thomas Franklin Schneider used a three-room plan in a long row of grand houses he built on the 1700 block of Q Street in 1889, using a small lightwell to illuminate the reception hall (discussed in chapter 6). In 1905, Nicholas T. Haller designed a row of bay-fronted houses at 138–62 Tennessee Avenue NE. The three-room plans, plus back building, used wide doorways to bring natural light to the reception hall. By putting the stairway in the middle room, the entrance hallway could be narrower and the parlor wider than would otherwise be the case in these 18-foot-wide houses.[16]

English-Basement Plan

"English basement," in American parlance, meant something very different a century ago than it does today (see fig. 13). While today it refers to a separate dwelling unit on the first floor, usually a few feet below grade, in the late nineteenth and early twentieth centuries it described a plan that had a reception room on the first floor and the drawing room or parlor at the front of the second floor, stretching across the building. Also called a "reception-hall plan," the English basement's most characteristic feature, a newspaper article noted, "is the location of the drawing room, dining room and library on what is in reality the second floor . . . The first or ground floor is devoted to an entrance hall, with kitchen, furnace and other service rooms in the rear." The plan, common throughout Europe, placed the principal rooms on a raised story called, in Italian, the *piano nobile.* An article in the *Evening*

Figure 13. "Three English Basement Residences." Architect T. F. Schneider designed these English-basement row houses with entrances at grade level and the public rooms on the upper stories, illuminated by oriels. (From *Selections from the Work of T. F. Schneider, Architect* [Washington, DC, 1894], DC History Center, NA712.S37)

Figure 14. Row houses, 100 Block of North Carolina Avenue SE. Architect Charles Burden designed 32 row houses on the square bounded by North Carolina Avenue, 2nd Street, and E Street SE. The oriels at the second floors denoted the parlor space in this English-basement design. (Daniel D. Reiff, photographer, 1970)

Star, reprinted from *Harper's Bazaar,* describes a similar arrangement in a townhouse in London and notes, "We are of course speaking of the usual London residence, known in this country as an English basement house."[17]

In 1892 John F. Waggaman, a self-described "real estate expert," commissioned 32 English-basement row houses to be built a few blocks south of the Capitol (see fig. 14). On a triangular square, he placed 15 houses on North Carolina Avenue, 13 on E Street, and 4 on Second Street SE. Waggaman had been in the real estate business for only a few years when he started this development, but he had met with some success. At about the same time he was developing this property, he was also subdividing the Tunlaw Farm in Northwest Washington into Wesley Heights, where he built a few houses. The depression of 1893 prevented him from fully developing that site, however.[18]

Charles E. Burden, an architect who had a thriving practice for a few years until his business also was affected by the depression, designed Waggaman's Capitol Hill houses.[19] For this development, Burden provided fanciful rows with oriels and balconies, windows with round arches and ogee arches, mansard and flat roofs covered with slate and tin, Palladian windows and swags and garlands. The most prominent feature, the second-floor oriel or balcony, denoted the most important room, the drawing room. On this triangular square, the depths of lots ranged from just under 50 feet to about 90. The houses were 18 feet wide on the shorter lots and 17 feet wide on the longer ones, and were either 36 or 38 feet deep. They adhered to the English-basement plan, with entry into a reception room with a corner fireplace and an L-shaped stairway leading to the second floor (see figs. 15 and 16). Behind the stairway was the kitchen. On the second floor, a parlor or drawing room stretched across the front, graced by an oriel or balcony, and a dining room behind. Bedrooms were on the third floor; this was a plan that necessitated a third floor, because bedrooms would not be on the same floor as the drawing room, where guests would be entertained. The three-fixture bathroom was on the third floor, and stoves, not central heat, heated these houses.

Sales were apparently not as brisk as Waggaman would have liked. On September 18, 1893, he advertised a number of properties "For Sale—Snap Bargains—Panic Prices," including the following description, which more than likely refers to these row houses: "$5,500 to $6,000, $50 cash and easy payment, buys a new three-story 7- and 8-room house; splendid construction and finish; unsurpassed location on broad avenue; two blocks from Capitol." Ten years after construction, one investor, Cecilia M. Coughlin, owned twenty-five of the thirty-two row houses, indicating that they had failed to sell to individual homeowners. Even when sold to individual owners, most of the houses remained rentals for several decades, occupied by government clerks

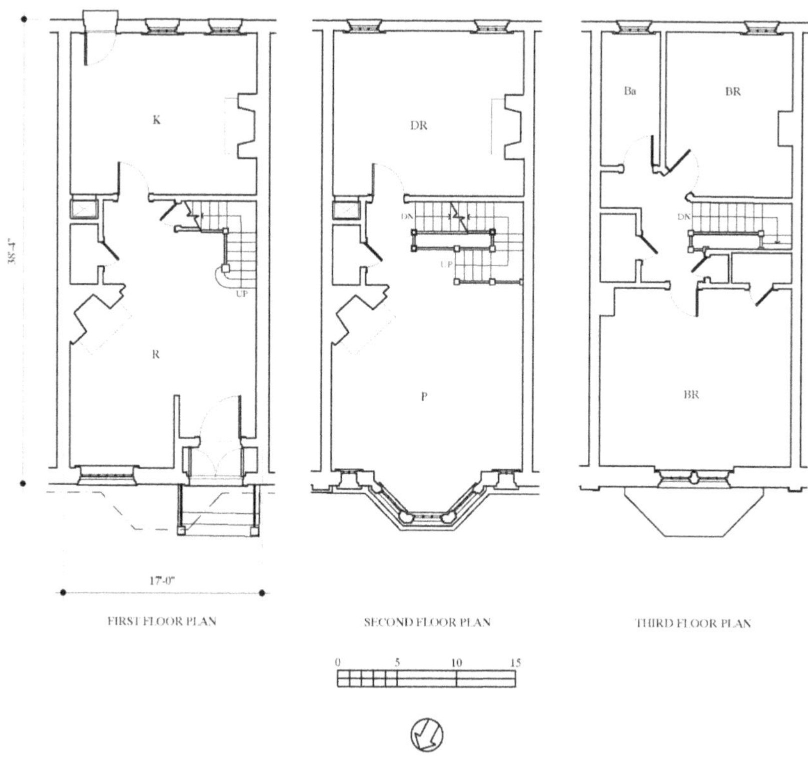

Figure 15. Row house, 129 North Carolina Avenue SE, plans. Contrary to current usage of the term, the "English-basement" plan had an at-grade entrance into a reception room (R), with the kitchen behind. On the second floor, the parlor was in the front with the dining room behind. The third floor had two bedrooms and a bathroom. (Conjectural original plans, Mark Schara, delineator, 2020, Library of Congress, Prints and Photographs Division, HABS)

Figure 16. Row house, 129 North Carolina Avenue SE. The prominent second-story oriel on the facade of this English-basement house delineates the most important room, the drawing room. A small reception area on the first floor provided a space in which to greet guests. (Jarob Ortiz, photographer, 2020, Library of Congress, Prints and Photographs Division, HABS)

and skilled laborers. The house at 129 North Carolina, for example, was owned and occupied by Oscar Bussart, an electrical engineer, and his wife, Jane, in 1910; then rented to Austin Garner, a clerk, in 1916; then owned and occupied by Adelbert Jorden, a clerk, in 1920; then rented to Hugh Hartley, a librarian at the Coast and Geodetic Survey, and his wife, Evelyn, in 1930; and rented to Charles E. Gift, a machinist at the Navy Yard, and his wife, Bessie, in 1935.[20]

The English-basement plan had a brief surge of popularity for speculative row houses aimed at the middle class in neighborhoods such as Capitol Hill. Usually located on cramped sites where back buildings were not feasible, this was, in essence, a two-room plan, ideal for shorter lots. The location of the kitchen a floor lower than the dining room was not ideal, however, for households with few or no servants, reminiscent of the basement kitchen that the back building had helped eliminate. As a newspaper article admitted,

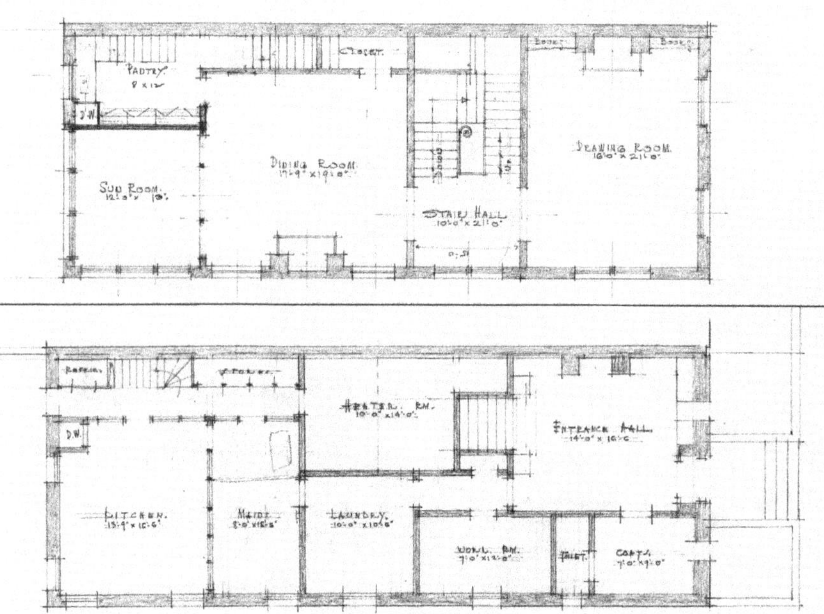

Figure 17. Row house, 1823 Twenty-Third Street NW, basement and first-floor plans. George Ray designed a grand pair of English-basement houses in 1924. At the basement level, guests would enter through a central doorway into a large hall with fireplace and stairway. A coat closet and toilet were off to one side, but the rest of that floor was dedicated to work spaces for servants—kitchen, laundry, work room. On the raised first floor, the drawing room was in the front of the dwelling, and the dining room was on the other side of the stairway. A sun room and pantry, with dumbwaiter, were at the rear of the house. The second and third floors had bedrooms for the family and servants. (George N. Ray, architect, 1924, Library of Congress, Prints and Photographs Division, ADE Unit 267, no. 26)

"the location of the rooms necessitates the employment of more servants than otherwise would be the case."[21]

Perhaps as a result, the English-basement plan's longer-term popularity rested in tonier neighborhoods such as Dupont Circle and Kalorama. In 1924 George Ray, serving as both architect and owner, designed four-story row houses in an English-basement plan at 1821–23 Twenty-Third Street NW (see fig. 17). Entry was in the center bay, into an entrance hall with a coat room. A wide stair led to the second floor, and the rest of the first level, denoted a "basement" despite being slightly above grade, was not meant for visitors: work room, laundry, heater room, maid's room, and, in the rear, the kitchen. On the main floor, a spacious drawing room stretched across the front. Behind the stairway was a dining room and, at the back of the house, a sun room and pantry, where the dumbwaiter was located. On the third floor, the "living room"—clearly for family only—was in the front, with two bedrooms behind, each with their own bathroom. On the top floor, two bedrooms were in the front, sharing a bathroom, and three servants' rooms were in the rear, sharing their own bathroom. The estimated cost of construction for these two houses was $60,000—a large sum for a row house, even for a three-servant household.[22]

The market for high-end English-basement houses is evident in a 1916 discussion of remodeling old row houses: "Many large homes of the old-fashioned basement type have been remodeled into what are generally referred to as English basement houses; high front steps have been removed . . . and entrances have been provided on the street level. One or perhaps two small rooms have been provided on either side of the entrance hall and an attractive stairway built to the second or main floor of the house. The basement dining room of years ago has given way to the entrance hall and adjoining rooms and what was once called the 'back parlor' is now the dining room."[23] The plan worked well with various architectural modes, being found in Romanesque-inspired row houses of the 1890s and classical row houses of the 1920s.

Admirers of the English-basement plan pointed to its suitability for entertaining. In a series of articles in the *Evening Star* in 1887, architect E. C. Gardner surveyed possibilities for row houses and concluded that the English-basement plan was the best. He mentioned indoor stairs, instead of a high flight outside, a large parlor, and "a sort of reception room, in which there may be comfortable chairs and, in cold weather, a cheerful hickory fire, a convenient place for outer wraps, a table holding a hospitable punch bowl, if one believes in punch, or a steaming coffee pot." Another observer, writing in 1913, noted that the house was "best suited for people who maintain an extensive establishment," and that "in the territory between Connecticut and Massachusetts avenues scores of homes of this type have been erected."[24] For residents in other neighborhoods and without numerous servants, though, the next plan—a compact dwelling for a servant-less household—was far more suitable.

Quadrant Plan

In 1922, Oliver and Edna Perry bought the house at 2214 Cathedral Avenue NW, in Woodley Park, facing Rock Creek (see fig. 18). They had been married for four years and this three-bedroom house would have been a good place to start a family. Oliver was a salesman for the Ford Motor Co., and in 1924 he built a two-car garage on the back of their property. But Edna, a clerk in the pension office, died the next year. In 1929, Oliver remarried and moved to Rockville, Maryland, renting out his row house.[25]

Figure 18. Row houses, 2200 Block of Cathedral Avenue NW. In 1922, developer Charles H. Small built a row of ten houses at 2208–26 Cathedral Avenue NW, in the quadrant plan. The houses had the characteristic front porch, along with a 20-foot width. The house at 2214 is at the center of this photograph. (Justin R. Scalera, photographer, 2019, Library of Congress, Prints and Photographs Division, HABS)

The house was one of a row of ten built by developer Charles H. Small.[26] The row had a rhythmic variation to the facades, but the houses all had the same plan of four rooms on the first floor, with the kitchen behind the entrance hall and the dining room behind the living room (see fig. 19). Each 20-foot-wide house originally had a porch across the front and two levels of porches in the rear. By the 1920s, this quadrant-plan house with front porch was a common type, built by the hundreds east of Rock Creek, as well as in this neighborhood. Architect George Santmyers, a prolific architect of row houses, designed this row as well as seventy-one row houses lining the 2700 block of Woodley Place, just a block away, for another developer, J. B. Shapiro. The house at 2214 Cathedral had some features that placed it on the higher end of the scale of quadrant plans: the living room had a fireplace in the corner, glass doors separated the main rooms on the first floor and, in addition to the three-fixture bathroom on the second floor, a half bath opened directly off of the primary bedroom.

Generally, the plan had a brilliant simplicity. Dividing the first floor into quadrants, the plan provided for an economical use of space and light. At 20 feet, a little wider than most row houses had been, the plan could squeeze two rooms beside each other, and from 1906 to 1912, 20 feet was by far the most popular width for new row houses. Developers soon realized that this plan would work with houses that were as narrow as 17 or even 16 feet wide,

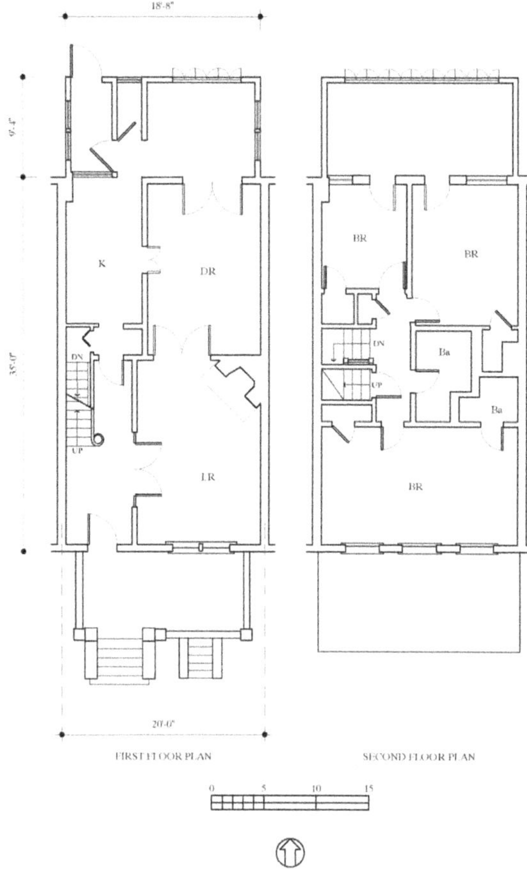

Figure 19. Row house, 2214 Cathedral Avenue NW, plans. The quadrant plan had an elegant simplicity: front hall, with kitchen behind, and living room, with dining room behind. Front and back porches, including a sleeping porch on the second floor, increased the livable space. This row was fancier than most, with a fireplace, French doors between some of the first-floor rooms, and a half bath off of the primary bedroom, in addition to the bathroom off the hall. (Conjectural original plans, Monica P. Ortiz-Cortes, Jocelyn C. Johnson, and Robert R. Arzola, delineators, 2019, Library of Congress, Prints and Photographs Division, HABS, redrawn by Mark Schara)

so that in 1924, for instance, more row houses were built with widths of 16, 17, or 18 feet than 20.[27]

The location of the kitchen is significant. No longer was it banished to the basement or back building. This was clearly not a plan intended for a family with servants. Instead, a family member, presumably the wife and mother, would prepare meals and serve them to her family only steps away. The plan also reflects the introduction of central heat, in that rooms did not have to be closed off to preserve warmth. The informal nature of this openness suggests that this is a house for a family, in contrast to the English-basement plan, which was designed for a formal lifestyle that included entertaining.

With porches front and back, the quadrant plan engaged the outdoors. Skylights ventilated and illuminated the second-floor bathrooms, and all of the other rooms had windows to the front or back. The wooden sleeping porch, which stretched across the back of the house at the second level, was a standard feature of row houses in this plan. Sleeping porches were enclosed with screens or glass and provided a cool space for people to sleep in the summer. In 1910, the newspaper noted that sleeping porches were just catching on, responding to health concerns (discussed in chapter 4). By 1928, fearing that the wooden porches posed a fire hazard, a government official proposed to eliminate them. A group of builders objected, noting that they "wished to speak in behalf of Government clerks, many of whom could own only row houses and desired to augment the quarters with inclosed porches."[28] The government backed down.

The front porch, a distinguishing feature of these quadrant row houses, had to remain unenclosed, with only an open balustrade, per building regulations. The front porch was a popular place for congregating and lounging. One ad claimed, "A lady who is considering one of these houses said she would not give the porch for a hundred bay-windows and stone stoops." The front porch had a fairly brief reign, though. In 1925 the Commission of Fine Arts apparently discouraged the construction of front porches, and the next year, architect Louis Justement declared, "The better types of home, whether row or detached, are discarding the front porch because it is lacking in privacy and because it usually distracts from the appreciation of the building." Although the front porch might have provided a cool place to relax, "the use of the automobile makes it possible to secure relief from the heat in ways that were not possible a few years ago." In addition, "the proper place for the porch is at the back of the house, facing what should be an attractive garden rather than the usual commonplace back yard."[29] Justement suggested a fundamental rethinking of the backyard, from work area to leisure space, which would affect the form of the row house after World War II.

The quadrant row house had a gently sloping roof, often hidden behind a small mansard roof that did not shelter an additional story, and sometimes not even a small storage space. These mansard roofs were covered with slate or sometimes tiles for a Spanish colonial appearance. Small windows lit the storage space or were there simply to imply that there was a third story. At 2214 Cathedral, the dormer windows lit an attic that was seven feet high in the front, sloping to two feet in the rear, whereas other quadrant plans had dormer windows with no usable space behind them. Justement, noting that these dormers in the mansard roof existed "purely for the effect of giving the impression of a three-story building," disapproved: "There should be no 'bluffing' in designing a building."[30]

The name "quadrant" is a current term, not employed at the time. When these row houses were being built, freestanding houses with essentially the same plan were popular; they were often referred to as "foursquare" or "square" houses. These square houses were usually two stories and often appeared to be cube-shaped, topped with a pyramidal roof. Washington's row houses were not square, however. Although beginning in 1913 this type of row house was called “daylight” in Baltimore, referring to the increased window exposure, that name did not catch on in Washington. Instead, here they were referred to as “colonial,” with their primary colonial feature being the white columns supporting the front porch. But the massing was also vaguely colonial, allowing for the constraints of a row house. Rather than the sprawling projections and corners and ells, as well as the verticality, of the Queen Anne and other late nineteenth-century modes, this new row house was compact, with flat walls both front and rear and the massing pulled inward. The houses were also referred to as “six-room houses,” as shown in a discussion of construction in Petworth in 1915: “The six-room type of house has been featured by practically all the builders operating in that locality. Six rooms, with front and rear porches and cellar under the entire house, has been found to be the most popular combination in home-building operations of this character.”[31]

The quadrant is essentially a plan of the Progressive Era, reflecting concerns for efficiency and expertise. The progressive house plan eschewed single-purpose rooms such as libraries and pantries, had smaller rooms overall, and facilitated informal living. The new science of home economics examined kitchens in particular, seeking effective layouts of new appliances and utilizing built-in cupboards, in a smaller footprint. The quadrant-plan row house’s narrow, 7-foot-wide kitchen was a model of efficiency. In addition, the quadrant plan represented the movement of the working class into the middle class, as their houses acquired important features of modernity. Previously occupying ill-equipped nineteenth-century row houses, Washington’s white working class flocked to row houses with the quadrant plan. As detailed by Thomas Hubka, the elements of the house that became standard at this time included three-fixture bathrooms (sink, toilet, bathtub), fully equipped kitchens, utilities, dining rooms, private bedrooms, closets, front porches, and garages; they were also larger houses overall, compared to the working class’s previous housing.[32] The quadrant-plan row house provided all these amenities.

The quadrant plan, introduced in Washington row houses in 1906, remained popular for several decades. By the late 1920s the front porch was discarded and the tiled “rooflets” replaced by parapets, but the plan persisted through the 1940s. It was, adopting Hubka’s argument, how the row house became modern.

Kitchen-Forward Plan

The row houses of the 1950s were radically different from their predecessors. While their modernist exterior simplicity was striking, their plans were truly novel. The redefinition of the rooms, the large windows and glass doors, and the placement of the kitchen reflected new technology and new attitudes toward the outdoors. Chloethiel Woodard Smith designed several house types for the first development in Capitol Park in Southwest Washington, built between 1959 and 1963, which introduced several of these concepts (see fig. 20).

One variant, the house at 813 Third Street SW, is small, 15 feet 8 inches by 32 feet 4 inches, on two levels, for a total of a little more than 1,000 square feet (see fig. 21). On the first floor, entrance is into a hallway with a straight-run stair and a room Smith called a "study" in the front, separated from the hall by an accordion door. The 8-by-8-foot kitchen is behind the study, and behind that is a "living room–dining area" that stretches across the back. On the second floor are two bedrooms with a 5-by-7-foot bathroom in between. Aside from the simplicity of the plan, some of the spaciousness derives from natural light: all of the windows are 4 feet wide, and the sliding glass doors in the living room are 8 feet wide.

Bringing the kitchen and bathroom to the interior of the plan also enabled the more lived-in spaces to have all the windows. The central kitchen reflects its importance to a servant-less household. The cook, presumably

Figure 20. Row house, 813 Third Street SW. In the late 1950s and early 1960s, Chloethiel Woodard Smith designed 323 row houses in the urban renewal area of Capitol Park in Southwest Washington. All were modernist in design, and most were modest in size. (Photograph by the author, 2018).

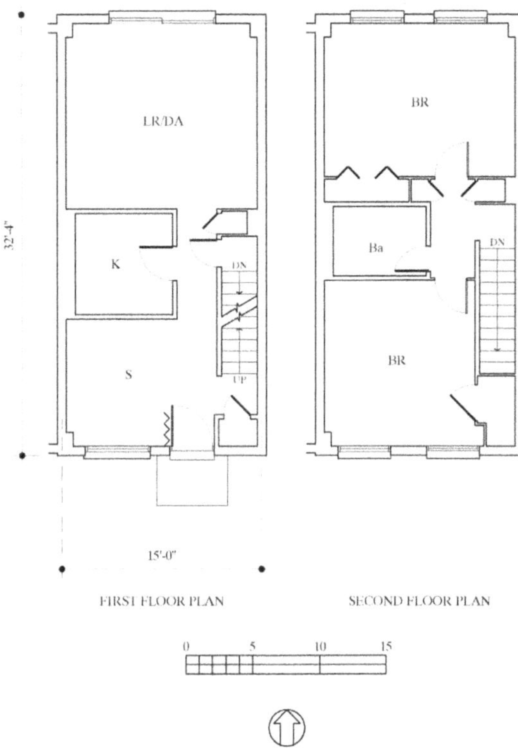

Figure 21. Row house, 813 Third Street SW, plans. In most of the Capitol Park row houses, Smith moved the kitchen from its traditional placement at the rear of the house. Here, she placed it in the middle of the plan, with a living room/dining area to the rear of the house and a room labeled "study" (S) in the front. On the second floor, a 5-by-7-foot bathroom separated the two bedrooms. (Redrawn by Ruben Melendez, Onairis Perez, and Mark Schara from original drawings by Chloethiel Woodard Smith, architect, 1958, Library of Congress, ADE C. W. Smith Collection, Sheet A-4 [Floor plans S7-S9])

the housewife, would not be banished to the rear, and goods such as ice and groceries were no longer delivered to the kitchen door. The dining room also disappeared. Referred to here as a nebulous "dining area" and not separated on the plan, the dining room could have been assigned to the room labeled "study." The fact that the developer and architect did not feel it was necessary to provide a designated dining room reflects the informal family life of the postwar period.[33]

The plan also shows the importance of access to and views of the outdoors. The backyard was now the prized outdoor space, suitable for ornamental gardens or children's play. The term "patio town house" appeared in discussions of Capitol Park, linking the new row house to a suburban feature.[34] Unlike decks, which became popular a decade or two later, patios and terraces were at grade, easily reached from the house. In this house, the first floor was at grade, so the terrace was a step away from the living room. The basement, entirely below grade and illuminated by light wells, housed a gas-fired furnace providing heat through forced air.

In the postwar period, the kitchen moved forward in the row house, either

Figure 22. The six typical plans of Washington row houses, shown at the same scale. While all the plans had variations, these plans show the general evolution of the common row house. (Onairis Perez, Ruben Melendez, and Mark Schara, delineators, 2020)

to the center or to the front of the house. With the kitchen in the front, the street front of the house became the utilitarian end, while the entertainment space was in the rear, upending the traditional perception of a house. This occurred in new construction away from Southwest, such as new, neo-Colonial row houses built by prolific residential developer Barrett Linde (who is discussed in chapter 5), as well as in rehabilitations of older row houses. In 1960, Donald Hudson Drayer proposed remodeling a two-story row house at 121 E Street SE, by moving the kitchen to the front and the living room to the rear. There was no dining room labeled as such, but the living room was 21 feet deep and stretched across the full 12½-foot width of the house. A new fireplace adorned the living room, which had French doors leading to the yard. Two bedrooms and two interior bathrooms were on the second floor.[35]

This plan continued to be opened up in the late twentieth century. As journalist Kate Wagner noted recently, "Prior to the last 25 years, an 'open floorplan' meant a living configuration without *doors;* now the term has come to mean a living configuration without *walls.*" In 2018 an article in *Architectural Record* described the renovation of an 1818 Georgetown row house, which involved "the reinvention of the main level as one large, contiguous space. Though the 119-foot length is defined by the parameters of the rooms—living, dining, and kitchen—you can see clear through from front to back. The effect is stunning . . . The introverted nature and fustiness have been replaced with an open, forward-looking sensibility."[36]

In the late twentieth-century row house, bathrooms rarely received windows, the kitchen moved to the middle or front of the house, and the kitchen increasingly was opened to the rest of the house. Entertaining guests occurred in the back of the house, either in the living room or in the backyard. In renovated late nineteenth-century row houses, kitchens were opened and extended, growing to include dining and lounging areas. Row houses continued to reflect larger trends in housing design, while still occupying a constrained space.

This brief overview of six typical floor plans of row houses in Washington, DC, has pointed to some themes that echo through the following chapters (see fig. 22). Despite the inherent constraints of the building type, change characterizes the story of the row house, including the shift of the kitchen from the basement to the rear to the front; the concomitant change in kitchen labor, from servants to householders; new technologies, from roofing material to kitchen appliances; and evolution of the backyard from utilitarian space to show place. People associated with the row house changed as well, including the shift in occupants, from renters to boarders to owners; the shift from small builders to large; and racial change in houses and neighborhoods. The remaining chapters examine these changes and others.

2

Constraints

Washington's built environment is framed, facilitated, and controlled by its plan and regulations. Government officials placed public buildings on prominent sites, influenced their classical designs, and financed their construction. The city's more modest private building fabric, though, was equally guided by decisions that were made by politicians and government officials, from the inception of the city in 1791 to the present day. George Washington, Thomas Jefferson, and Peter Charles L'Enfant, usually associated with more monumental decisions about the new capital, also concerned themselves with privately built dwellings and assumed that a good number of them would be row houses.

The Constitution mandated that there be a federal district, separate from the states, to accommodate the government. Once Maryland and Virginia agreed to cede their control over land that might be selected, the Residence Act of 1790 gave George Washington the authority to determine a site on the Potomac River. Located where the Anacostia River (then called the Eastern Branch) flowed into the Potomac, the District included in its ten-mile-square the towns of Georgetown, Maryland, and Alexandria, Virginia. Most of the rest of the land had been divided into nineteen plantations, most using enslaved labor. Before the arrival of English colonists in the seventeenth century, the land had been inhabited by Nacostines, an Algonquian-speaking people.[1]

Washington appointed three commissioners to oversee the survey, arrange the purchase of the land, and supervise construction of government buildings. The landowners, called proprietors, agreed to give the government the land it needed for roadways and to receive compensation for the land taken for public buildings. The remaining land would be divided into squares and lots, with half belonging to the government and half to the proprietors.[2] Sales of the lots, then enhanced in value, would compensate the proprietors for their donation, while the government would use the sales of its half of the lots to finance the construction of public buildings.

Washington engaged the French-born designer Peter Charles L'Enfant

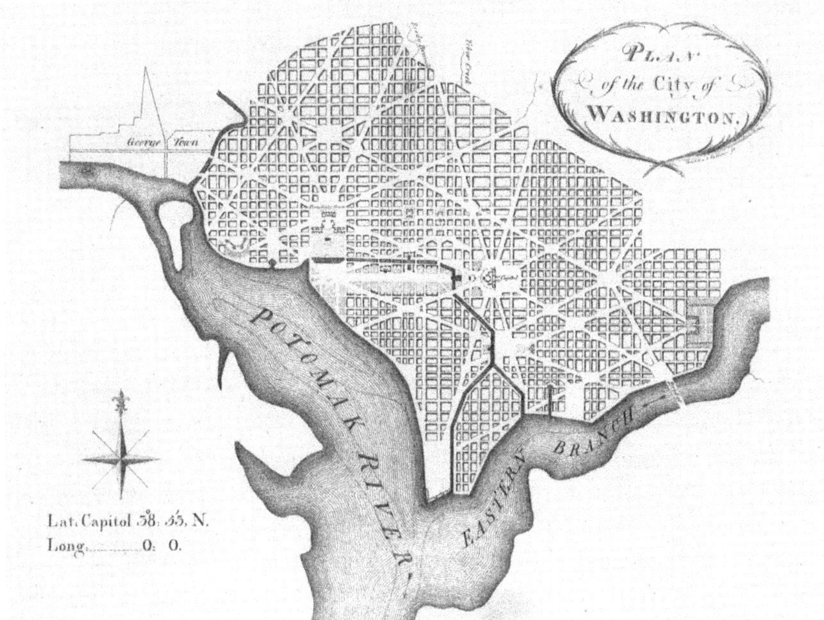

Figure 23. L'Enfant plan of Washington. The plan consisted of an irregular grid of streets overlaid with diagonal avenues, placed at the juncture of the Potomac River and the Eastern Branch. Canals helped drain the city. (Thackara and Vallance, 1794, Library of Congress, Geography and Map Division)

to plan the new city. L'Enfant arrived in Georgetown on March 9, 1791, and began work, producing by August a design for the city, which covered a little less than ten of the one hundred square miles designated for the government. The plan was a brilliant expression of the new democracy written on the land (see fig. 23). L'Enfant placed the president's house and the congressional building on separate hills, one and a half miles apart, in view of, but clearly not beholden to, each other. The street system was an irregularly spaced grid overlaid with dramatic diagonal avenues. At the intersections of avenues, L'Enfant planned for public spaces with statuary serving as visible punctuations of vistas.[3] But it was on the grid streets that most of residential Washington would be built.

After L'Enfant was summarily fired in 1792, Andrew Ellicott laid out the streets and squares. The width of these streets and avenues—most streets were 90 feet wide, and avenues ranged from 110 to 160 feet wide—affected the building fabric over time. (By contrast, in Philadelphia, laid out in 1682, most of the streets were 50 feet wide, with the two major ones being 100 feet wide. The streets in Alexandria, laid out in 1749, were all 66 feet wide.) Washington's wide roadways would prove to be a headache to city engineers trying to pave all that space, but they also provided room for bay windows that would, in the late nineteenth century, give the city's row houses their distinctive character.

Row houses were clearly in the minds of Washington, Jefferson, and L'Enfant, as they were in the minds of most people familiar with other cities in the new republic and in northern Europe. London had row houses by the early fourteenth century and, by the middle of the seventeenth they were an integral part of the urban fabric. In many American cities, individual attached houses, as well as arrangements of attached houses produced by one builder at one time, appeared when urban areas became dense enough that such intense usage of the land made sense economically. New York City, the nation's capital before 1790, was a densely packed arrangement of attached houses. Philadelphia, the largest city in the new nation and home of the national government from 1790 to 1800, was also familiar to those who were planning the new capital city. Its grid plan facilitated row houses, and after the earliest period of settlement they characterized the city. Closer to home, the Potomac River ports of Alexandria (founded in 1749) and Georgetown (founded two years later) were both laid out in grid plans and by the late eighteenth century had attached houses. In Alexandria, the cohesive row at 207–15 Prince Street, consisting of three-story brick buildings with gabled dormer windows built in the 1780s, or similarly in Georgetown the row houses at 3001–03 M Street, built in 1788, demonstrate the elegance that this building form had attained.[4]

Unlike these other American cities and towns, where row houses were built organically, Washington's founders planned it to be a city of row houses. This chapter examines that intention, expressed through regulations and other means, as well as subsequent regulations and governmental interventions that encouraged and enabled row-house construction. These public policies influenced Washington's six typical row-house plans.

Urban Plan and Early Regulations, 1790–1860

Once L'Enfant completed the plan of the new city in August 1791, Washington and the commissioners were anxious to begin selling lots in order to produce income. L'Enfant argued that it would be better and ultimately more profitable to wait until more of the infrastructure was in place, but he was overruled. He foresaw dense, attached buildings in what he envisioned as the business area between what would become the White House and the Capitol, south of Pennsylvania Avenue. He noted that "the stimulate [stimulus] to builth [build] houses in those part[s] being so great it is not to be doubted that they will be erected contigious [contiguous] to each other" and would provide a density conducive to business, as well as accommodations for congressmen and public employees.[5]

L'Enfant was not the only one who foresaw row houses. Concurrently with the sale of lots, George Washington released building regulations on October 17, 1791. The regulations, which carry implications for the form of privately built structures, applied only to construction in the area that L'Enfant had designed, which would become known as the City of Washington (see the appendix).

Beginning with the one most pertinent to row houses, the fourth regulation guided the erection of party walls, permitting and even encouraging row houses. It allowed a municipal official to "enter on the land of any person to set out the foundations and regulate the walls to be built between party and party," and explained how party walls would be determined and paid for—the second builder to reimburse the first for half the cost of the wall and government officials to oversee the process. This regulation, taken almost verbatim from a 1721 Philadelphia law, was the longest-lasting of the original regulations, being repeated in the city's building regulations into the twentieth century.[6]

The first regulation, "That the outer and party walls of all houses within the said City shall be built of Brick or Stone," reflected the desire for a fireproof and substantial, not ramshackle, city. Thomas Jefferson, who had a great interest in the new capital, met with the commissioners on September 8, 1791, to discuss some questions Washington had about the regulations he was considering. One of his questions, "Ought there to be any wood houses in the town?" Jefferson answered, on behalf of the commissioners, in the negative. Jefferson's experience in Paris led him to envision a solid, handsome, coherent capital, but the requirement for masonry dwellings was immediately seen to be impractical and even harmful, preventing construction of the cheap dwellings necessary to begin settlement. New residents did not flock to the new capital, nor did the workmen and artisans necessary to build it. One of the objections was that there was no housing, so imposing a requirement that made new construction more time-consuming and expensive was counterproductive. On June 22, 1796, Washington suspended this requirement until December 1800, permitting the construction of frame houses if they were less than 320 square feet and no more than 12 feet high and located no closer than 24 feet to a masonry house.[7] The suspension was renewed periodically until 1820, with the same provisos.

The second and third regulations concerned the appearance of houses. The second, which encouraged variation of the building line, specified "That all buildings on the Streets shall be parallel thereto and may be advanced to the Line of the Street or withdrawn therefrom at the pleasure of the Improver." Washington asked an open-ended question of Jefferson and the commissioners: "What sort of brick or stone houses should be built—and what height—especially on the principal streets and avenues?" Jefferson's response was "Liberty as to advancing or withdrawing the front." Historians have noted that this had long been an interest of Jefferson's, who had written previously, "I doubt much whether the obligation to build the houses at a given distance from the street, contributes to its beauty. It produces a disgusting monotony; all persons make this complaint against Philadelphia. The contrary practice varies the appearance, and is much more convenient to the inhabitants."[8] Despite this encouragement of variety, few builders seem to have taken advantage of it, preferring to align the fronts of their buildings with the property line.

The third regulation read "The wall of no house to be higher than forty feet to the roof in any part of the City, nor shall any be lower than thirty five feet on any of the Avenues." This requirement for houses to be of a consistent height also reflects Jefferson's ideas in particular. When Washington asked his open-ended question of Jefferson and the commissioners, the response included not only advice about varying the fronts of houses, but also this: "but some limits as to height would be advisable. No house wall higher than 35 feet in any part of the town, none lower than that on any of the avenues." Restrictions on height were not unusual; Paris limited building heights to about 51 feet (8 toises) in 1667.[9] The height limit had both safety implications, in that fire would be more easily controlled on shorter buildings, and aesthetic ones, in that a low city was envisioned. But the height minimum on the avenues was clearly an aesthetic choice, seeking an almost-uniform cornice line. Jefferson's derision of the "disgusting monotony" of a consistent building line was balanced by his desire for a consistent cornice line of 35 feet on the avenues. President Washington permitted a 5-foot leeway, so that avenue buildings could range from 35 to 40 feet high.

Like the first regulation, the third was almost immediately suspended, given that it tended to "impede the settlement in the city, of mechanics, and others, whose circumstances do not admit of erecting houses of the description authorized by the said regulations."[10] The regulation was repeatedly suspended, and in 1822, when a new municipal government adopted George Washington's 1791 regulations, the height minimums and maximums were quietly dropped. Limits to buildings' heights did not reappear until the end of the century, and no attempt to insure a height minimum on the avenues was made again.

Drawing on a Philadelphia law from 1782, the seventh regulation prohibited projections beyond the building line, including "vaults . . . stoops, porches, cellar doors, windows, ditches, or leaning walls," unless permission were obtained. Requests for steps seem to have been routinely granted, but this was nevertheless the first regulation to be altered. In 1794 the commissioners, with Washington's approval, changed it to allow vaults and areas of specific dimensions and materials in order "to tend to the convenience and safety of the inhabitants and their property and add to the beauty of the city." In 1845 this provision was extended, so that steps, vaults, areas, and porticoes were permitted, although tightly defined.[11]

The sixth regulation is one of the more puzzling regulations, and it has to do with the meaning of the word "square." The regulation addresses "the way into the squares" and declares that it is a public space, although adjacent property owners could arch over it or erect gates, if the commissioners permitted. L'Enfant used "square" in two senses: in one part of the written explanation that accompanied his plan, he noted that the orthogonal lines "make the distribution of the city into streets, squares, etc.," implying that a square is a city block, the solid to the street's void. But in another part of the explanation, he mentions "The Squares colored yellow," which are open spaces at the intersections of avenues, where he was hoping that each state would erect "Statues, Columns, Obelisks" and so on. He also specifically mentions a square east of the Capitol where East Capitol Street begins, and where "the pavement on each side will pass under an Arched way under whose cover Shops will be most conveniently and agreeably situated."[12]

One interpretation of this regulation conforms with the latter definition of square—public places, akin to plazas, surrounded by multistory buildings arcaded at ground level, accessed by roadways that go through the buildings.[13] Another possible explanation is more prosaic, although compatible with a set of regulations that was directed at private construction throughout the city. Perhaps L'Enfant was considering access to the interiors of city blocks, and that the narrow passageway to the interior could be built over at the upper stories. As will be seen, the squares (meaning city blocks) that L'Enfant divided into lots and alleys had narrow access roads, opening up into a wider alley in the center. He wanted this interior alley to remain free from nuisances and obstructions. The regulation was directed at the owners of property abutting the access roads, permitting construction over them, compatible with a row-house neighborhood.

With these regulations, Washington laid out a vision for private property in the new city. He wanted substantial, masonry buildings with even cornice lines on the dramatic avenues. Although the front facades of the buildings did not have to be at the building line, they could not project beyond it. They would be row houses, providing a flat front, even height, and sense of permanence. Washington's vision, though, soon clashed with reality. By the time the government moved to the city in 1800, the requirements for masonry structures and height minimums had been scrapped, areas in front of houses were permitted, and no one had built grand arcaded plazas. With the retention of the regulations regarding party walls, though, the stage was set for row houses.

The division of the squares into lots and alleys also suggested row houses.

Before he was dismissed from his job at the end of February 1792, leaving it to Andrew Ellicott to reproduce his plan from memory and make some minor adjustments, L'Enfant had a hand in subdividing several squares in preparation for the October 1791 sale. No map survives from this sale, but more than a decade later surveyor Nicholas King cited the squares where the sales had concentrated: "No. 78, 79 or 101, 105, 107, 126, and 127." All of these were located around Pennsylvania Avenue between the White House and Georgetown, and King noted that "plats of that portion of the city, were shown to the purchasers."[14] King was apparently mistaken in naming Square 79, because all of the rest share an unusual feature: diagonal alleys. Each of the remaining squares contains a narrow access road (usually 10 feet wide) in the middle of the long side, perpendicular to a broad hyphen (usually 20 feet wide) in the middle of the square, and four diagonal roadways (usually 10 feet wide), stretching from the ends of the hyphen into the corners of the square, providing alley access to every lot. L'Enfant's fondness for diagonals, a majestic feature of his city plan, apparently extended into the interiors of city squares (see fig. 24).

Washington and the commissioners held two more public sales of lots with disappointing results. Squares seem to have been subdivided on an ad

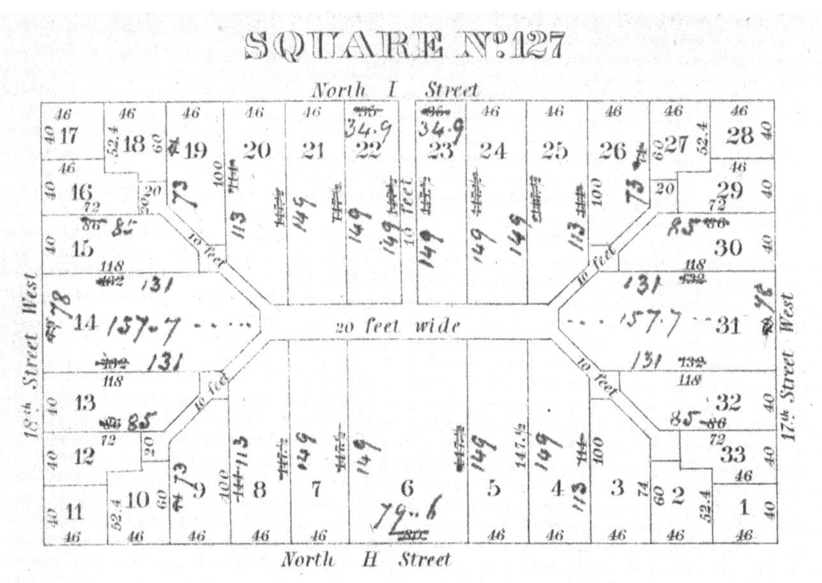

Figure 24. Square 127, showing lots and alleys. One of the squares subdivided into lots for sale in 1791, Square 127 had a 20-foot-wide alley reached from I Street, with diagonal offshoots so that nearly every lot had access to the alley. L'Enfant himself bought Lot 30. This plat, as printed, reflected L'Enfant's original measurements; the handwritten numbers represent Dermott's adjustments in 1793. (From *Maps of the District of Columbia and City of Washington and Plats of the Squares and Lots of the City of Washington* [Washington, DC: A. Boyd Hamilton, 1852])

hoc basis. Finally, in April 1793, the commissioners ordered a systematic survey of the lots, and the job fell to James Reed Dermott in the surveyor's office, who completed the task over the course of three years. Of the more than 1,200 squares, he delineated alleys on 487 of them. Embedded into the squares, these alleys were usually 30 feet wide in the shape of an H or an I, and reached by a narrower roadway, usually 15 feet wide. In the many squares without alleys, developers often added them when they subdivided their property, which sometimes did not occur until late in the nineteenth century.[15]

Alleys permitted row houses to function. With a solid frontage along the street, completely enclosing a city square, there would be no way to reach the backyard, other than going through the house itself. For emptying privies and disposing of ashes, this was not a desirable situation. Some rows included narrow passageways along the shared lot lines to permit backyard access, but the alleys of Washington provided for a public roadway for horse-drawn carts to enter the interior of a square.

While alleys suggest that the squares were planned for row houses, the width of the lots did not. In general, the size of lots throughout the city was about 55 to 60 feet wide by 120 to 130 feet deep, although the varying shapes of the squares means that there is no standard lot size. In the squares that L'Enfant subdivided, the lots usually had frontages of 40 to 45 feet, and even this is wider than a row house would be. Yet the 45-foot frontages could be subdivided into 15-foot lots, the 55-foot frontages could be subdivided into lots that were slightly more than 18 feet wide, and the 60-foot lots divided nicely for 20-foot-wide lots.

With the failure of the public sales of lots, the president tried another approach: a deal with a developer. In 1793 Washington and the commissioners sold 3,000 lots to James Greenleaf, an entrepreneur who implied he had Dutch financing. Greenleaf bought these lots, as well as a subsequent 3,000, on credit on the condition that he would build ten houses a year until 1800. He formed a partnership with financiers John Nicholson and Robert Morris, then sold out to them in 1795, leaving them with such debt that all three of them went to debtors' prison. When Greenleaf sold 500 lots to Thomas Law for four times what he had paid for them a year earlier, Washington, who had been trying to avoid speculation on vacant lots, was furious.[16]

Nonetheless, Greenleaf and his partners did construct some buildings. One of the first ventures was begun by Greenleaf, who bought twenty lots on South Capitol Street from proprietor Daniel Carroll on July 8, 1794, on the condition that he build twenty brick houses, each 25 by 40 feet, two stories high. Ownership of this land fell to Morris and Nicholson, who rushed to complete the stipulated houses, constructing them of brick. On September 26, 1796, they celebrated their completion with "a barbecue on the spot" for "a

Figure 25. Six Buildings, 2100 block (north side) Pennsylvania Avenue NW (a seventh row house, shown at the far right, was built later). Developers James Greenleaf, John Nicholson, and Robert Morris built several rows of houses in the mid-1790s, including this one. (Photographer unknown, 1890s, DC History Center, General Photograph Collection, CHS 02364)

few of their acquaintance, the architects, workmen and laborers—being nearly two hundred in number." The twenty row houses occupied "the whole front on South Capitol Street; and greater part of the front on South N Street." They were, the newspaper noted, "the first and only entire front built on any square in the City."[17] They were, however, not exactly finished. With Morris and Nicholson's bankruptcy, the buildings were abandoned and left to ruin.

Greenleaf and partners were also responsible for Wheat Row, discussed in chapter 1, and for two rows on Pennsylvania Avenue, west of the White House. Six Buildings, between Twenty-First and Twenty-Second Streets, and Seven Buildings, between Nineteenth and Twentieth Streets, were both handsome rows of three-story brick buildings (see fig. 25). The houses of both rows had three-bay facades, round-arched doorways, splayed lintels, and dormer windows in the gable roofs. The plans were two rooms deep with a curving stairway at the end of the side hall. As with the Twenty Buildings, Greenleaf initially bought the lots, and Morris and Nicholson were obligated to construct the buildings. They apparently sold them, unfinished, in 1796, and the new owners completed construction.[18]

Despite the construction in the 1790s of these several rows of handsome, masonry row houses, as well as some other rows and individual buildings, the city was slow to develop. By the spring of 1800, when the government moved to the city, the commissioners reported 109 brick houses in the city and 263 of wood. But people were building furiously; six months later, 84 more brick houses had been built and 151 of wood. That year, the census counted 3,210 people (about a quarter of them enslaved) in the city, part of the 14,093 that lived in the District. The houses were strewn across the city but also were gathered at various nodes such as the Capitol and the Navy Yard. As one observer noted in 1796, "Were the houses that have been built situated in one place all together, they would make a very respectable appearance, but scattered about as they are, a spectator can scarcely perceive any thing like a town."[19]

In 1820 the government of the District was reorganized, with Washington City and Georgetown each having an elected mayor, board of common council, and board of aldermen. The new local governments had the power to issue building regulations, with the approval of the president; consequently, in 1822 Washington City's government issued regulations that recognized those promulgated by George Washington in 1791, including the suspension of the first regulation requiring masonry construction.[20]

The city's slow development meant that speculators made profits by trading land, but not building. Congressmen, in town for only brief sessions, lived in boardinghouses. Major public buildings impressed visitors, who were equally struck by the scattered, village-like appearance of the private city. Alexander Mackay, a Scot, visited Washington in 1846 and described the view from the Capitol dome as a collection of "incipient country villages, with here and there a few scattered houses of wood or brick." Also in 1846, after several years of lobbying by Alexandria residents, Congress retroceded the Virginia portion of the District—the 31 square miles south and west of the Potomac—back to Virginia. It was at about this time, though, that the population began a dramatic increase, and the buildings became more densely packed. The 1840 population of the city of a little more than 23,000 grew to 40,000 in 1850, and to 61,000 in 1860. By then, the population of the District as a whole was 75,000 (3,185 of them enslaved and 11,131 of them free Blacks).[21]

The slow development of the city did not demand row houses, a practical building form in dense urban environments. At the eve of the Civil War, few squares were fully built, other than those downtown, between the White House and the Capitol. Houses built out to the front and side building lines stood all over the city, but not necessarily attached to others. The two-story two-room-plan row houses of the early decades grew to three-story ones in the 1850s, and gable roofs gave way to flat roofs behind elaborate cornices. Washington's streetscapes of modest privately built houses were beginning a transformation to a denser urban environment in which row houses would proliferate.

Modernizing the City, 1860–1900

The Civil War transformed Washington from a town to a city. With the onset of hostilities, people flooded into the capital: not only military men, but also clerks, entrepreneurs, family members of soldiers, and escaped enslaved people, and after the war many of them stayed. The population of the District grew by 75 percent between 1860 and 1870, for a total of 131,700; in that same time period, the African American population increased by 200 percent, composing about a third of the total. The inadequacy of the city's infrastructure to handle this influx was glaringly obvious, with overcrowded conditions and unpaved streets. As novelist Anthony Trollope observed on a visit to the city in 1861–62, "Washington is but a ragged, unfinished collection of unbuilt broad streets, as to the completion of which there can now, I imagine, be but little hope." After the war, several states petitioned Congress to move the capital west, closer to the center of the country.[22] Although the city was able to discourage these attempts, District leaders realized that the physical infrastructure needed to be modernized.

Black males gained the franchise in 1867, helping elect a Republican, Sayles Bowen, as mayor the next year; Bowen, in turn, appointed African Americans to political posts. Among his other actions, Bowen began to address the infrastructure needs of the city and found that the great width of the streets posed a paving challenge. As the Board of Public Works' report noted, the streets consumed half of the real estate; Washington's roadways were "of greater width than those of any other city in the world, and, with the alleys, comprise an area equal to about one-half of that contained within the entire city limits." Paving them from building line to building line would involve "bankrupting the people."[23]

The Bowen administration devised a solution to this problem, which was to narrow the roadway and turn the area between the sidewalk and the building line into "parking," or cultivated green spaces improved by the adjacent property owners (see fig. 26). In effect, although the front yards of private residences would not be owned by the homeowners, they would be fenced and maintained by them. In 1870 Congress approved a law that authorized the city to set aside "parks, to be adorned with shade-trees, walks, and enclosed with curb stones, not exceeding one-half the width of any and all avenues and streets . . . leaving a roadway of not less than thirty-five feet in the center of said avenues and streets."[24]

On January 16, 1871, just weeks before the territorial government was authorized by Congress, Washington's city council passed a law "authorizing the extension of bay windows to a distance of four feet beyond the building line."[25] That was the extent of the regulation; no permit was required, and

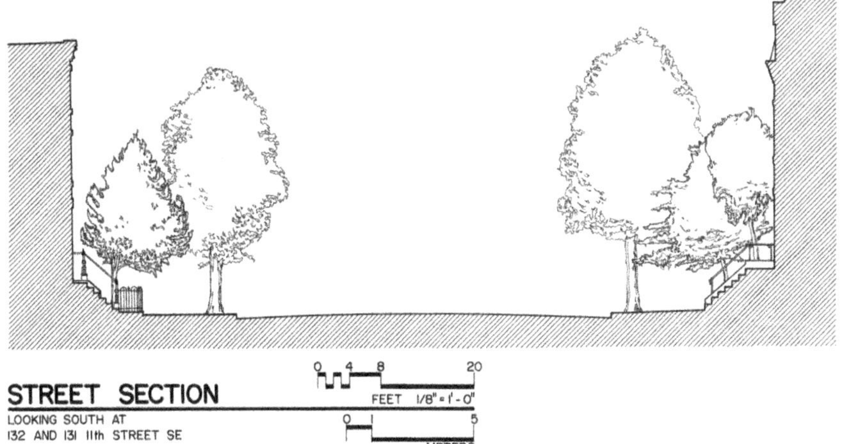

Figure 26. 100 block of Eleventh Street SE, sectional drawing. For this 90-foot-wide roadway, only the middle 50 feet are paved. Trees line the street, and a sidewalk runs between the trees and the steps to the houses. The public space includes everything up to the front of the house. (Joel R. M. Gagnon and Dennis E. McCarthy, delineators, 1989, Library of Congress, Prints and Photographs Division, HABS)

no limits on the width or height of the bay window were specified. But it was a radical change: row houses could project onto the public space. And many did; one-story, wooden bay windows were attached to the fronts of brick row houses (see fig. 27). The bay window offered several advantages to row-house residents, including increased floor space, more light and air, and an opportunity to be fashionable.

Alarmed at the growing political power of African Americans in the Bowen administration, the old guard reacted by persuading Congress to replace the elected municipal government with a territorial government and to supply a steady stream of federal funds adequate to remake the city—although this last provision was dropped.[26] Installed in 1871, the new government, whose jurisdiction covered the whole District, included a democratically elected House of Delegates, but also a presidentially appointed governor and upper chamber. With this consolidation, the cities of Washington and Georgetown were no longer governed separately from the County of Washington—all were Washington, DC. The most important arm of government, given the city's needs, was the presidentially appointed Board of Public Works. The territorial governor was the ex officio president, but Alexander Shepherd, who had masterminded the political usurpation, was the board's vice-president and from that position wielded tremendous power.

Shepherd proposed a Comprehensive Plan of Improvement at a cost of $6.6 million, most of which was to be obtained by a loan. The spending was immediate and the improvements notable: in less than three years, from 1871 to 1874, the board paved 150 miles of city streets, paved and curbed 200 miles of sidewalks, planted 60,000 trees, installed 3,000 streetlamps, and laid

Figure 27. Row houses, 22–24 Sixth Street SE. Bay windows such as these wooden ones were permitted to extend beyond the building line beginning in 1871. (Photograph by the author, 2018)

120 miles of sewers, 30 miles of water mains, and 39 miles of gas lines.[27] The work initially concentrated in downtown, then spread northwest.

The attention given to the city's streets, while important for commerce, development, and the overall appearance of the city, also had an indirect effect on the form of privately built houses. Shepherd's Board of Public Works adopted Bowen's "parking" scheme in its Comprehensive Plan of Improvements and explained: "The most feasible plan suggested was so to narrow the carriageways as to render the use of improved pavements practicable. This would place the surplus width inside the footwalks, where it could be parked and otherwise beautified at slight expense to the public and, in many instances, at the expense of the property bordering upon it, the owners of which, for the privilege of the use of the ground, would gladly beautify and adorn it."[28] The board was right; homeowners happily beautified the space that they perceived as their front yards, defining them with wrought-iron fences and planting ornamental shrubs and trees, and they continue to maintain their front spaces today. Through this device, as well as a concerted effort to plant street trees between the sidewalks and the curbs, many streets in Washington cultivated a leafy, green, park-like appearance (see fig. 28).

Figure 28. Row houses, 1000 block (north side) of Massachusetts Avenue NE. On Massachusetts Avenue, which is 160 feet wide, the 50-foot-wide roadway is flanked by 15-foot-wide sidewalks and a 40-foot-deep space that has been turned into front yards by the adjacent homeowners. (Photograph by the author, 2019)

The territorial government's Board of Public Works issued the city's first comprehensive building regulations on August 18, 1872. Distinguished architect Alfred B. Mullett sat on the board, occupying the position reserved for an engineer, but the regulations were authored by architect Adolf Cluss, whom the board had appointed inspector of buildings. Cluss had been born and educated in Germany before immigrating to the United States in 1848. He worked for the U.S. Coast Survey, the Navy Yard, and the Treasury Department, where he was in charge of one of the rooms in the Office of the Supervising Architect. During the Civil War he returned to the navy but also began a private practice. In 1874 he claimed to have "planned and supervised all public buildings now owned by the District of Columbia." Franklin School and Eastern Market are among the municipal buildings he designed; he was also the architect of the Smithsonian's Arts and Industries Building and a number of houses for wealthy clients. During an illustrious career that helped alter the built landscape of Washington, the development of these building regulations looms large.[29]

The new regulations, which applied only to the cities of Georgetown and Washington (i.e., the city defined by the L'Enfant plan), established order and provided for supervision. As Cluss noted, the previous guidance was "absolutely obsolete, imperfect, and defective." He took the "wise original provisions" of George Washington's order and subsequent amendments and put them into "one well systematized compilation."[30] The regulations evinced a concern for safety, both from fire and from unstable buildings. Coming soon on the heels of the devastating fire in Chicago, the regulations demonstrated a concern for one of the great dangers of city life. The regulations also provided for bay windows projecting onto public space, adopting the recent initiative of the Bowen administration.

The regulations required written applications for permits for construction and alterations of buildings. All projections beyond the building line—bay windows, steps, areas, and so forth—required a separate permit. The regulations established thicknesses of masonry walls, depending on the size of the building, and governed recesses and openings in them. All party walls had to be brought up six inches above the roof, and all roofs had to be "slate, tin, or other noncombustible roofing material." Wooden buildings were permitted, except in specified districts, but not within 24 feet of any masonry building and not taller than two stories. Wooden dwellings in rows more than 40 feet long had to have brick partition walls carried up through the roof. Reflecting public health concerns, the regulations prohibited dwellings with windows "on one side only," and every room intended for human habitation or sleeping had to be at least 8 feet high.[31]

Despite some success, "Boss" Shepherd gained enemies, and he increasingly used jobs and contracts for political advantage. Charges of corruption resulted in a congressional investigation, but Shepherd's greatest miscalculation was simple overspending: the city ran out of money in 1873. When Territorial Governor Henry Cooke resigned, President Grant appointed Shepherd to his post, but the Panic of 1873 (triggered in part by Henry Cooke's brother, Jay, a financier who went bankrupt) sent the city's finances into a tailspin. By then, Shepherd's improvements had cost nearly $21 million. Congress investigated again and in 1874 replaced the territorial government with a commission government, wholly appointed by Congress. In recognition of the strain the federal government put on local infrastructure, Congress also promised to bear half of the city's expenses. Although intended as a temporary measure, the commission form of government was made permanent in 1878, and Washingtonians lost a democratically elected government for a century.

After the ouster of Shepherd and the Board of Public Works, the commission government reissued Cluss's regulations with some minor changes but applied them to the whole District of Columbia. Taking effect on January 1, 1877, the regulations further controlled bay windows: if they extended more than three feet above the floor of the second story—in other words, were two or more stories high—they could not be wood. Brick bay windows, integrated with the brick wall of the house, became characteristic of Washington's larger row houses. Structures above the roofline, such as towers and dormer windows, had to be made of a noncombustible material. Wooden buildings were banished from all of the old city of Washington and were permitted only in part of Georgetown and in the rest of the District.[32]

The commissioners issued new building regulations four times in the 1880s. For the most part, the changes regarding row houses were minor. The 1887 regulations showed some concern for public health, requiring not only that rooms intended for human habitation be 8 feet high, but also that no permits be granted for buildings less than 12 feet wide or that fronted on an open space less than 20 feet wide. Oriel windows, defined as "a projection for a window above the first floor," were mentioned for the first time, and the regulations permitted bay windows, oriels, and towers to be of frame construction if they were covered with a fireproof material, but cornices had to be constructed entirely of noncombustible materials.[33] An inexpensive option for a fireproof cornice was brick corbeling, which was frequently employed.

Despite detailed restrictions on projections, a court case brought Congress's attention to these encroachments on public space. Mrs. Annie Cole owned a house near Thomas Circle, at the intersection of Massachusetts Avenue and M Street. She applied for a permit to put a sizeable addition on her house that would extend it to cover the adjacent triangle of land; the building inspector granted it on September 7, 1888. Although projections could not be more than 14 feet wide, one continuous projection ran 26 feet 6 inches along Massachusetts Avenue, around the apex of the triangle (where it maintained a 5-foot distance from the building line), and 29 feet along M Street, on the theory that the apex of the triangle formed a third building line from which projections could be calculated (see figs. 29 and 30).[34] Only 14 feet of

Figure 29. Annie Cole House, intersection of Massachusetts Avenue and Eighteenth and M Streets NW, site plan. Cole proposed an addition, on the right, that projected beyond the building line at every opportunity, taking the permission to project onto public space to extremes. (From Building Permit #468, September 11, 1888, National Archives and Records Administration, RG 351, annotated by Mark Schara)

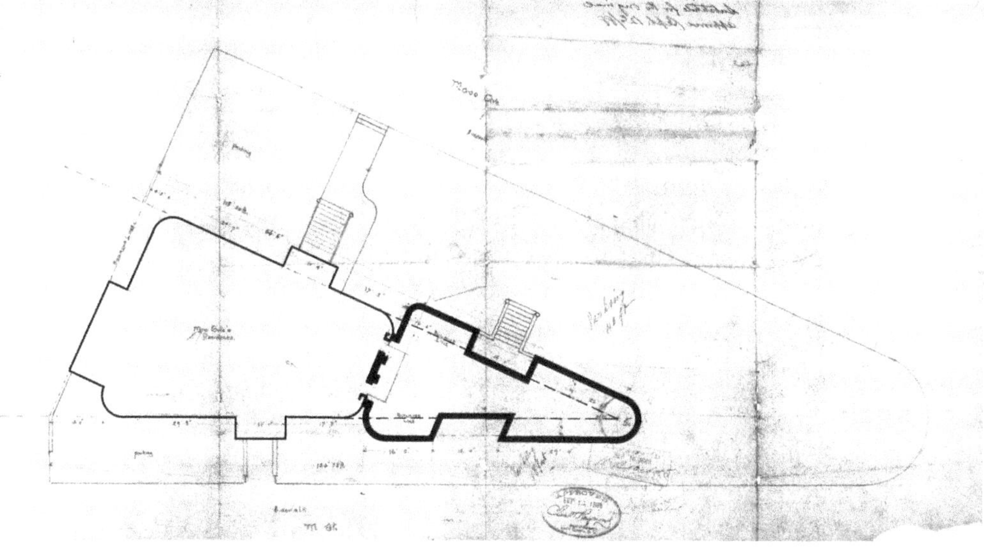

Figure 30. Annie Cole House. The three-story house's tower, bays, and oriel were the subject of litigation and legislation but were eventually allowed to stand. (Photographer unknown, ca. 1927–35, General Photograph Collection, DC History Center, CHS 12291)

the building remained at the building line along the 52-foot frontage on Massachusetts Avenue, and about the same on M Street, but Cole then asked the building inspector if she could put an oriel on the north side of the building and a glass conservatory on the south side. Her neighbors objected to the excessive projections and persuaded the U.S. government to sue Cole, the District commissioners, and the inspector of buildings.

The court ruled against Cole and the commissioners on December 23, 1889. While affirming the District's right to make and enforce building regulations and to permit projections beyond the building line, the court took issue with the projections of Cole's building that did not spring from the building line. Cole fought back by exerting influence in Congress, which enacted legislation benefiting her. Congress "ratified, without prejudice," permits for projections beyond the building line that the commissioners had granted—including Cole's. But henceforth, all projection permits had to be approved by the secretary of war, as well as the commissioners, increasing the time involved in gathering permits as well as adding a level of uncertainty. Meanwhile, to correct its vagueness, the District commissioners adopted a schedule of projections, which included restrictions for eleven kinds of projections, from height to width (depending on the width of the house) to depth (which differed for business streets and those with or without the parking strip and depended on street widths). It also included diagrams for angled walls, bowed projections, and corner towers.[35]

Building regulations continued to be issued, but the changes pertaining to houses were fairly minor. By the end of the century, separate regulations for plumbing, electric wiring, and elevators accompanied the building regulations. Lots could not be built on in their entirety (except for commercial structures); ten feet of the rear of the lot had to be left open, unless the lot faced on a wide alley. The regulations decreed that no dwelling could be less than 16 feet wide, but the ensuing outcry from owners wishing to subdivide 60-foot-wide lots into five smaller lots caused the commissioners to accommodate them, permitting houses that were only 12 feet wide, but only if they were on lots that had been previously platted.[36]

The city's form was set: it would be one of bay-fronted row houses. Nearly every new house built after the late 1870s hugged the front building line and many of them took advantage of the free public space in the form of a bay window. Narrower row houses aimed at working-class buyers might have forgone bay windows, but most new row houses 16 feet or wider sported a brick bay window extending the full height of the building. The gain in space was attractive to developers; the owner of a 16-foot-wide corner lot could add almost 25 percent to the size of the house through the judicious application of bay windows. And there were a lot of new houses; the city grew at a steady clip through the end of the nineteenth century, more than doubling in size between 1870 and 1900, with African Americans still forming about a third of the population of 278,718.[37]

These quarter-million people lived in a city that had acquired a modern infrastructure and a polished appearance. In 1887 another writer reflected on the Shepherd legacy: "In ten years from the time the Board of Public Works began its improvements, the city was transformed. The streets were covered with an almost noiseless, smooth pavement; fifty thousand shade-trees had been planted; the old rows of wooden, barrack-like houses had given place to dwellings of graceful, ornate architecture; blocks of fine business buildings lined Pennsylvania Avenue and the other prominent thoroughfares; blossoming gardens and luxuriant parks were to be seen on all sides; the squares and circles were adorned with the statues of heroes, and bordered with costly and palatial mansions; splendid school-houses, churches, market buildings, newspaper offices had been erected. The water-works and sewer system were unequaled in the country. Washington had risen fresh and beautiful, like the Uranian Venus, from stagnation and decay."[38]

Progressive Reform and Zoning, 1900–1945

By the end of the nineteenth century, the L'Enfant-designed city was fairly well built out, and developers looked beyond its boundaries, especially to the area north of present-day Florida Avenue (then Boundary Street). Subdivisions had been established in the county after the Civil War, first facilitated by horsecars, and then after 1888 by electric streetcars. Congress and the commissioners attempted to control this development and make it accord with the L'Enfant plan, most effectively with the 1898 Highway Act, which authorized the creation of a plan for extending L'Enfant's design into the former county but exempted those subdivisions that had been planned before 1893.[39]

Congress and the commissioners also enacted legislation to control the height of buildings in the District. In 1894, in response to the construction of the 165-foot-high Cairo apartments, the commissioners decreed that buildings in residential areas could be no higher than the width of the street on which they faced. Congress passed similar legislation in 1899, then in 1910 adopted legislation that restricted buildings' height to the width of their street plus 20 feet, except for Pennsylvania Avenue downtown, where a 160-foot height was permitted.[40] The height act had an indirect effect on row houses, eliminating tall apartment buildings as a solution for housing a burgeoning population. Instead, row houses would spread into the District beyond the old city of Washington.

The District's population growth continued, ballooning during World War I. Congress imposed rent controls on housing (mostly because the congressmen themselves could not a find affordable housing), which lasted from 1918 to 1925. The city's population grew by a third in the 1910s and again in the 1930s, when the expansion of the federal government due to Franklin D. Roosevelt's New Deal and the buildup to World War II brought many people to Washington. Again, they faced a housing shortage, and again Congress imposed rent control, which lasted from 1941 to 1953.[41] Beginning in 1937, redlining of federally backed mortgages, which labeled most African American neighborhoods as undesirable, discouraged reinvestment and increased racial segregation. In 1950, the District reached its population peak of a little more than 800,000, with African Americans still forming about a third of the total. Until the late 1920s, row houses continued to be a popular option for new residences.

Shortly after the turn of the century, the new row houses began to look dramatically different from the old ones, due to yet another regulation. The change derived from concerns about adequate light and air for residents. Consistent with Progressive Era exposures of unsanitary and unhealthful

Figure 31. Bethune House, 1318 Vermont Avenue NW. Built in 1875, long before regulations limited the size of open courts, this house had a court that was 6 feet wide and 33 feet long. (Jack E. Boucher, photographer, 1993, Library of Congress, Prints and Photographs Division, HABS)

living conditions, which is discussed in more detail in chapter 4, the focus in Washington dwelt on narrow courts that did not permit light and air to penetrate occupied spaces and thus aided in the spread of disease. The climate was another concern; as the newspaper wrote of dwellers in apartment buildings with small interior courts: "There are no front door-yards or parkings in which the occupants of such a dwelling can refresh themselves in summer. They must vacate their apartments for the parks or the street cars and return later to sleep in hot and stuffy rooms."[42]

The solution, as put forth in a December 1, 1905, regulation, was to restrict the total coverage of the lot and to limit open courts to a minimum of 4 feet wide. On row houses, an open court was the space created by the back building (see fig. 31). The width of the court had to increase if the building was taller than 20 feet, or if the court was longer than 20 feet. For example, the house at 1524 T Street NW was 30 feet tall, so its 4-foot-wide court would have had to be one foot wider to conform to the new regulation, narrowing the already-narrow back building (see fig. 10).[43]

The application of this open-court regulation to row houses, as well as apartment buildings, caused a rethinking of the row-house form. As the newspaper noted, this regulation affected "houses on narrow lots, which usually have back buildings," because it would "make it impossible to put a back building on a narrow lot." Recent changes in expectations for buildings—which included more rooms, the elimination of the basement dining room, and "the need, or supposed need, of having the kitchen on the main or first floor instead of in the basement"—had resulted in more rooms on the first floor.[44] But the change in regulations meant that a back building, which is where additional rooms would usually be accommodated, was impractical, especially in a house 16 or 17 feet wide.

Detached and semi-detached houses were the preferred alternatives, although more expensive. Many new detached houses were bungalows, which by 1916 the newspaper had declared "among the most popular types of detached residences, and that each spring sees more and more of them built in and around the National Capital." The bungalow had initially met with doubts, with naysayers arguing that "they never would prove popular with Washington people . . . because bungalows didn't have upstairs living rooms and English basements," a reference to the English-basement plan.[45] By the time the bungalow caught on, the basement kitchen was on the way out.

But row houses, too, tried to accommodate the new regulations. The solution was a wider lot and a quadrant plan, which dispensed with the back building and court (see fig. 32). Porches in the front and sleeping porches

Figure 32. Row houses, 612–42 Princeton Place NW. Developers built quadrant-plan row houses by the hundreds in the early twentieth century. (National Photo Company, ca. 1919, Library of Congress, Prints and Photographs Division)

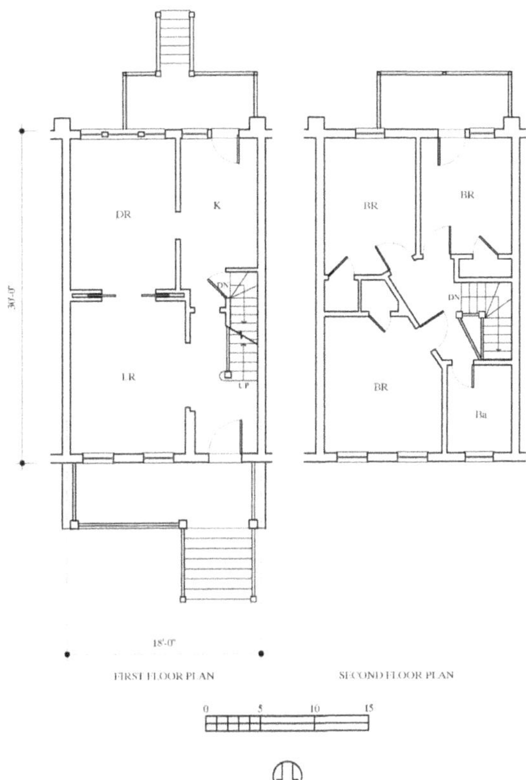

Figure 33. Row house, 1317 C Street NE, plans. In this quadrant-plan house, built by developer Harry Kite in 1913, the second-floor bathroom is in the front of the house, ventilated by a window. (Ruben Melendez, Onairis Perez, and Mark Schara, delineators, 2019)

in the rear characterized these quadrant-plan row houses, which were built by the hundreds between 1906 and the late 1920s. Front porches that projected beyond the building line, which were not mentioned in the building regulations until the 1891 schedule of projections addressed them, could be 4 or 5 feet deep, depending on the width of the street, and they could be almost as wide as the house.[46]

Another aspect of this new type of row house was the placement of the second-floor bathroom. Initially, regulations required bathrooms to have a window to the outside, so builders located the bathroom on an exterior wall, either in the front or back of the house, which left room for one bedroom next to the bathroom, and two on the opposite wall (see fig. 33). In 1909, the building regulations allowed bathrooms to be ventilated by operable skylights, markedly changing the row-house plan.[47] Then the bathroom could sit between the two bedrooms on an interior wall, so that one bedroom stretched across the whole width of the house, usually the front, and two smaller ones were located on the back wall (see fig. 34). By the 1920s bathrooms in row houses were routinely placed in the interior, ventilated and lit by skylights.

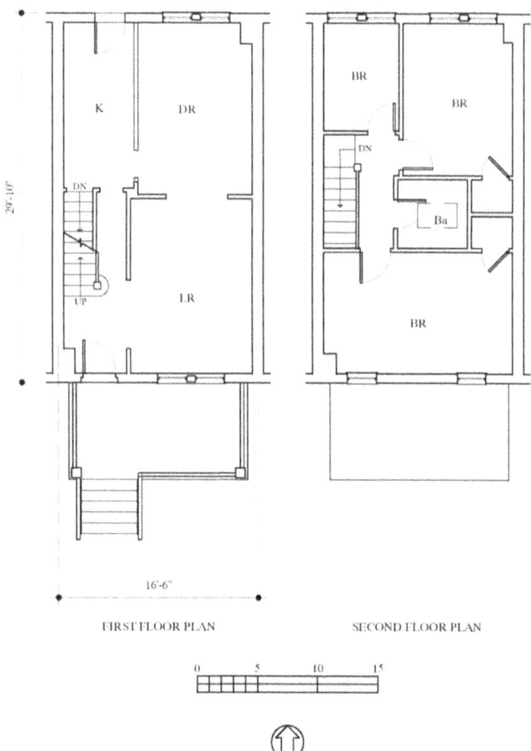

Figure 34. Row house, 1430 D Street NE, plans. This quadrant-plan house, built by developer B. H. Gruver in 1924, places the second-floor bathroom on the interior, ventilated by a skylight. These are conjectural original plans; the bathroom has been enlarged and the closets removed. (Ruben Melendez, Onairis Perez, and Mark Schara, delineators, 2019)

In 1911, the *Evening Star* noted the change in row houses, from an L-plan to a quadrant plan: "In recent days the back building has practically vanished along with the basement dining room. The building lots are wider, even for houses of moderate cost."[48] Lighter-colored brick, one-story porches with white columns, and compact dimensions of about 20 by 30 feet characterized the new row house, which spread across the new subdivisions just beyond the old city boundaries. Developers built longer rows, so that they stretched the full length of a square. In the 1910s thousands of these row houses sprang up, changing the face of the city. But soon objections arose.

The prejudice against row houses showed that they had become associated in the public mind with cheapness and lower-class dwellers. In 1912 the *Evening Star* reported somewhat warily that Harry Wardman, prolific developer of row houses, was training his sights on Chevy Chase Terrace in far Northwest Washington, where, if he were to develop it into row houses, it "will mark the farthest advance in this direction from the center of the city of houses in rows." With one exception, "the entire section north of Cleveland Park has been built up in the suburban manner with detached houses," and that consistency of appearance and class, it was implied, would be marred by the introduction of row houses. Opposition also arose to the construction of row houses in Dahlgren Terrace and Michigan Park in Northeast Washington. A decade later, the newspaper, in heralding a development of 140 detached houses on Jefferson and Kennedy Streets between Georgia Avenue and Fourteenth Street NW, suggested an aesthetic objection to row houses: "Instead of long rows of dwellings reaching uninterruptedly from block to block the streets would have a broken skyline of pleasing variation, with lawns and shrubbery separating the properties."[49]

Defenders of row houses pointed out their chief asset, which was that they were affordable. Economies of scale in building long rows meant that the houses would be cheaper, and narrow lots meant lower land costs for the developer and lower tax assessments for the homeowner. As a result, "the salaried employe can now own his own home on very reasonable terms . . . in a choice location." And row houses continued to be built. In 1926, when the *Evening Star* featured nine demonstration houses, two of them were row houses.[50]

A new way of regulating row houses appeared, and that was the zoning code of 1920. New York City had adopted the nation's first zoning code, which regulated use and density, only in 1916. Washington's zoning code, developed by noted planner Harland Bartholomew, controlled development through three overlays: Area (i.e., lot coverage), Use, and Height. The zoning commission regulated row houses through the Area designation by requiring that buildings in Area A have at least one side yard, effectively ruling out row houses. As mapped, this meant that "row houses cannot be put up in any part of town which they have not already invaded," as the newspaper summarized it. In 1920, the city had 39,000 row houses (which accommodated 71 percent of the city's population), compared to 13,000 detached and semi-detached houses, 7,500 flats, and 830 apartment buildings. By 1936 the residential designation had been subdivided into seven categories, restricting row houses further. As one report described the area in which row houses were permitted, it "surrounds down-town and is an old settled district." The limited area in which row houses were permitted reflected the undesirability that they had attained.[51]

A loophole of a sort was built into the zoning regulations, and developer Harry Wardman was there to exploit it. The 1920 zoning regulations included a definition for a "Community House: A group of not more than three buildings so designed as to give the appearance of a single building and erected simultaneously" (see fig. 35). The regulations allowed a community house to waive the requirements of side yards in Area A provided that the two side yards for the three houses were each at least 10 feet wide, enabling rows of

Walter A. Dunigan
Community Group Houses
Located at Marietta Park—
5th and Longfellow
Sponsored By The Star

The public is invited to come out and view these houses in their present stage of construction.

A Demonstration of Home, Beauty and Efficiency will be staged when these houses are completed.

Announcement Soon

Walter A. Dunigan
925 15th St. Main 4555

Figure 35. Advertisement for community group houses, Fifth and Longfellow Streets NW. As defined by the 1920 zoning code, community houses were three attached dwellings built at the same time and designed to look like one building. They were allowed in areas designated for single-family homes. This design was named one of the *Evening Star*'s Model Homes in 1926. (*Evening Star*, June 26, 1926, p. 35, reprinted with permission from the DC Public Library, Star Collection, © Washington Post)

three houses to be built in areas where longer rows were not permitted. In 1924, when the Zoning Commission considered changing this loophole, neighborhood groups in Woodley Park, Takoma Park, and Manor Park, all in Northwest, argued that "community houses are merely small groups of row houses" and that they "mar the appearance of detached neighborhoods and reduce values." Harry Wardman, who had built eighteen community houses in a neighborhood he called English Village at Thirty-Fourth Street and Woodley Road, objected, claiming that he was an altruistic benefactor. Unless he was permitted to build community houses on his land, "young married couples would not be able to get cheap rent but would be compelled to live in the crowded downtown section in one-room apartments instead of four or five rooms farther out." Wardman's lawyer called him "a philanthropist on whose activities depended the health and happiness of thousands of residents of Washington." Citizens' groups were unmoved and contended that "community houses are merely row houses broken into groups of three," but the Zoning Commission declined to act.[52]

The issue arose again a few years later, when Wardman opposed the rezoning of part of Manor Park to exclude semi-detached and community houses. He again positioned himself as selfless, invoking Commerce Secretary Herbert Hoover, who advocated better-quality and less expensive housing; Wardman claimed to be "actuated by the same incentive, to give wage earners homes at reasonable prices." He also argued that "the community group of three houses will only serve to break the monotony in the neighborhood." Herbert Wilson of the Manor Park Citizens Association inquired, "Who made the monotony?" and Wardman responded, "I made it, but you were the cause of it."[53] Apparently the parties reached a compromise, because Wardman built only semi-detached houses in the area in dispute.

The zoning code was so effective at restricting the areas in which row houses were permitted that it drove up the price of that land. In 1925 the Operative Builders' Association, composed of residential builders, alleged that "there is not enough row-house property at this time available through the zoning laws to keep the price of the property reasonable, despite the fact that three out of every four houses built are row houses." As a result, "residents will be deprived of the benefits of living within the District, or if they do, they will have to live in apartments." The shortage of land zoned for row houses continued; twenty years later, in the midst of the post–World War II housing shortage, "Few of the row-type or 'group' houses now are being built in the District area owing to the scarcity of land on which such building is authorized by zoning regulations."[54]

Urban Renewal and Historic Preservation, 1945–2000

The federal government's impact on private housing in the last half of the twentieth century was profound. In addition to furthering programs begun in the 1930s, such as mortgage insurance and public housing, the government also undertook highway construction and urban redevelopment, helping to remake the American landscape. The programs tended to favor suburban, single-family houses and encourage the turn away from aging, urban row houses. In Washington, plans focused on moving some federal agencies to the suburbs to disperse the population, and highway construction facilitated commuting from suburbs to center city and back out again. Shoring up the existing building stock and its residents was not on the federal agenda. The city's total population fell, with the white population dropping by about a third in the 1960s and again in the 1970s, while the African American population grew by 40 percent in the 1960s and by 50 percent in the 1970s. By 1960, with a population of 763,956, Washington was a majority-Black city, and in 1976, Black people formed 77 percent of the population.[55]

Although many of the federal programs affected row houses by shifting populations and federal support away from them, one program in particular had ramifications for Washington: the urban renewal of Southwest Washington, an undertaking that both took row houses away—demolishing them by

Figure 36. Southwest, looking northeast toward Capitol. This community of small row houses drew the interest of urban renewal advocates. Its proximity to the U.S. Capitol was part of its attraction as a demonstration area. (David Myers, photographer, 1939, Library of Congress, Prints and Photographs Division, Farm Security Administration)

the thousands—and introduced new row houses in a reworked landscape.[56] By 1945, urban planners saw Southwest Washington as a slum, with several surveys to prove it. This neighborhood within sight of the Capitol promised to be an excellent demonstration ground for new government programs. The area was clearly definable, located south of the Mall, west of the old canal, and north and east of the river. The removal of a largely African American and poor population was effected seemingly without qualms on the part of many.

Early assessments of the area found it to be a charming, if dilapidated, row-house neighborhood (see fig. 36). In a 1942 study that looked at a portion of Southwest Washington for wartime housing, Arthur Goodwillie of the Home Owner's Loan Corporation described the area: "Streets are wide, and well shaded. Water, light and sewer mains, sidewalks and pavements are in place, paid for and well maintained. Side by side with decrepit frame structures are some 2,900 substandard but basically sound brick buildings, usually in rows, virtually all of which can be saved and are well worth saving." In 1951 landscape architect Elbert Peets, commissioned by the National Capital Planning Commission, developed a plan that advocated preserving and rehabilitating many of the houses, maintaining the street plan, and also preserving the socioeconomic character of the neighborhood. The Redevelopment Land Agency thought this was not bold enough, however, so it contracted with architects Louis Justement and Chloethiel Woodard Smith, who proposed vast demolition, innovative rebuilding, and a shift to middle- and upper-middle-class residents. Planner Harland Bartholomew, who had maintained his connection with the city after developing the zoning code in 1920, produced a compromise plan that drew on aspects of both, but even that was altered as circumstances shifted. Beyond revitalizing a neighborhood, the goals were to bring back middle-class residents who had fled to the suburbs and thereby increase the tax base.[57]

Southwest was the site of some of the oldest buildings in the District, located along the Potomac and Anacostia Rivers. Like the rest of the old city, Southwest filled with row houses in the last half of the nineteenth century. The population was racially mixed, with a large Jewish component. As development intensified in the late nineteenth century, Southwest's blocks also filled with alley dwellings, cramped dwellings not equipped with running water. By 1950 the neighborhood's population of 23,416 was 69 percent African American, mostly unskilled laborers. When the Redevelopment Land Agency surveyed the buildings in 1951, it found only 4 percent of them in "good" condition, 40 percent "obsolescent," and 56 percent "blighted." In the first area to be redeveloped, Area B (bound by Fourth, I, and South Capitol Streets and the freeway then in the planning stages), 80 percent of the housing was substandard, with 58 percent dependent on outside toilets, 31 percent without running water, and 29 percent without electricity. Despite impoverished conditions, the neighborhood was home to growing families and a vibrant culture. After the 1954 Supreme Court decision *Berman v. Parker* reaffirmed the government's right to seize property for urban renewal, residents were relocated across the city. Earlier plans for rehousing old residents in the new construction had been dropped in favor of upscaling the neighborhood.[58]

The new Southwest, constructed between 1956 and 1970, involved ten separate complexes with different architects and developers. The 5,900 dwelling units were spread among high-rise apartments and row houses (called town houses), along with a few two-story apartment buildings and larger low-rise, three- and four-story apartment buildings. The architectural appearance was, with one exception, modernist, complemented by landscape designs. As architectural historian Richard Longstreth has claimed, "No better embodiment of urban design ideals of the mid-twentieth century can be found in the United States."[59]

The role of the row house in this modernist utopia bears examination. Chloethiel Woodard Smith, first in partnership with Nicholas Satterlee and then as head of her own firm, was charged with the design and development of Area B. Smith produced five apartment towers and 323 town houses in an ensemble called Capitol Park, completed between 1959 and 1963. The town houses were clustered in groups, some in U-shaped arrangements around parking lots, with the backs of the houses facing each other across common green spaces, or in quadrangles with open corners. The superblock, with only Third and G Streets remaining between Fourth, Delaware, I, and the freeway, was divided into clusters of town houses with pathways, passageways, and breezeways among them, producing changing views and an interesting pedestrian experience (see fig. 37). The careful separation of pedestrian and automobile, as well as the common open spaces, suggested new approaches to urban living. The modern architecture was angular; brick walls were painted in one of six light shades and crowned with sharp-edged cornices and restrained ornament, such as shutters or iron railings (see fig. 38). The eighty-one houses in the first section, west of Third Street and adjacent to the first apartment building, had six different designs, mostly 16 feet wide and 30 or 32 feet deep, two and three stories (see figs. 20 and 21). A few were 18 feet wide and had garages on the first floor.[60] Most houses had paved terraces in the rear, demarcated by shrubbery, while some had balconies.

In an application for a 1964 award, Smith described the design problem, in part: "To develop a group of two and three story units for families who want to live in the center of the city, want the advantages of town house living but prefer to rent. . . . To provide several two and three bedroom plans and attempt to give sufficient variety in arrangement and design to counteract the

Figure 37. Capitol Park, Southwest Washington. In this redeveloped area, row houses (called town houses) are grouped so that their backyards form intimate courtyards. (Photographer unknown, ca. 1960s, Library of Congress, Prints and Photographs Division, PR13 CN 2010:100, C. W. Smith container 211, folder 37)

Figure 38. Capitol Park, Southwest Washington. The modernist row houses are angular, with restrained ornament, and painted in pastel colors. (Photographer unknown, ca. 1960s, Library of Congress, Prints and Photographs Division, PR13 CN 2010:100, C. W. Smith container 211, folder 36)

growing public resistance to the standard red brick garden apartment and at the same time keep cost low enough so that rents will attract a major market." Her explanation of the design solution included this description: "Six basic units, all air conditioned, were developed, and fenestration, balconies and sun control devices varied for different orientation and location. Sliding doors and windows were used throughout. . . . The large glass doors, balconies with spiral stairs, terraces and varied exterior colors had not been tried in this city before, and it appears that these plus the extensive landscaping are important elements in attracting families back to the center of the city." The brochure to market these dwellings advertised, "Your private entrance courtyard leads to a home with spacious rooms for living and entertaining. Wide sliding glass doors open on your private garden, screened with holly hedges and handsome flowering shrubs. Floor-to-ceiling picture windows look out across the sweep of park, fountains and handsome sculpture."[61] The emphasis on the outdoors—gardens, parks, and sliding glass doors to provide access and views—seemed aimed at suburbanites who might have valued large yards, while the mention of a variety of designs and colors, as well as the short rows, tried to distinguish this complex from stereotypical row houses.

The development was critically well received. One sharp journalist noted: "This new town will have the advantages of Georgetown, the old town within the City with its pleasant individual town houses with quiet gardens near parks and schools yet close to the shops and galleries. It is especially interesting that Mrs. Smith and Mr. Satterlee, both members of the firm of Satterlee & Smith . . . are residents of Georgetown and live in houses of traditional design."[62] Many descriptions of Southwest likened it not to its previous row-house building fabric, but to Georgetown, where a new wave of white residents were "rediscovering" the attractions of small row houses and urban density. Georgetown also implied a social acceptance that old Southwest had lacked.

The other complexes in Southwest Washington provided a variety of concepts and designs. One of the bolder ones, River Park, was designed by Charles Goodman and completed in 1963. That site, bounded by N, O, and Fourth Streets and Delaware Avenue, contained an apartment building and 134 town houses. The complex was sponsored by Reynolds Metal Co., and the buildings displayed a free use of aluminum, including dramatic barrel-shaped roofs on the town houses. On the more conservative end of town-house design, Town Square, located west of Capitol Park, included an apartment building along with town houses designed by Macomber and Peter, completed in 1967. The developer described these two- and three-story town houses as "in the Federal manner, with a 'Georgetown flavor.'"[63] Many of these brick town houses had mansard roofs and raised first floors over habitable basements.

The rest of the developments tended to feature a combination of apartment buildings and town houses in a modernist vein. While the apartment buildings housed most of the population, the town houses provided an intimate feel to the neighborhood, grouped in rows of fewer than a dozen and oriented to each other perpendicular to the street, as well as facing the street. Only a handful of houses had been saved from demolition, and those were incorporated into new developments, including the 1790s ensemble Wheat Row, which became part of Harbour Square, designed by Chloethiel Woodard Smith.

The evolution from "row house" to "town house" reveals the changing reputation of the building form. By the mid-twentieth century, row houses had come to be associated with monotony, shabbiness, and lower-class dwellers. Yet they had obvious virtues: besides being less expensive than detached houses, they also gave each family its own entrance and yard. The term "town house" was a way to obscure the suspect reputation of the row house and market it to a new generation. Although "town house" had traditionally referred to an in-town mansion, in contrast to a country one, it became synonymous with the row house. As one newspaper article noted, "You might say that the town house is a row house with class."[64]

By the time the new Southwest was completed in 1970, 5,900 new units of housing had been constructed. Although policy makers hoped for racial integration in the new housing, the neighborhood's population of nearly 70 percent African American before the redevelopment had flipped to about 70 percent white by 1970. The socioeconomic class had also changed, with the median household income tripling with the new population. In subsequent decades, though, these numbers shifted again, as the neighborhood became majority Black by 2000 and housing prices remained moderate in comparison to the rest of the city.[65]

Yet one of the Southwest redevelopment's scarring legacies is that twenty-three thousand people, mostly poor Black residents, had been ousted from their homes, and a 550-acre neighborhood had been razed.[66] A redevelopment of this magnitude was never attempted again. The racial implications of redevelopment, here and elsewhere, were clear, with the bitter analogy of "urban renewal" to "Negro removal." Southwest's redevelopment helped fuel civil rights protests in Washington, where segregation, highway plans, and inferior treatment boiled over into a violent uprising in 1968. The high-handed treatment of the majority-Black residents by presidentially appointed white commissioners could not stand, and in 1967 President Lyndon Johnson appointed a mayor-commissioner and a city council, the majority of whom were Black. Finally, in 1974, District residents achieved limited home rule, with a popularly elected mayor and city council, although citizens remain without full representation in the House and Senate.

Inner-city ills and the aspirations of the Black middle class pushed and pulled African Americans to the suburbs; between 1970 and 1980 the African American population of Prince Georges County, Maryland, adjacent to Washington, grew by 170 percent. This outmigration contributed to Black people again becoming a minority in Washington in the 2010s. The city's population, which had peaked at 800,000 in 1950, fell below 600,000 by 2000; it has since rebounded to nearly 700,000.[67]

Another governmental effort in the second half of the twentieth century affected row houses, elevating them in reputation as well as value. A historic preservation movement that focused on neighborhoods, not just individual buildings, inevitably addressed row houses and the way that they created a sense of place in certain in-town areas. The Old Georgetown Act of 1950 created the first historic district in the District. The portion of Washington that predated the creation of the District, Georgetown had a reputation as a colonial village, although most of its buildings date from later in the nineteenth century. Bypassed by intensive development in the late nineteenth and early twentieth centuries, Georgetown had lost industrial and commercial preeminence and gained a significant African American population. In the 1920s and 1930s, an influx of white government workers had settled in Georgetown,

Figure 39. Row houses, 2900 block of N Street NW. Small row houses line narrow streets in Georgetown, the site of the first historic district in the city, created in 1950. (Photograph by the author, 2022)

finding its row houses charming rather than dilapidated (and providing an acceptable analogy for town houses in Southwest) (see fig. 39). The political power of these new residents resulted in the designation of a historic district, in which alterations and demolitions would be reviewed by the U.S. Commission of Fine Arts. African American residents of Georgetown attributed these preservation efforts to their displacement, decimating a once-vibrant Black community.[68]

Like many communities that experienced a loss of historic fabric due to redevelopment and highway construction in the 1950s and 1960s, white Washingtonians sought to put the brakes on demolitions through historic preservation. The National Capital Planning Commission established the Joint Committee on Landmarks in 1964 to designate landmarks and refer them to the National Register of Historic Places, but it was DC Law 2–144, the DC Historic Landmark and Historic District Protection Act of 1978, that put teeth in the landmark process. By this law, all applications for permits for demolition and alteration of designated buildings had to be reviewed by the DC Historic Preservation Review Board, which had the power to deny the permits. In the face of development pressures, this was a way to preserve the scale and history of historic row-house neighborhoods. Today the city has sixty-nine historic districts encompassing more than twenty-eight thousand historic buildings, many of them row houses.[69] The list includes nineteenth-century neighborhoods such as Capitol Hill and Dupont Circle and twentieth-century ones such as Woodley Park and Foxhall Village.

Over the past half century, row houses in some neighborhoods have become desirable and expensive. Historic preservation law protects visible exteriors, emphasizing the street face and *tout ensemble* of row houses. The interiors have met with much more change. A move toward restoration in the 1960s, with young homeowners stripping paint from oak balusters, uncovering sealed fireplaces, and patching plaster walls, has evolved into contractors gutting interiors and removing original fabric in order to install central air-conditioning and open plans. Gentrification in Washington is so widespread—with the population shifting back to minority Black by 2015—that it cannot be attributed to historic preservation alone, but the rising price of real estate in the city means that gentrification is economic, and row houses in in-town neighborhoods are increasingly out of reach for middle-class residents. Gentrification is also clearly racial; with FHA-backed mortgages not available to Black people in neighborhoods into which they had been restricted (as is explained in chapter 4), Blacks had fewer opportunities for the kind of wealth accumulation that would have enabled them to buy into gentrified neighborhoods.

Government programs affected privately owned buildings in every American city. Washington may have been subject to more of this than most cities because of its unique role as a city that the federal government sees as its own backyard in which to experiment or model programs. But governments intervene in different ways in different cities, so that local architecture develops differently in response to the constraints that governments impose. Most obviously, in Washington the bay fronts resulted from the wide streets of L'Enfant's plan and ordinances permitting projections onto it, but other constraints—such as the size of courts or the zoning for community houses—have also influenced Washington's row houses. The next two chapters flesh out the row houses that resulted from these constraints.

3

Facades

With the two-dimensional plans having been laid out in the first chapter, and the regulatory constraints in the second, the next two chapters examine row houses in three dimensions, outside and in. This chapter focuses on the facade of the row house, that sliver of a public statement that connects a building's plan and internal workings to its neighbors and neighborhood, to its builder's and owner's aspirations, and to architectural fashion (see fig. 40). With a row house's form tightly circumscribed by its adjoining neighbors, the designer uses the front facade to demonstrate style, suggest the plan, and attract buyers. With the facade the designer can evoke status, hierarchy, intent, and a host of meanings, while at the same time providing one of the hallmarks of modern real estate business, "curb appeal." This chapter begins by examining fashions expressed in the facade in the context of influences and constraints on the plan. Next, the chapter delves into two departures from the prevailing aesthetic: first, an instance where one architectural mode was deployed to attract certain residents and counteract the row house's reputation as being lower class and undesirable, and, second, a few experiments with modernism, a starkly different approach. Finally, the discussion turns to the dominance of the Colonial Revival facade for row houses in the mid-twentieth century and its wide-ranging effects on their gentrification and preservation.

Most of the row housing built for the middle and lower classes was built speculatively, for an investor, not for a specific future occupant, and for this class of housing, architects and consumers played a less influential role in design than builder-developers. The facade was essential to appeal to buyers and renters, even if subconsciously. The person most conversant with architectural trends, the architect, had a relatively small role in the design of speculative row houses, except in a few cases such as the ones discussed below. Often the builder or owner listed himself as the architect on the building permit or left the "architect" line blank, indicating a fluid understanding of the role of the architect, especially in the nineteenth century.[1]

Client-driven row houses were, of course, a different situation, one in which the homeowner was often heavily involved and the architect responded to the homeowner's erudition and taste. Noted architects, who saw every commission as bearing on their reputation, designed a few speculative row houses with reference to architectural trends and publications, and some even published in the latter. For example, *The Brickbuilder* published a photograph and floor plans of a row of six houses at 1810–20 Nineteenth Street NW, in 1906 (see fig. 41). Prominent architects Wood, Donn and Deming designed varied exteriors in a vaguely Spanish Colonial mode for these elegant row houses with similar floor plans.[2] Many speculative row houses, though, were designed by journeyman architects who followed rather than led, and who will be discussed more thoroughly in the next chapter.

Figure 40. Row houses, 1520–32 T Street NW. This row of seven houses, built as an investment in 1891, has elaborate facades arranged as an ensemble, but the houses were not large, each offering just 1,650 square feet of living space. See also figs. 9 and 10. (Justin Scalera, photographer, 2018, Library of Congress, Prints and Photographs Division, HABS)

The consumer was an uncertain factor in the design of speculative row houses, so developers tended to adhere to conservative modes that the investor knew would be successful in the marketplace. Outlandish or avant-garde forms of expression faced the prospect of not selling. And while the facade of a building undoubtedly had a subconscious effect on potential occupants, especially the first time they encountered the house, buyers and renters were far more concerned about factors other than exterior appearance when they were considering a place to call home. In a study of a late nineteenth-century row-house neighborhood in Boston, Margaret Supplee Smith and John C. Moorhouse found that lot and house size and neighborhood characteristics accounted for most (74 percent) of the increased value. Architectural style and features accounted for 14 percent, but the buyers' concern was more for ornament that would differentiate a row house from its neighbors than for ad-

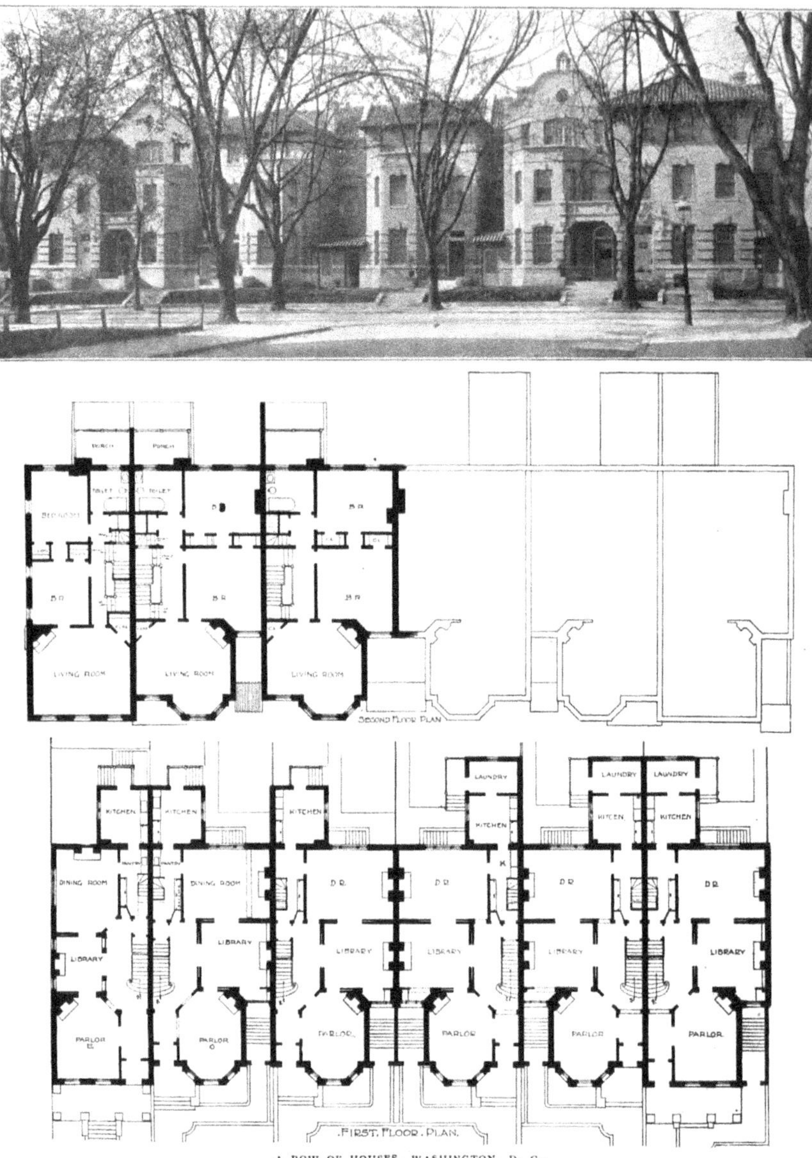

Figure 41. Row houses, 1810–20 Nineteenth Street NW. The prominent architectural firm of Wood, Donn and Deming designed a row of six houses near Dupont Circle in a Spanish Colonial style. (*The Brickbuilder* 15, no. 11 [November 1906]: 234, courtesy of the University of Virginia Library)

herence to a stylistic standard. Similarly, in a smaller study in Washington, Marcia McAdoo Greenlee found that African American residents were drawn more to the large size of a house than to its aesthetics, describing their block as, for instance, "they were just row houses."[3] A house's style was rarely promoted in late nineteenth-century advertisements, whereas its material—brick or especially stone—was seen as a selling point. In early twentieth-century ads, "colonial" was widely used to denote a light-colored brick house with a front porch and quadrant plan and, as this chapter discusses, Old English was promoted in opposition to that. Mostly, though, consumers were not interested in exterior appearance except as it conveyed a general respectability.

Builders, who were either owners of speculative row houses, or who answered to investors, undoubtedly had the most involvement with the appearance of their creations. They were not inclined to be dogmatic followers of architectural trends and styles. As Thomas Hubka has pointed out for modest houses more broadly, builders tended to reach a local consensus on design, usually based on common floor plans. For row houses, the few floor plans that serve as the organizing principle for this book reflected this consensus among builders. Builders began with the floor plan then current, adjusted it for the width of the lot by adding or subtracting a side hall and widening or narrowing a bay window, for example, and then they considered the front of the house, using ornament to differentiate their rows and sometimes to make houses in a row seem more individual. The use of brick corbeling, pedimented rooflines, chamfering at the corners of otherwise-rectangular bay windows, stained glass in the upper portions of windows—these and other flourishes served to make one builder's row house, he hoped, superior to or at least distinctive from others.[4]

Builders were not constrained by the materials available to them. From its founding, Washington had timber nearby, soil suitable for brickmaking, and the ports of Georgetown and Alexandria to receive shipments of other materials. Within a few decades, the Chesapeake and Ohio Canal and a number of railroads increased the shipping and receiving capability. As early as 1809 a glassmaking factory on the Potomac River in Foggy Bottom advertised window glass. By 1850 Washington had three iron foundries and one lumber mill powered by water, and a few years later, a steam-powered sash and blind factory offered those critical components for houses. As one observer claimed in 1885, "There are many brickyards in this vicinity, and a superior sort of brick is made in them, the clay of the region being particularly adapted to brickmaking. The brick has a bright red color, very pleasing to the eye." By 1887 Washington boasted 22 brick dealers and brickmakers, 20 lumber dealers, and 21 stone and marble yards. Several decades later, the newspapers continued to praise local materials, including not only high-quality brick but also concrete, with broken stone barged in from quarries and combined with locally dredged sand and gravel. Other building materials, such as lumber, stone, and steel, were easily shipped in. The newspaper claimed that "California redwood and Oregon pine can be brought to [Potomac River] wharves for a song in the way of freight rates."[5]

Architectural Fashion to 1920

Despite the fact that speculative row houses were not rendered in high style, and were not intended to be, by consensus they followed larger architectural trends. Within their tightly constrained forms, row houses reflected current fashion in their plans, materials, and ornament. A brief review of the general architectural trends of the nineteenth and early twentieth centuries shows their influence on the common understanding of what a row house should look like. Most of that was expressed in one place—the facade—but the plan also evolved as styles changed.

The classicism that ruled when the city was established proved a challenge for row-house builders because it relied on symmetry, which did not adapt easily to row houses, as a basic orientation. Most row houses were three bays wide, and the door was in an end bay, so that the hall would be to one side of a main room. This immediately upset any hope of symmetry. One effort to achieve balance in row houses was seen in Wheat Row, where four row houses were gathered under one hipped roof with a pediment over the four central bays. In addition, the window and door arrangement was flipped, achieving balance and symmetry (see figs. 3 and 4).

Architectural historians have called the three-bay, side-hall plan "two-thirds Georgian"—a somewhat awkward phrase indicating a Georgian center-hall house without the rooms on one side of the center hall.[6] While it might have been stylistically derived, the side-hall two-room plan was a functional solution for a row house, allotting as much width as possible for a parlor, with a narrow circulation system to one side. On row-house facades, cornices were modestly ornamented. Splayed lintels and keystones over the windows gave way to more delicately molded trim in the first decades of the nineteenth century. A columned portico could be reduced in size to frame a doorway for an elegant row house, but in speculative row houses this might be expressed by pilasters. Overall, smooth brick walls with white-painted wooden ornament and a harmonious repetition evoked the classicism in early nineteenth-century Washington (see fig. 42).

In the middle of the nineteenth century, architectural fashion made an abrupt shift toward the picturesque, which valued irregularity, asymmetry, rough textures, and dark colors. The publication in 1850 of Andrew Jackson Downing's *The Architecture of Country Houses* articulated this trend, while introducing new modes to American domestic architecture. Gothic cottages and Italian villas were depicted as detached houses on verdant, landscaped grounds. Washington row houses adopted some elements of these new trends, settling for an approximate Italianate, expressed by heavy bracketed

Figure 42. Cameron Row, 1000–02 Independence Avenue SW. Gilbert Cameron, a master stonemason working on the construction of the Smithsonian Museum across the street, built these two houses in about 1848. Aside from the oriel on the side, which was added later, these buildings serve as a good representation of the Greek Revival style applied to the row house, with thin columns framing the doorways. The houses, each with a two-room plan with side hall, were demolished in 1941. (John Brostrup, photographer, 1937, Library of Congress, Prints and Photographs Division, HABS)

cornices and a desire for asymmetry (see fig. 43). This worked well with the row-house plan, and the already asymmetric floor plan—side hall, main rooms opposite—added a wing out the back to create the L-shaped plan, furthering the imbalance. And when bay windows, which were also promoted by Downing, were permitted in Washington beginning in 1871, they amplified the asymmetry. Wooden bay windows with bracketed cornices could be applied to either wooden or brick facades. Critics liked the visual interest that bay windows provided, in contrast to the monotony of flat-fronted row houses. As one noted in *Harper's New Monthly Magazine* in 1875, "The old square barrack houses of brick have in many cases been pulled down and rebuilded in lighter forms, with Mansard-roofs, crotcheted pinnacles, airy verandas, and such a plentitude of bay-windows in all forms as to show the geniality of a climate and people and open-air habits."[7]

To emphasize the bracketed cornice and hoodmolds over the windows, a flat wall worked best. Pressed brick—a denser brick with a smooth finish—with thin mortar joints provided a flat surface on which the ornament's shadows would be cast. The heavy cornice also complemented another feature of

Figure 43. Row houses, 500 block (north side) Independence Avenue SE. Built before 1874, these typical Italianate row houses had flat fronts with bracketed cornices and hoodmolds over the doorway. Most of them had L-shaped plans. (Carol M. Highsmith, photographer, 2010, Library of Congress, Prints and Photographs Division, The George F. Landegger Collection of District of Columbia Photographs in Carol M. Highsmith's America)

Italianate row houses, which was the "flat" roof, sloping gently toward the rear. The cornice provided a termination of the facade, rendering the roof invisible.

The 1870s also saw a brief flourishing of the Second Empire style. Referring to the reign of Napoleon III in France, the Second Empire employed flat wall surfaces and contrasting ornament, like the Italianate mode, but with heavier ornament and more of it. The Second Empire was most recognizably denoted by the mansard roof. Although most mansard roofs sloped in four directions, a single mansard slope in the front of a row house was sufficient to evoke the style. In 1873, Adolf Cluss, the architect who drafted the first comprehensive building regulations in Washington, designed a prestigious row of Second Empire houses on K Street, at the corner of Connecticut Avenue (see fig. 44). The row consisted of three stone houses with mansard roofs, a corner tower, and two-story bay windows. Dormer windows, iron cresting on the rooftops, stone balustrades, and elaborate hoodmolds added to the busyness of the facade, bursting out of its constraints. Cluss himself owned the house in the middle, while Alexander Shepherd lived in the corner building. A more common adaptation of the Second Empire is found at 1318 Vermont

Figure 44. Shepherd's Row, K Street and Connecticut Avenue NW. An example of the Second Empire, Shepherd's Row had a prominent mansard roof, while dormers, bays, and other projections enlivened the facade. Territorial Governor Alexander Shepherd occupied the corner house, and the architect, Adolf Cluss, owned the house next door. Built in 1873, the row was demolished in 1952. (Photographer and date unknown, DC History Center, James H. Goode Capital Losses Slide Collection, GC06.20)

Avenue NW (see fig. 45). Here, a wooden bay window was affixed to a brick house, two stories tall with a prominent mansard roof. The house, 23 feet wide with a side-hall plan and back building, was built speculatively in 1875 and occupied in the twentieth century by African American activist Mary McLeod Bethune.[8]

In the late 1880s the Washington row house flourished, with more than a thousand built in most of the years between 1885 and 1892.[9] With building regulations requiring masonry construction, Washington became a red-brick city, a fitting material for the darker colors that were preferred by the Queen Anne and other late Victorian modes. Pushing irregularity and asymmetry, this fashion accommodated Washington's irregular street plan. Every acute-angled intersection or trapezoidal lot provided an opportunity for a tower; every front yard derived from the "parking" suggested a bay window and cast-iron stairs; and every alley alongside a house deserved an oriel. In an effort to avoid the monotony of earlier rows, a particular interest arose in ensembles, rows that differentiated among their constituents with a higher tower in the center house, or different shapes of bay windows. Examples include the seven buildings at 1520–32 T Street NW, modest two-story brick bay fronts, with the center and end houses marked by pediments and pyramidal roofs atop

Figure 45. Bethune House, 1318 Vermont Avenue NW. A more modest example of a mansard-roofed row house, this house built in 1875 in an L-shaped plan also had a one-story bay window. Civil rights activist Mary McLeod Bethune occupied this house as her home and office in the twentieth century. See also fig. 31. (Jack E. Boucher, photographer, 1993, Library of Congress, Prints and Photographs Division, HABS)

their bays (see fig. 40). In addition, the second-floor windows are segmental-arched in the featured buildings and elliptically arched in the others. The variation was superficial, though; the sizes and floor plans were identical, so the difference in cost was negligible.

Even if differentiation within the row was not possible, the row as a whole could be quirky and idiosyncratic. Queen Anne row houses attempted to assert their individuality by breaking through the confines of the box that is the usual rectilinear house. Bay windows were a natural for this, and with a change in the building regulations in 1882, multistory bay windows had to be masonry. While square bays made the most use of the allotted space, square bays with chamfered corners gained a little more ground, and the chamfering provided an opportunity for decoration. Flat expanses of wall were enlivened with molded brick panels. Windows received stained-glass transoms or small panes of glass. In 1885 an observer noted that "some of the latest houses erected have a good deal of ornamentation produced by means of brick-work. Bricks are constructed for the purpose after special designs. Large bricks, fan-shaped, octagonal, and in other forms, are set in the walls and in the arches over the windows and doors, giving variety and richness, and some very fine effects are produced in this way." While brick ornamentation might have been acceptable, wooden was not, according to one 1885 critic, who described the typical Washington house as a building "covered in meretricious ornamentation, its wooden and metal mouldings bedraggling cornice and lintel, and perching upon wooden bay-windows which were stuck into walls without a thought of harmony"[10] (see fig. 46).

Walls no longer ended in consistent cornices, but broke through to place a pediment or a visible roof—conical or pyramidal—on a bay. These flourishes gained little space in the attic, and behind them roofs were still flat, but they enlivened the streetscape (see fig. 1). The 1877 building code regulated a profusion of projections from the roofline, suggesting the options: "domes, cupolas, pavilions, towers, spires, pinnacles, buttresses, lanterns, louvres, lutheran or dormer windows, sky-lights, scuttles, ventilators, cornices and gutters."[11]

Inside, the Queen Anne row house's floor plan was as busy as its exterior. Colorful tiled foyers introduced the visitor to dark hallways. Bays, nooks, and fireplaces with decorative surrounds and overmantels broke out of the box of rectangular rooms. Rooms were separated by wide sliding doors to amplify the sense of space, and ceiling heights increased for a style that encouraged verticality. The reintroduction of the "great hall," echoing down the ages from medieval England, appeared in row houses as a reception hall. In the three-room plan, the entrance hall led past the parlor into this wider room, in which the opposite wall held a stairway with multiple turns and wood panel-

Figure 46. Mount Vernon Row, K and Tenth Streets NW. When a critic complained about "mouldings bedraggling cornice and lintel," he may have been thinking of these row houses, built in 1873 and since demolished. (Photographer and date unknown, DC History Center, James H. Goode Capital Losses Slide Collection, GC06.24)

Figure 47. Hay-Adams Houses, Sixteenth and K Streets NW. These two abutting houses were designed by the preeminent architect H. H. Richardson for Henry Adams and John Hay in 1884. With contrasting rough- and smooth-faced walls and a unifying hipped roof, the houses offered a more coherent design than the typical Queen Anne row houses. The Hay-Adams Hotel now occupies this site. (Photographer and date unknown, DC History Center, General Photograph Collection, CHS 13611)

ing. Behind this middle room was the dining room, so that the great hall was illuminated only by light borrowed from its neighboring rooms and perhaps a skylight over the stairs.

The excesses of the late Victorian modes of expression were not loved by all. Although he put his criticism in the voice of a fictional character, architect E. C. Gardner disapproved of the eclectic decoration of the Washington row house in 1887: "No matter how pinched the countenance may be, the face of the house must have windows and bay windows, dormer and oriel windows, cathedral windows and convent doors; it must have iron balconies, stone balconies and carved brick balconies; turrets and pinnacles; Norman arches and Queen Anne ellipses; gothic points and Elizabethan rectangles and curves; brass railings and copper crestings—anything and everything but simple dignity and evident fitness."[12]

In the 1890s, row houses took elements from the Romanesque-inspired vocabulary promoted by H. H. Richardson (see fig. 47). Rough stone exteriors were favored, although for speculative row houses, even a stone veneer was often prohibitively expensive, so stone was more often used as a facing for just the basement level of the front facade, or perhaps the lintels above the openings. At the same time, more coherent forms took over, so that square bays that jutted out from the facade were more likely to be replaced by rounded ones that flowed smoothly into the wall. Much of the applied ornament was discarded in favor of round-arched windows, doorways recessed in round arches, and an overall restraint.

At the dawn of the twentieth century, classicism reappeared and took hold. Builders of speculative row houses did not use Beaux-Arts styling often, but row houses began to display a new sense of order along with their modillioned cornices and restrained classical ornament. A sophisticated classical mode gained favor with elegant owner-occupied commissions, particularly in Northwest neighborhoods such as Kalorama, but this was less common in speculative row houses.

In the 1910s, builders and realtors gave the name "Colonial" to the majority of speculative row houses, which had light-colored brick, front porches with wood columns, tiled pent roofs, and the quadrant plan (see fig. 48). Ads read: "FOR SALE . . . 10 fine renting houses; colonial style; 20-foot front each; lots 140 feet deep; 6 rooms and bath; furnaces; houses about one year old," or "FOR RENT—39 V St., N.E., New 6 r. and b. colonial home," referring to the quadrant plan.[13] The colonial connection was murky—perhaps the white columns, or maybe the Spanish Colonial Revival evoked by the tile roofs—but the radically different plan did hearken back to English colonial styles. With its four rooms in the main mass of the house, and no projections out the front or rear, the quadrant plan's simplicity and straightforwardness returned to the "two-thirds Georgian" with a wide side hall and cohesive massing.

Not always welcomed, these row houses were built by the hundreds in

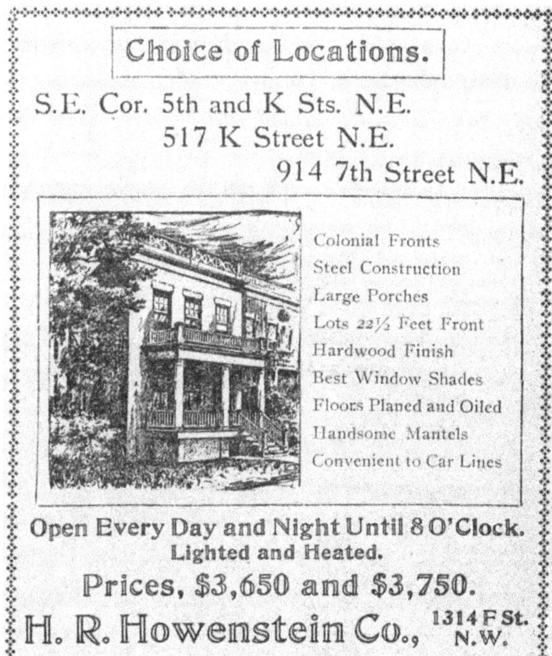

Figure 48. Advertisement, Northeast Washington. This ad for row houses at Fifth and K Streets NE heralds "Colonial Fronts" as a prominent feature. The illustration shows a balustraded porch and roofline. (*Evening Star*, January 3, 1910, p. 3, reprinted with permission from the DC Public Library, Star Collection, © Washington Post)

numbingly long rows in new neighborhoods in Northeast and eastern Northwest Washington. Their economical construction became a drawback when they became associated with lower-class dwellers. Their appearance also drew criticism, as in the description in the 1937 guide published by the Federal Writers' Project of the Works Progress Administration, which called them "disheartening rows of two-story houses with identical porches and faked tile 'rooflets.'"[14] Because of their association with the lower ranks of society and their monotonous appearance, row houses met with opposition from city planners and homeowners in the 1920s. Washington's new zoning code in 1920 severely limited the areas in which they could be built, as noted in the previous chapter. In response, there were several efforts to recast the row house into something more palatable. The developments of English Village and Foxhall Village in the 1920s illustrate some of the strategies employed by developers.

Old English

Developer Harry Wardman, whose career is discussed more fully in chapter 5, launched English Village in 1922 (see fig. 49). Located on four blocks southeast of the intersection of Woodley Road and Thirty-Fourth Street NW, the development was situated close to Wardman's eponymous hotel, built at Connecticut and Calvert in 1917, his own house at Connecticut and Woodley, and his other developments in Woodley Park. At English Village, Wardman

Figure 49. Advertisement, English Village. This ad for Wardman's English Village promoted its old English character and also promised modernity by including the image of a motorcar. (*Evening Star*, June 4, 1924, p. 3, reprinted with permission from the DC Public Library, Star Collection, © Washington Post)

Figure 50. Row houses, 3216–20 Klingle Road NW. In English Village, Wardman arranged row houses in groups of three to satisfy zoning requirements and decorated them with half-timbering, dark brick, and small-paned windows. (Photograph by the author, 2022)

signaled in three ways that this was not like his row-house developments east of Rock Creek. First, it was racially restricted, a subject that is discussed more fully in chapter 5. Like much of this section of Northwest, the deeds for English Village carried a clause prohibiting sale or rental of the land to "any negro or person of African blood."[15]

Secondly, Wardman made stylistic adjustments to appeal to the higher-class buyers he was seeking. The houses' facades evoked old English dwellings, with dark red or brown brick walls trimmed with limestone or concrete and complemented by faux half-timbering on some upper stories (see fig. 50). Quoins in contrasting materials were found at the edges of doorways or walls. Steep gable roofs covered with slate and terminating in stone coping also added to the feel. The windows had small panes, but the sashes were metal, as noted in the neighborhood's advertising, in order to be as modern as possible. Small bays and oriels were added for decorative effect, not in order to project beyond the building line, because these houses were well behind it. The landscape and architectural elements combined to foster an impression of buildings of ancient origins in an informal village. English-born Wardman did not define what he meant by an English village, except to note that he had recently been in England and had "gathered much important data and many ideas that will be used in the development."[16] By attaching the neighborhood through its architectural ornament and name to England, Wardman was suggesting that not just any whites, but those of English extraction or those who aspired to be, would be most welcome here. At a time of national concern over the influx of immigrants after World War I, and in the midst of the imposition of restrictions on immigration, Wardman tried to appeal to those who cherished America's English origins.

The third strategy, also addressing the appearance of the neighborhood, entailed avoiding association with row houses, which were prohibited by the newly imposed zoning in this area. So Wardman built "community houses," groups of three attached houses with 10-foot-wide side yards, which were permitted in Area A, the same area that the Zoning Commission designated for detached houses. The dwellings in English Village were designed to be as densely packed as possible while not actually being row houses.

The first phase of development, built in the summer of 1922, consisted of eighteen dwellings: three detached houses on Woodley Road, two blocks of community houses on Thirty-Fourth Street, and three blocks of community houses on the south side of Klingle Road. The architect was listed as Wardman himself, along with his chief architect, Eugene Waggaman, although historians suspect that a more accomplished architect in his office, Mihran Mesrobian, was the real designer. The newspaper called the development "a novel English village, with all the quaintness associated with such places in the old world" but, the advertising copy always hastened to explain, with "all the conveniences and necessities required in modern home building." As a subsequent article clarified, "These homes will be modern in every detail and will contain many new and attractive features. They will have breakfast and sleeping porches, hardwood floors and trim throughout, large back yards, metal window sashes and built-in garages." Wardman also touted the "unusual display of every electrical contrivance for comfort, convenience and ornamentation," and showed a car—a stylish roadster, no less—in an ad, signaling the suburban setting as well as modernity.[17]

Despite the Old World ornament and modern technology, the floor plan of the community houses was very familiar to Washingtonians—the quadrant. At 3216-18-20 Klingle Road, the end houses were a little more than 21 feet wide, while the middle one was 20 feet wide by 37 feet deep. The kitchen was behind the entrance hall, and the dining room was behind the living room, so the dwellings had both the size and plan of the quadrant row houses Wardman was building elsewhere in the city. The groups of three row houses broke up the massing of long rows, and some were also designed with projections and setbacks within each block. Thus, 3216 Klingle was set back 27 feet from the road, 3218 was 28 feet, and 3220 was 26 feet. The change in planes and recessed doorways mean that the block is not immediately read as a three-unit structure.[18]

Three of the houses in the first phase of construction sold before they were completed in the fall, and Wardman embarked on a second phase, which included four blocks of community houses on the north side of Klingle Road. Ultimately, by the end of 1924 he had built eighteen community houses, for a total of fifty-four dwelling units, intermixed with detached and semi-detached houses. The hilly topography, the lack of long rows, and the sense of privacy created by a slight rise from the street added to the exclusive feel of the neighborhood.

Another neighborhood that traded on the English village theme was Foxhall Village, where development began in 1925 (see fig. 51). Located on the

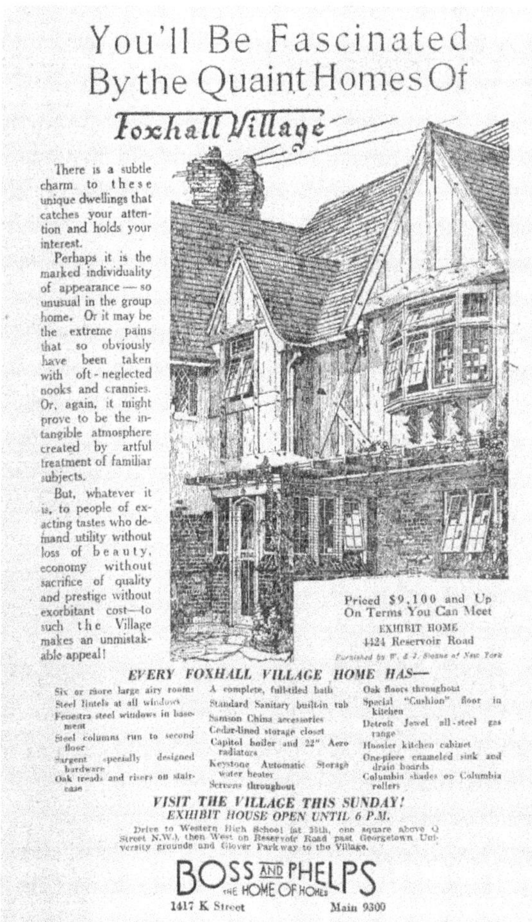

Figure 51. Advertisement, Foxhall Village. An ad for Boss and Phelps's Foxhall Village also pictured half-timbered walls and small-paned windows. (*Evening Star,* December 19, 1925, p. 7, reprinted with permission from the DC Public Library, Star Collection, © Washington Post)

west side of Glover Archbold Park, across Foundry Branch from Georgetown, this development also endeavored to minimize the effect of row houses. Despite the fact that its rows of houses were longer than those of English Village, Foxhall Village managed to dilute their impact. The community also exuded exclusivity, not only writing racial restrictions into the deeds—"not to be used or occupied by . . . any negro or colored person or persons of negro blood or extraction"—but also promising that management would interview every potential homeowner personally to insure a "judicious selection of village residents."[19]

The name of the community derived from a prominent previous owner, Henry Foxall, who moved to Georgetown in 1799 and established a foundry on the stream that would later be known as Foundry Branch. He built a summer house on the west side of the stream, near present-day Foxhall Road and P Street; the spelling of Foxall's name was corrupted sometime in the nineteenth century. In 1890 Charles Carroll Glover started buying land along Foundry Branch and in 1894 built a summer house called Westover at the north end of the stream, near Massachusetts Avenue. In 1923 Glover, an ardent supporter of parks, donated seventy-seven acres along Foundry Branch for a park. He also persuaded his neighbor, heiress Anne Archbold, to donate twenty-eight acres near her newly built summer home on the east side of the stream. Together, their donations became known as Glover Archbold Park.[20]

Boss and Phelps, a real estate firm formed in 1907 by Henry K. Boss and H. Glenn Phelps, acquired property abutting the west side of this new park. Apparently inspired by a recent trip to England, Boss hired an architect with a specialty in Old English character. James E. Cooper was well trained, having worked for Baldwin and Pennington of Baltimore and Warren and Wetmore of New York, while studying at the Maryland Institute of Design and the Ecole des Beaux Arts Ateliers in New York. With his own firm in the 1920s, Cooper's practice included houses and apartment buildings in the Old English mode.[21] For Boss and Phelps, Cooper laid out lots for row houses, an efficient use of land. He also allocated space for parks—unusual in row-house developments—and positioned the row houses to address the open space in varied ways.

The first dwellings to go on the market, in October 1925, were fifteen row houses on Reservoir Road. Parallel to and south of Reservoir, the developers changed the name of the street from Dent Place—which would have been the name had the road carried over from east of the park—to Greenwich Parkway, giving it a suitably English connotation. The developers' argument for the change was specious, though; they claimed that Dent did not "harmonize with the alphabetical nomenclature for this territory," ignoring the fact that Greenwich did not either. The parkway had a median strip, which widened into an oval park in the center and accommodated dwarf elms, a ring of five hundred American box bushes, and an outer border of English ivy.[22] South of this minipark and perpendicular to Greenwich Parkway ran Surrey Lane—more English nomenclature—which terminated in a circle at its intersection with Q Street. East of the circle on Q was another oval park (see fig. 52).

These circles and ovals helped to break up the lines of row houses, which recessed or advanced as the road widened and narrowed around the parks. A newspaper article claimed that the circle at Surrey Lane and Q Street was "carrying out the idea of the famous Crescent at Bath, England." Bath was notably Neoclassical in design, not Old English, but the connection may not be as farfetched as it seems. Harry Boss kept a photographic album of a trip to England that he took in the 1920s, and one of the photographs shows him in front of the Crescent.[23] At any rate, framing the circles and ovals with row houses produced a coherent streetscape, viewed obliquely.

By the end of 1928, Boss and Phelps had lined Greenwich Parkway, Surrey Lane, and Q Street with row houses, then turned their attention to Forty-Fourth Street overlooking the park, continuing construction there into 1931. But another developer, Waverly Taylor, outbid them on adjacent land. Taylor constructed houses on the east side of Forty-Fourth Street, blocking the view of the park for Boss and Phelps's houses. Taylor built on Forty-Fourth down to P Street and along Volta Place in 1930–32. Taylor, who called his development "Foxall Village," perhaps needling Boss and Phelps for their ahistorical spell-

Figure 52. Map of Foxhall Village, Foxall, and Colony Hill. Foxhall Village, with two oval parks and one circular one, is in the center of this map, while Waverly Taylor's Foxall is to the left. Unlike these two communities, which were row houses in the Old English mode, Boss and Phelps developed Colony Hill, on the right, with single-family Colonial Revival houses. (Dunlap, delineator, 1932, reprinted in Richard Conn, "Foxhall Community at Half Century" [1979], 21)

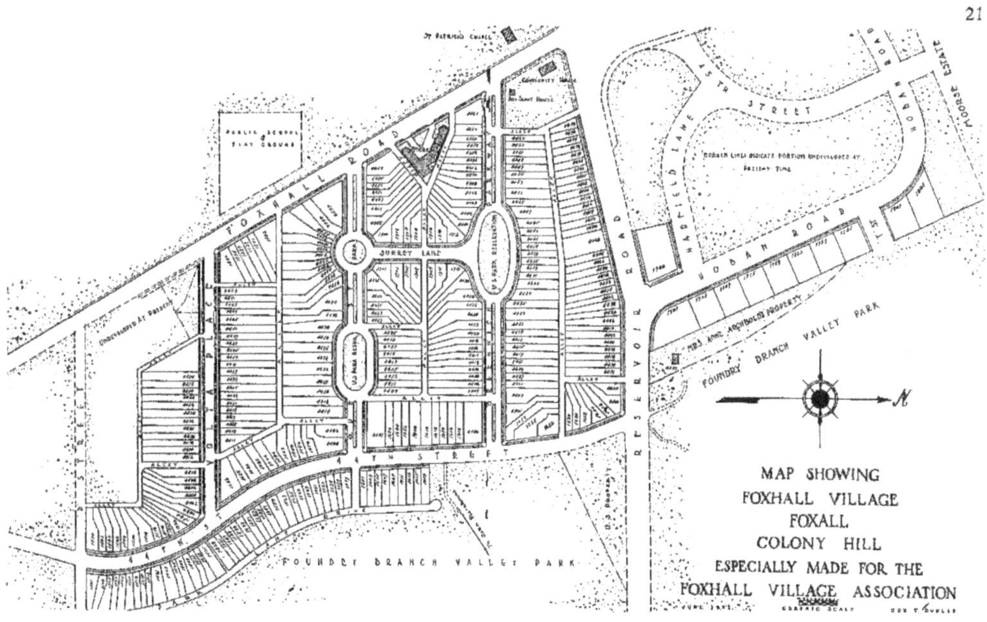

Figure 53. Row houses, 4400 block (north side) Greenwich Parkway NW. Arranged in long rows, the houses in Foxhall Village have unique facades and varying setbacks. (Photograph by the author, 2022)

ing, carried on with the Old English mode, so that the two developments seem as one. Boss was so miffed, however, that he initially refused to let residents of Taylor's houses into the Foxhall Village Citizens Association or garden club.[24]

Initially, Boss and Phelps envisioned Foxhall Village as a development of moderately priced row houses. The first houses they built on Reservoir Road and Greenwich Parkway in 1925 were modest two-story houses priced under $10,000 (see fig. 53). Measuring 18 by 30 feet, they were similar in size and plan to the quadrant row houses in other parts of the city. Unlike the usual quadrant plan, however, entry was directly into a living room, instead of a hallway, and arched openings set off the transverse stairway (see fig. 54). The rest was more familiar: the dining room and narrow kitchen occupied the back half of the first floor, and three bedrooms and an interior bathroom were on the second floor. Four years later, when Boss and Phelps built the three-story houses on Forty-Fourth Street that they termed the Gloucestershire Group, the prices ranged from $17,750 to $24,500. Located on the northwest corner of Greenwich Parkway and Forty-Fourth Street, these were exceptionally well equipped, with "five master bedrooms and three tiled baths," oil-burning furnaces, electric refrigeration, gas-fired hot-water heaters, and fireplaces with marble mantels and hearths. Boss and Phelps built a total of 190 row houses in Foxhall Village, while Waverly Taylor added 106 in the same Old English mode.[25]

Particularly striking about Boss and Phelps's village is the variety of the houses. No two facades are identical, steeply pitched slate roofs vary between side and front gables, walls are clad in brick and faux half-timbering, bay windows and oriels break up the massing. Other features intended to make the viewer think of old England include chimney pots, parapets, concrete heraldic shields applied to the walls, and banded windows with small panes. The interiors included fireplaces, window seats, semi-elliptical arches between rooms, and wrought-iron stair railings. The variety of facades, their staggered alignment, the irregular street plan, and the rolling site combine to create an informal and picturesque settlement that achieved the developers' goal of "a village in the city."[26]

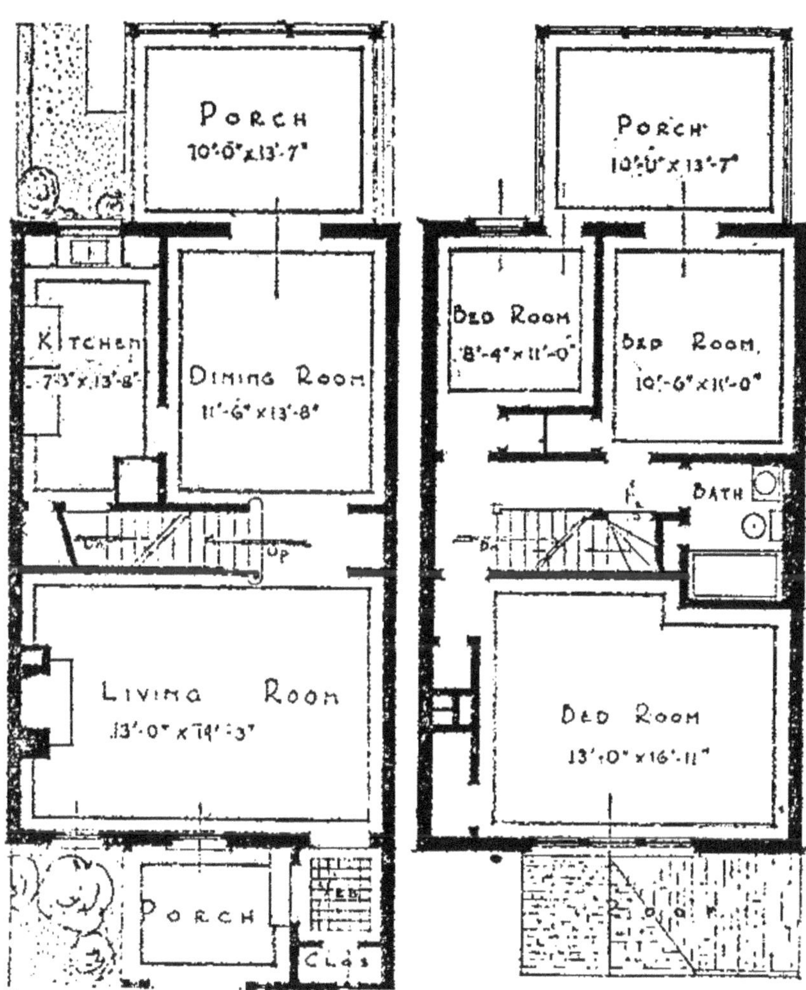

Figure 54. Row house, 1573 Forty-Fourth Street NW, plans. Adjacent to Boss and Phelps's development, Waverly Taylor developed row houses with a similar transverse stairway. Built in 1929, the houses measured 20 by 32 feet. (Plans reproduced in Richard Conn, "Foxhall Community at Half Century" [1979], 18)

Part of the prestige of Foxhall Village was that the buildings did not look like row houses, which lacked the social standing that the developers coveted. The 1920 zoning regulations permitted row houses in this area, so no strategies such as "community houses" were necessary, and row houses' economical use of the land appealed to developers. Repeatedly, though, newspaper articles and company brochures tried to deny the fact that these were row houses. For example, "An illustration of row houses that are not 'row houses' in the formerly generally accepted sense is seen in the English group dwellings at 1616 and 1618 Forty-fourth Street, Foxhall Village." The article goes on to explain: "The feature of these adjoining houses that makes them 'group' houses rather than row structures is that roof and façade lines are differentiated so as to give each building a different aspect, materials employed in the facades are varied and the layout of the separate houses also is varied." The term "group house" avoided the apparently unsavory associations of row houses. Another article pointed to "a distinct innovation in group home construction" and maintained that "it is difficult to believe these homes are all in one row, so artistically distinctive is the effect of each house."[27]

The combination of Old English styling and row houses varied in facade and site plan proved to be a successful strategy for Wardman as well as Boss and Phelps. Old English row houses appeared in other neighborhoods, such as Burleith and Glover Park, where developer B. H. Gruver advertised "Beautiful English-Type Homes," "The Quaint Charm of English Architecture," and "New English-Village Homes" in the late 1920s and early 1930s. The "English Village" appellation became so popular that residents of Wardman's development called it "Wardman's English Village" in classified ads, apparently to distinguish it from its rivals.[28]

Modernist Influences

Old English aside, Washington's row houses in the 1920s were overwhelmingly "Colonial," with front porches and quadrant plans.[29] In the 1930s and 1940s, the facades underwent some shifts reflecting a growing modernist sensibility. The front porch fell out of fashion, replaced by a large concrete stoop, or nothing at all. The visible tile or slate roof disappeared, and walls terminated in modest cornices or in parapets shielding the roofs from view. The brick walls were unadorned, except for a concrete shield here or classical swag there. The quadrant plan persisted, as row houses became plainer, simpler, and smaller as the Depression deepened.

A few dramatically different row houses espoused an uncompromising modernism. According to owner and builder J. B. Tiffey, he was the first to "introduce as many architecturally modern homes to the Washington public

Figure 55. Row houses, 4116–36 Arkansas Avenue NW. Architect Joseph H. Abel designed these modernist row houses, built in 1940 for developer J. B. Tiffey. Despite their unconventionality, they sold immediately. (From *Architectural Forum* 75, no. 1 (July 1941): 68, courtesy of the University of Virginia Library)

at one time." In 1940 he built ten modern row houses at 4116–36 Arkansas Avenue NW, just one block off of Sixteenth Street and across from Piney Branch Park (see fig. 55). Designed by architect Joseph H. Abel, the houses were shockingly different from the usual Washington row house. Eschewing cornices and window trim, they had recessed entrances, glass-block walls, porches across the front, and blocky chimneys on the front facade. Faced with a steeply rising slope, Abel placed the main entrance in the basement; the main floor was at the level of the rear entrance. The basement accommodated a recreation room or "second living room" with corner fireplace. The main floor had the living room, dining room, and kitchen in a traditional arrangement, with the kitchen in the back building, but no halls or doorways separated these rooms. Instead, two steps demarcated the living room and the dining room. The third floor had three bedrooms and two bathrooms (see fig. 56).[30]

Tiffey had no trouble selling these unusual houses. In the first month that they went on the market, five thousand people visited the model home, and all ten sold within four months. Tiffey embarked on the construction of seventeen more the next year. Tiffey's advertising used terms and phrases such as "utterly new in principle," "streamlined living," and most of all "modern," but he also felt the need to reassure: "Don't misunderstand. They're not mod-

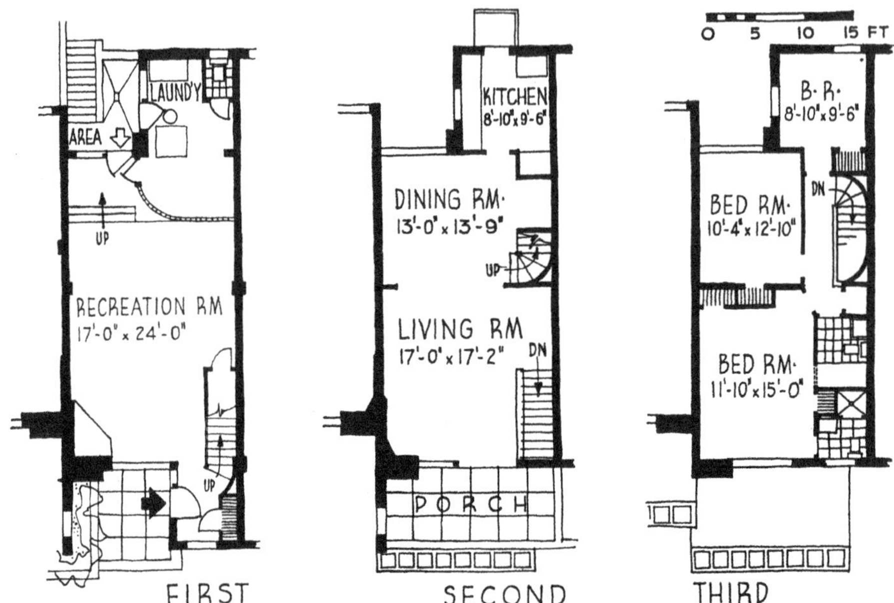

Figure 56. Row house, 4116 Arkansas Avenue NW. The plans accommodated the steep site by locating the entrance in the basement level, along with the recreation room and laundry. Upstairs, the kitchen was in the back building. (From *Architectural Forum* 75, no. 1 (July 1941): 69, courtesy of the University of Virginia Library)

ernistic, not futuristic. Just modern." The rationale for deciding on a modern appearance was due to the steepness of the site; Abel argued that to counteract the extremely tall appearance of the houses, the horizontality of the modern was necessary.[31]

In 1943 Joseph Abel designed another long row of modernist row houses. This time the developer was Shapiro, Inc., which built thirty-one dwellings at 1701–61 Harvard Street NW (see fig. 57). Faced with an even steeper site, Abel put the houses on the crest of the hill. These three-story houses were smaller than the Arkansas Avenue ones, measuring 16 by 25 feet compared to 18 by 42 feet.[32] Cantilevered door hoods and cornices as well as banded windows added a horizontal pull to counteract the height of these buildings. As dramatic as the Harvard Street and Arkansas Avenue rows were, modern row houses were the exception, not the rule, in 1940s and 1950s Washington until the rebuilding of Southwest in the early 1960s.

Colonial Revival in the Mid-Twentieth Century

The Colonial Revival had a lasting effect on Washington row houses in the middle of the twentieth century, in terms of new construction, but also concerning their preservation and renovation.[33] Georgetown was both the leader and the model in historic preservation, sparking a renewed interest in row houses. Although in the early nineteenth century Georgetown was an important port and site of industry, by the twentieth century its waterfront had silted in and its industries were no longer as viable as they had been. Rock Creek, separating Georgetown from the rest of the city, had become an open sewer. Georgetown's population was increasingly African American, constituting nearly 30 percent of the population in the early twentieth century. With the flow of people into Washington during World War I, new white residents settled in Georgetown, attracted by its convenient location, row houses, and charm. In the 1920s, this new population, led by housing reformer John Ihlder, used its growing political power to downzone the neighborhood to prevent an incursion of apartment buildings and preserve its low height. Rock Creek was redeveloped into a parkway. Georgetown began to acquire a reputation among the educated elites as a desirable place to live, and it attracted even more of them during the influx of government workers into the city in the 1930s.

A large part of the attraction of Georgetown was undoubtedly its history. As a colonial-era port town, Georgetown predated the rest of Washington.

Figure 57. Row houses, 1700 block (north side) Harvard Street NW. In 1943, Joseph H. Abel designed these modernist row houses for Shapiro, Inc. Three stories tall, they measured just 16 by 25 feet. (Photograph by the author, 2022)

With the rise of the Colonial Revival movement beginning in the late nineteenth century and gaining steam through the early twentieth, Georgian and Federal dwellings associated with the nation's founders gained popularity. While much of the Colonial Revival movement can be attributed to the desire of old-stock elites to hold onto power and influence in the face of new fortunes created by large industries and a burgeoning urban immigrant population, some of the appeal of the Colonial Revival was aesthetic. Victorian dwellings fell out of fashion, derided as dark and ungainly. The clean lines and simplicity of the Georgian and Federal buildings, along with their associations with a seemingly noble past, held great appeal. In the 1920s in Georgetown, three freestanding houses, all built around 1800, were stripped of their Victorian additions and restored to their early nineteenth-century appearance—or, to some degree, to an imagined past appearance. The houses also acquired new names and are known today as Dumbarton Oaks, Dumbarton House, and Evermay.[34]

Along with grand houses, more modest row houses experienced renovations, also with Colonial Revival aspirations. But Georgetown was not, in fact, a colonial town; most of its building stock dated from long after the Republic was formed. In 1939 a reporter for the *Washington Post* felt she had to explain to readers that "every house in Georgetown is not Eighteenth Century." Still, it was the colonial and early republic character that resonated with the more recent homeowners. In 1960 the real estate editor for the *Evening Star,* Robert J. Lewis, applauded "the kind of house remodeling used to gain the simplicity of a more-or-less Georgian exterior through use of small-paned windows, six panel doors, wrought-iron handrails, appropriate hardware and other details." He rationalized the radical interventions by pointing to the dictionary definition of "restoration," which included "putting back into an unimpaired, or much improved condition," thereby justifying the kinds of drastic renovations that were taking place.[35]

Part of the appeal of Georgetown's row houses was that they were small and simple—many of them working-class housing—and lent themselves to interpretation as Federal-style dwellings. Alley dwellings also fit this description (see fig. 58). At Bell's Court the city government condemned the deteriorated alley dwellings, forcing out the African American tenants. The owners, Russell Eldridge and Graham Lytle, took the opportunity to rehabilitate the dwellings into Colonial Revival rows, rename the alley "Pomander Walk," and rent the homes for ten times what they had cost before. Throughout Georgetown, newcomers bought up old rental dwellings, displacing the African American population. Just as the diversity of building eras was erased through aggressive "restoration," so too was the diverse population through displacement. Among whites, though, Georgetown gained the repu-

Figure 58. Alley dwellings, Pomander Walk, Georgetown. These late nineteenth-century alley buildings in Georgetown were some of the first that were renovated into Colonial Revival dwellings after World War II. Bell's Court was renamed Pomander Walk to enhance its appeal. (Emil A. Press, photographer, 1961, DC History Center, Emil A. Press Slide Collection, PR 0569A)

tation as a place that was romantic, historic, and colonial. As the 1937 Federal Writers' Project guide described it, "in the residential section are occasional quaint cottages, small fine homes, and pretentious mansions. Here and there a street is still laid in ancient cobblestone, and a sidewalk in smooth, worn brick. Gabled roofs, tiny dormers, inviting doorways, and brass knockers are reminders of a vanished past." This charming antiquity was rooted in its colonial past, or even a century or two before its founding: "To many, the community's origin appears shrouded in mists as ancient as those which hover over Jamestown or Plymouth Rock."[36]

After World War II, the interest in preservation spread to other neighborhoods, with the preference for the Colonial Revival persisting. While the preservation movement may be unsurprising today, at the time it seemed unlikely that private individuals could, or would, reinvest in urban dwellings in any meaningful way. Bringing tax-paying, middle-class white families back to the city they were deserting, aided by federal government policies, was the goal. Far better to achieve this, some argued, was full-scale urban renewal, in which neighborhoods were demolished wholesale and then rebuilt. As Robert Lewis wrote in the *Evening Star* in 1960, "A persistent viewpoint of a number of government housing and planning officials somehow fails to understand the value of the private restoration movement, underestimates its significance and too often accords it hindrance rather than help."[37]

Capitol Hill was one of the first neighborhoods outside of Georgetown to experience interest in its historic architecture. An article in the *Evening Star* heralded a "Capitol Hill Comeback" in 1949. The Capitol Hill Restoration Society formed in 1955, and by 1960, more than a thousand houses on Capitol Hill had been "restored." But with Victorian styles having fallen out of favor, the trend among early renovators was to remodel them into something resembling a colonial dwelling, at least on the facade. One example is the house at 13 Fourth Street SE, which was included on the Capitol Hill Restoration Society's house tour in 1960. Built sometime between 1857 and 1874, long after the colonial period, this house and its adjacent neighbors received the full Colonial Revival treatment in their renovation, with shutters, coach lights, small-paned windows, and, in the case of the house at number 11, fluted pilasters framing the doorway. Photographs of the houses illustrated an article titled "The Neat and Orderly Colonial Façade," in which Lewis praised colonial architecture for its order and homelike qualities, while listing its characteristics: "small-paned windows, shutters, wrought-iron porch railings, entrance lanterns, and an occasional modestly pedimented doorway," along with "door knockers and entrance handles of brass in Colonial design."[38]

Foggy Bottom also received early attention from preservationists, due to its location adjacent to Georgetown and, like Georgetown, its supply of modest working-class row houses that could be interpreted as Colonial. In 1956 the Foggy Bottom Restoration Association held its first house tour, showcasing "what one group of independent home builders and owners has been able to do in partially rehabilitating one Washington slum area." The four featured houses were "all typically Georgetown in character." While the exteriors might have had Georgetown appeal, with shutters and iron railings, the interiors were brand new: in one, the homeowner gutted the interior and added a large kitchen and second bedroom; in another, the homeowner installed pastel green wall-to-wall carpeting and air-conditioning.[39]

Some of the early preservation activity in Foggy Bottom was in alleys. Not only because alley dwellings were small, outdated, and cheap, but also because multiple alley dwellings were generally owned by one person, it was easier for redevelopers to acquire several at a time. Eleanor Dulles, sister of Secretary of State John Foster Dulles, renovated three alley dwellings in Green's Court, Ben and Dorothy Burch renovated houses in both Green's Court and Hughes Court, and Jean and Jonas Robitscher took on twenty-two alley dwellings in Snow's Court (the last is discussed in more detail in chapter 6). Although all of these houses dated from the late nineteenth century and were thus only about sixty years old, their renovators turned their exteriors into Colonial Revival dwellings, adding carriage lamps, staircases with iron railings, and shutters in "authentic Williamsburg colors," while the interiors received modern conveniences and decor. Similarly, on Capitol Hill, homeowners had begun renovating houses in Terrace Court, one block east of the Supreme Court, in 1946. Six owners acquired the eight alley dwellings and renovated them, adding indoor plumbing and electricity. They also added green shutters and coach lanterns, producing "a colonial atmosphere," although the houses had been built in 1889.[40]

As the slums of Washington, alley dwellings had been targeted for removal for decades, beginning in 1914. By the time their prohibition was scheduled to go in effect in 1954, white professionals had begun to acquire and renovate alley dwellings, as these examples in Foggy Bottom and Capitol Hill show. In Georgetown, where newcomers had begun renovating alley dwellings before the war, by 1953 they claimed to have remodeled 100 alley dwellings, representing an expenditure of $2 million. The investors successfully advocated for the repeal of the Alley Dwelling Act, which ordered the removal of all alley dwellings. For four decades, reformers had been trying to eliminate alley dwellings, but now they received a permanent reprieve. Today, middle-class homeowners in the old city occupy 108 surviving alley dwellings.[41]

Appreciation for Victorian styles emerged in the 1960s. The publication of an influential article in the journal of the local historical society, Henry Glassie's "Victorian Homes in Washington," in 1965 led to a reappraisal of row houses that had long been termed dowdy and out of fashion. As Glassie extolled, "Late Victorian had flights of exuberant fancy, wild and lavish color, and above all, comfort. Ceilings were high. Windows were large. No one who has ever lived in a corner tower room with a circle of windows opening onto the upper branches of a tree could ever feel this style was gloomy." Neighborhoods such as Capitol Hill, Dupont Circle, and Logan Circle began to celebrate the houses that characterized them. In 1974 the *Washington Post* carried an article about *The Old-House Journal,* illustrated by line drawings of row houses in different styles.[42] Understanding the innate character of specific row houses and alterations appropriate to the time period became more important than forcing row houses to conform to some ideal of "old."

The Colonial Revival movement had hardly expired. It now exerted its influence on row houses in another way in mid-twentieth-century Washington, and that was through new construction. Although the old city—equivalent to Washington's L'Enfant city—had long been written off as a bad investment for new middle-class housing, some developers saw opportunity there in the 1960s. One of the preeminent developers of new row houses in Washington's old city was Barrett Linde, who favored a Colonial Revival mode. Educated at Harvard and the University of Pennsylvania's Wharton School, Linde began building new row houses on Capitol Hill in the early 1960s. Within a few years, he was wildly successful, selling houses before construction was completed. Linde described one development of nine houses at Seventh and G Streets SE as "the largest number of new houses built at one time on Cap-

Figure 59. Lafayette Row, 536–52 Seventh Street SE. In 1965 Barrett Linde built Federal-style row houses with first-floor garages, accessed from the street. The nine 15-foot-wide row houses all sold before construction had even begun. (Photograph by the author, 2021)

itol Hill since the turn of the century" (see fig. 59). The "Federal-front town houses" measured 15 by 40 feet and had garages on the first floor, entered from the street, not the alley. Each house had a "patio and garden, 2 fireplaces, 2½ baths, large all-electric kitchen, laundry room and two zones for heating and air conditioning with thermostatic controls." He called the development "Lafayette Row."[43]

Two years later he built 17 row houses at Eighth and C Streets SE, in the "Federal" style. Houses in the "Capitol Square" development had first-floor garages, three and four bedrooms, and "stepdown living-rooms that lead into patio-gardens (walled, of course)." By then, Linde had built 95 houses in Washington, 60 of them on Capitol Hill. Elsewhere, Linde built in Dupont Circle, the Palisades, Glover Park, and Mount Pleasant. When permission for curb cuts for front garages became difficult to obtain, he put separate apartments on the first floor, appealing to homeowners who wanted the extra income from a rental unit.[44]

Linde's row houses (always called "town houses") had a similar appearance; even he admitted they were "'fairly' formulaic." One critic called it "Architecture by Xerox. He found a model that worked, and he kept replicating it all over." His houses tended to be of a light brown-red brick, with modest ornamentation such as pilasters and pediment framing the doorway, a plain cornice, non-operable shutters on windows with six-over-six lights and splayed lintels, and an occasional slate side-gable roof. The plans usually placed the kitchen in the front, the bathroom in the interior, and a fireplace in the living room. Iron railings, step-down living rooms, and patios were nods to contemporary fashion. But by the 1970s, when appreciation for Victorian architecture was mounting, the facile Colonial references of Linde's buildings began to grate. As Sarah Booth Conroy raged in the *Washington Post* in 1972, "Fie to the Fake Federal Front." She excoriated Linde's Corcoran Street houses, then under construction, and noted that "nothing about Corcoran Street ever was or ever has been Federal, either fake or true. Corcoran Street is sometimes Victorian and many times Edwardian and often Twenties, but never, ever Federal." Still, Linde's dubiously Federal row houses had great appeal. One architect observed: "This is a market where if you have a modernist house, it sells for less. People want all the conveniences, but tricked up in something traditional."[45] That something traditional was an enduring Colonial Revival.

Aided by an evolving preservation ethos that privileged the original fabric and character of the building, as well as a burgeoning number of historic districts protected by a strong preservation law, row houses in the old city experienced a lighter touch in their rehabilitation beginning in the 1980s. Stripping off ornament or transforming a house into one from a different time period became far less common. New construction still preferred traditional styles, although an enhanced sensitivity to context meant that they were more likely to look like their neighbors. At the more modest end of the scale, this could produce bland, vaguely Italianate or Queen Anne row houses or, at the other end, the exuberant neo-Victorianism of a project by architect Amy Weinstein. A Capitol Hill development of 134 housing units to replace a 1941 public housing project called the Ellen Wilson Dwellings consisted of row houses and duplexes in a mixed-income cooperative, with half of the houses market-rate and the other half subsidized (see fig. 60). "Townhomes

Figure 60. Townhomes on Capitol Hill, 600 block (north side) I Street SE. Architect Amy Weinstein designed row houses that took architectural cues from the neighborhood for this mixed-income development, which opened in 1999. The buildings replaced low-rise multifamily public housing blocks, dating from 1941, which in turn had replaced alley dwellings and other row houses dating from the late nineteenth century. (Photograph by the author, 2021)

on Capitol Hill," which opened in 1999, have a variety of sizes and materials, all within a coherent aesthetic.[46] Some houses have raised entrances with cast-iron stairways, three-story brick bay windows, brick ornamentation in the walls, and corbeled cornices; others have flat walls, hoodmolds over the windows, and wide bracketed cornices; and others have side-gable roofs and a low profile. The variety of sizes and styles works to belie the fact that these were built simultaneously, because they do not look like long rows of speculative row houses.

Nontraditional styles face an uncertain acceptance in the marketplace, so rows of modernist, contemporary row houses from the late twentieth or early twenty-first centuries are rare. Single instances of blatantly new row houses, set in a row of much older neighbors, can be found, but speculative rows tend to stick with the traditional. Interiors tend to be open and feature the latest domestic technology.

Besides offering the first impression to a visitor, facades contribute to the streetscape and neighborhood, offering order, identity, beauty, security, and a host of other qualities. The facade's relationship to the plan can be essential, by suggesting what lies within, or is inconsequential, by concealing an unexpected plan.[47] The next chapter shifts attention inside the row house, where concerns for health and comfort manifested themselves in the procurement of utilities, which also affected the plan.

4

Health and Comfort

The L-shaped row house at 1524 T Street NW that Grace Smith rented in 1900 was very different from the quadrant-plan row house at 2214 Cathedral Avenue NW that Edna Perry owned in 1922 (see figs. 9, 10, 18, and 19). Although not all that different in size—the three-bedroom houses provided 1,650 and 1,400 (plus porches) of square feet of space, respectively, on two floors—those spaces were arranged very differently. Grace Smith's L-shaped house had a back building, where the kitchen was located; the parlor and dining room were reached by a side hall; the outdoors was brought indoors by way of a bay window; and the row house had a width of only 17 feet. By contrast, Edna Perry's quadrant-plan house was 20 feet wide; the hallway did not give access to the dining room; the spacious front porch promised a leisurely lifestyle; and the kitchen was fully integrated into the mass of the house. While some of these differences can be attributed to changing building regulations and architectural fashion, they are also due to evolving ideas about health and comfort.

While health and comfort may seem like universal, immutable values, the means of securing good health and more comfort changed over time. In the nineteenth century, good health was strongly identified with good air. Because of the fear of disease being carried by air, late nineteenth-century Americans were particularly concerned with ventilation.[1] Scientific theories affected contemporary beliefs about threats from bad air, and while these beliefs were widespread, their translation into building regulations varied from place to place. In Washington, these beliefs ultimately influenced the arrangement of the row house.

Health and comfort are also tied to utilities—water, sewer, gas, and electricity—which facilitated sanitation, light, and heat. But each of these utilities, while providing convenience to residents, also brought threats to health inside the home. In addressing these concerns, building regulations affected the form of the row house, as noted in chapter 2. Access to each of these utilities—all of which became available in the last half of the nineteenth century—varied, depending on economic class as well as on geography, with some neighborhoods gaining utilities before others. The web of utilities connected row houses to each other and to the larger city.

Sanitarians and the Home

For most of the nineteenth century, homeowners desired a free flow of fresh air in order to dissipate poisonous air. Americans believed in the filth or environmental theory of disease, which held that diseases developed spontaneously in damp, dirty locations, such as swampy areas, damp cellars, or trash-strewn unpaved streets, and were spread by air. In 1857, when several people died mysteriously at the National Hotel in downtown Washington, the committee appointed by the city's Board of Health to investigate concluded that the cause was "poisonous miasma generated in the sewers, cesspools and sinks about the establishment."[2]

After the Civil War, a new breed of experts arose. Sanitarians were doctors, civil engineers, and others from allied fields who promoted public health. As one scientist said, looking back at the sanitarians and their filth theory of disease, "dirty clothes, bad smells, damp cellars, leaky plumbing, dust, foul air, rank vegetation, swamps, stagnant pools, certain soils, smoke, garbage, manure, dead animals, in fact everything physically, sensorially, esthetically, or psychically objectionable, were lumped together as 'unsanitary' . . . and were regarded as a sort of general 'cause of disease' to be condemned wherever found, 'for fear of epidemics.'"[3] The threat came from a dirty or smelly environment.

Enclosing sewers and draining swampy areas were the purview of the government, and Washington issued contracts to remove privy waste by 1820, plant and animal waste by 1856, and inorganic waste and ashes by 1900. While municipal officials considered offensive items in the yard to be a public health concern, sanitarians also directed attention to the home. Unventilated spaces and cramped quarters permitted "filth diseases" to spread; one source was the exhalations of their residents, especially during sleep. As noted sanitarian Dr. John S. Billings wrote, abundance of fresh air "is a necessity for the preservation of health and happiness." The flow of air in a home helped dispel the disease-causing air. The simplest solution was ample windows, but this was a constraint experienced by row houses; they could have windows in only two walls—front and back. The introduction of the bay window in the 1870s permitted air and light to enter, however minimally, from the sides (see fig. 61). The bay window was thus not only a sign of middle-class gentility, but also an important offense in the battle against disease. Aiding the passive

Figure 61. Bethune House, 1318 Vermont Avenue NW. Bay windows enabled breezes from several directions to ventilate the row house. Views up and down the street were another benefit. See also figs. 31 and 45. (Jack E. Boucher, photographer, 1993, Library of Congress, Prints and Photographs Division, HABS)

movement of air might be a skylight over the stairway, an interior window from the front bedroom into the stair hall, a jog in the wall to widen the aspect of the dining room window, and ceiling heights of ten feet on the first floor and nine on the second.[4] Grace Smith, renting the L-shaped row house at 1524 T Street NW, in 1900, benefited from all these features (see fig. 62).

Another domestic source of disease was oil lamps and gas lighting, which emitted carbon monoxide. In Washington, gas lighting began to replace oil lamps in 1848, when businessmen formed the Washington Gas Light Company. While much of the company's emphasis was lighting public buildings and streets, the company also had 1,700 residential customers by 1856 and more than 4,000 by the end of the Civil War. By the end of the century, Washington Gas Light Company had more than 26,000 customers, and Washington was a gas-lit city.[5] Grace Smith's L-shaped row house, built in 1892, was equipped with gas lighting, which, while more effective and efficient than oil lamps, also brought with it a greater danger to health

Figure 62. Row house, 1524 T Street NW. On the second floor, air flow was encouraged by the skylight over the stairs, transom windows over the doors, and a window from the hallway into the front bedroom. See also figs. 9, 10, and 40. (Justin Scalera, photographer, 2018, Library of Congress, Prints and Photographs Division, HABS)

(see fig. 63). The solution, again, was ventilation, not only when the lights were burning, but through routinely airing out gas-lit rooms.

Fireplaces were an effective mechanism for encouraging air flow. The fire drew oxygen from the room, ensuring a constant circulation. The replacement of fireplaces with stoves, beginning in the early nineteenth century, imperiled that function. While stoves were more efficient, burning less coal for greater heat, they did not draw air to the extent that open fires did, so the gain in comfort was offset by the loss in health. As one alarmist wrote, "since the invention of air-tight stoves, thousands have died of slow poison." Nonetheless, the Latrobe stove became a standard feature of row houses in the late nineteenth century. Patented in 1846 by John H. B. Latrobe, the son of the famous architect Benjamin H. Latrobe, the Latrobe stove was a cast-iron stove that fit into a fireplace opening. Distinguished from those for cooking, Latrobe stoves were designed for the parlor. By the late 1870s, if a row house did not have central heating in some form, the building permit often specified "Latrobes," as did the permit for Grace Smith's house (see fig. 64). [6] Fireplaces and stoves helped air in the home move passively.

Figure 63. Row house, 1524 T Street NW. When it was built in 1892, the row house had gas lighting, which some critics thought was harmful to good health. (Justin Scalera, photographer, 2018, Library of Congress, Prints and Photographs Division, HABS)

Figure 64. Row house, 1524 T Street NW. Despite its other modern amenities, this row house did not have central heating, but rather it was equipped with Latrobe stoves. (Justin Scalera, photographer, 2018, Library of Congress, Prints and Photographs Division, HABS)

Water and sewer systems were intimately connected with health through the implied sanitation effect, but they also required ventilation. Water and sewer service also increased the comfort of residents, who no longer had to haul water or go outside to use the privy or empty chamber pots. By 1892, when Grace Smith's house was built, running water was standard, and water closets were required.

Washington's water system developed with the city. Early residents obtained water from wells, springs, and cisterns; in 1819 pipes conducted water from a spring in Franklin Square to the White House. In 1850 Lt. Montgomery C. Meigs of the U.S. Army Corps of Engineers devised an ambitious plan that he promoted with the ringing declaration, "Let our Aqueduct be worthy of the Nation." The system, which was soon inadequate to meet the needs of the burgeoning city population, took water from the Potomac River at Great Falls, twelve miles upstream of the city, and delivered it by aqueduct and conduit to a receiving reservoir and then to houses in the city. Water began to flow through this system in 1859, and it was fully functional in 1863.[7]

Although the water system was an undeniable technological achievement, in practice it had its faults, especially in the quality of the unfiltered river water. In 1887 even the city's engineer admitted that it was "often muddy and uninviting in appearance," which was "usual for large portions of the year." In that year, the "disagreeably fishy smell" that usually arose from plant growth in the distributing reservoir was not present. But the engineer also mentioned "many instances of eels and fishes getting into the service-pipes and interfering with the flow of water, and putting householders to trouble and expense in getting them removed." One resident recalled, "Wise people in the [eighteen-]nineties never drank water which had not been boiled for at least six minutes . . . Others imported drinking water in huge demijohns from far off springs."[8]

Despite the uneven quality of the water, Washingtonians enthusiastically signed up for it. In 1876, nearly 12,000 of the 25,000 houses in Washington and Georgetown were "water-takers," or customers of the municipal water system; by 1887 there were more than 25,000 water-takers among the rapidly increasing population. Of the 12,000 water-takers in 1876, 10,000 of them had water closets, or toilets, and more than 5,000 had bathtubs. Running water was a selling point; the water-registrar noted that "in most of the old dwellings owners have been compelled to introduce water, or allow their property to remain idle . . . Tenants are not willing to forego the water-privilege, even at the expense of paying additional rent." Still, about a quarter of the households did not have running water in the late nineteenth century, forcing residents to take it from public hydrants.[9]

Even for those who signed up as water-takers, water was not always available. In dry periods the water level in the river fell so that some houses got no water at all, despite being billed for it. In 1879 residents complained so strongly about the erratic water supply that the city government had to refund $30,000 in water charges. Nonetheless, water usage was high; in 1875 the water-registrar reported that consumption, averaging 158 gallons per person per day, had doubled in the previous eleven years. That number included commercial and governmental users, but the registrar attributed the excessive consumption to other factors: "rapid growth of our city; by the luxurious manner in which nearly every modern house, so far as relates to water-fixtures, is furnished, and by the increased numbers of water-takers and population." He also claimed, "It is well known that over one-half the private houses in the city allow closets and spigots to constantly run, and it is estimated that near one-quarter of the daily supply is wasted therein." Residential use was not metered until 1906; rather, water-takers were charged a flat fee. By 1890, when the average use per person was 177 gallons per day, the third highest in the nation, the water charge for an average house in Washington was $4.50 per year, compared to $6.00 in New York City and $7.00 in Baltimore. A government official defined an average house in Washington as "seven rooms, hot and cold water in kitchen sink, bathtub with hot and cold water, and water closet," which was a pretty accurate description of Grace Smith's house.[10]

The erratic supply contributed to the uneven development of the city. The northwest portion of the city as well as areas lower than the distributing reservoir in Georgetown received water more readily. Engineers raised the dam at Great Falls to increase supply in 1882, but even then the city was irregularly furnished with water. One Capitol Hill resident, who asserted that the neighborhood "suffered more than any other part of the District," recalled installing a force pump in his house to get water to the second floor—which was effective only if the nearby Navy Yard was not using an excessive amount of water at the time. In 1890 the city's water department heralded the completion of a 48-inch main and noted that "water was turned on and the protracted famine on Capitol Hill came to an end." Finally, in 1902, a new reservoir at McMillan Park opened to serve the greater part of the city, and three years later a slow sand filtration plant opened there, treating the drinking water for the first time. The death rate from typhoid fever dropped dramatically, and the mortality rate fell even more when chlorination was introduced in 1920.[11]

To the sanitarians, who believed that filth and odors caused diseases, the toilet was a particularly dangerous element in the home. Sanitarians identified the specific danger as "sewer gas," a combination of all of the gases of the putrefying elements in the sewer. Sewer gas was invisible and could be odorless, heightening the danger, and it came into the house through drains in fixtures or from leaky sewer lines running underneath the house (see fig. 65).

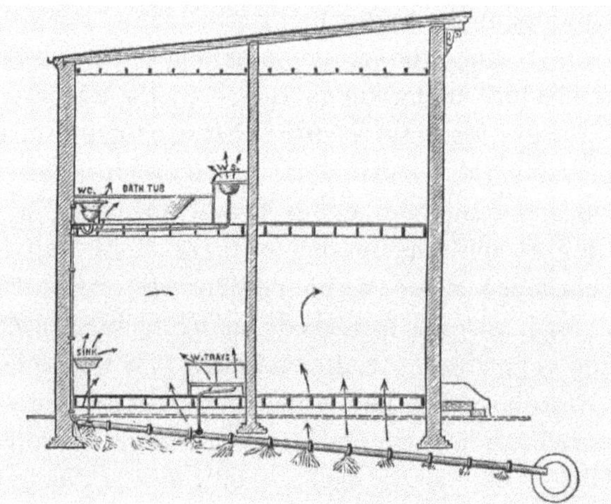

Figure 65. Row house, sectional drawing. The dangers of sewer gas were depicted in this section of a row house in Southeast Washington. Sewer gas—odorless and invisible—came into the house through the untrapped plumbing fixtures as well as a leaky sewer pipe below ground. (Reprinted from an article in *The Sanitary Engineer* by Harriette Plunkett, *Women, Plumbers and Doctors: or, Household Sanitation* [NY: D. Appleton, 1885], 234, courtesy of the University of Virginia Library)

As asserted in the 1881 publication *Sewer-Gas and Its Dangers,* in cities such as Chicago, "sewer-gas is the cause of more physical suffering and the cause of more diseases, than any other one thing."[12]

In the 1870s and 1880s, sanitarians advised the public on how to address the dangers of sewer gas. Sinks in bedrooms were considered a particular danger, because sewer gas could come up the drain pipe and poison oblivious sleepers. Another threat was when what was meant to be flushed lingered in pipes, emanating sewer gas. As one sanitarian said, "Not an atom of filth should be allowed to cling to the sides of the waste-pipes."[13] To achieve this, sanitarians recommended shorter runs of pipes in the house, because the shorter the pipe, the more likely it was to be flushed out completely after use. Accordingly, bathroom fixtures—sink, toilet, and bathtub—gathered in one room, and the three-fixture bathroom became the norm, based in large part on the fear of sewer gas, a theory of disease that was outmoded by the twentieth century.

The location of the bathroom was also important. Although the bathroom posed great danger, placing it in a distant part of the house negated the very convenience that having an indoor facility was supposed to provide. The best solution, argued E. C. Gardner in his book *The House That Jill Built, after Jack's Had Proved a Failure,* was "one bath-room for all chambers of the second floor, not too remote but somewhat retired, and having no communication with any other room." Stacking the second-floor bathroom above the kitchen not only saved on the cost of pipes, but further assured shorter runs of them.[14] Sanitarians also recommended that the pipes and fixtures be left open, not encased in wooden structures, as had been the norm, so that sewer gas could not build up in enclosed areas.

More than the pipes themselves, the whole bathroom needed ventilation. Every bathroom needed an opening to dispel the odors that were not just unpleasant but potentially deadly. In Washington, the 1872 building regulations required that bathrooms have an exterior window.[15] The most common placement of the bathroom in row houses with back buildings was in the back building close to the main block of the house, with a window onto the court, as illustrated by Grace Smith's house, which was unusual in having two bathrooms, one on each floor (see fig. 10). The placement of the bathroom on an exterior wall with a window continued well into the twentieth century, even as row-house plans changed, and the filth theory of disease fell out of favor.

Local officials did not doubt the virulence of sewer gas. In 1879 the Health Officer, Dr. Smith Townsend, attributed three cases of scarlet fever, two of diphtheria, and two of typhoid to sewer gas. He also identified the cause of another four cases of these diseases as "filth." Despite the danger of sewer gas, toilets were desirable, and they were also required, beginning in 1877, if water and sewer connections were available, and in 1902, in all new construction.[16]

Washington's sewer system, which began as a system to contain stormwater runoff, was a threat to health in itself. Given the city's topography, much of the water ran down toward the broad flat area at the foot of Capitol Hill and downtown. The first effort to contain this began in 1802, when Congress authorized construction of the Washington Canal, which channeled Tiber Creek (site of present-day Constitution Avenue), turned south in front of the Capitol, and channeled James Creek to empty into the Eastern Branch (present-day Anacostia River) (see fig. 23). The canal was only fitfully successful as a canal, but it served as a large drainage ditch. Once the aqueduct was online and providing ten million gallons of water to the city daily, the sewer system was even more stressed. Seven sewers drained into the Washington Canal, which had little slope to it and was plagued by a tidal backwash, so the sewage tended to remain there.[17]

In the early 1870s the Board of Public Works, directed by Alexander Shepherd, filled in the canal and built a sewer parallel to it. In less than three years the board built an additional 120 miles of sewers, concentrated in the downtown area. The work was alleged to be shoddy; lateral sewers that ran uphill to mains had to be rebuilt. Still, the change was remarkable; as one observer described it at the end of 1872: "If you will conceive a city, substantially without a decent sewer, its sewage carried off through the gutters by infrequent rains, and natural water-courses depended upon for similar service, you will have an idea of what Washington was substantially less than two years ago. Today there are seventy miles of sewerage in the ground." In 1881, of the thirty thousand houses in Washington and Georgetown, fewer than a third had sewer connections, but the requirement that new houses connect to the sewer, if

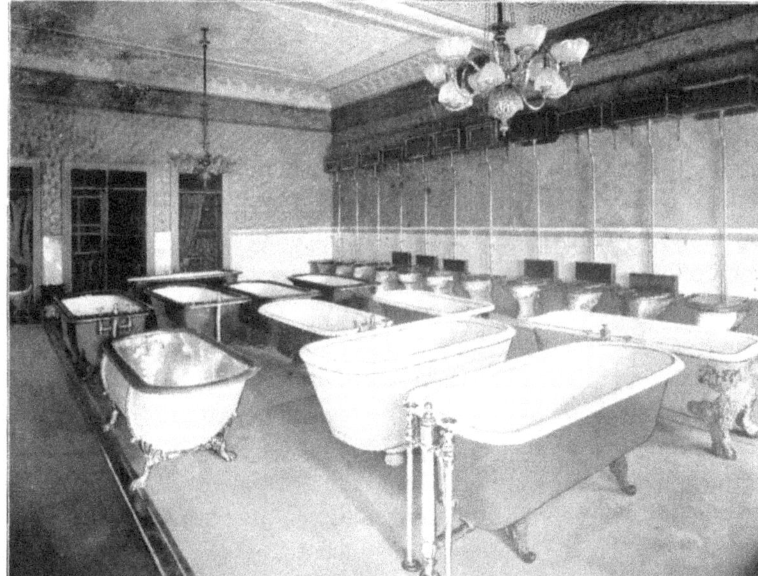

Figure 66. Advertisement, Henry McShane Mfg. Co., 423 Tenth Street NW, 1894. Footed bathtubs with rolled rims and toilets with elevated tanks are on display in this showroom in downtown Washington. (From *Selections from the Work of T. F. Schneider, Architect* [Washington, DC, 1894], DC History Center, NA 712.S37)

available, kept increasing that number. As the Inspector of Plumbing noted, "consequently even a small house is generally fitted up with a kitchen sink, a water closet, and sometimes a bath tub, while in a more expensively built residence, arranged with a more costly system of plumbing, we find, in addition to the above, stationary wash stands, near sleeping apartments, a number of bath and dressing rooms, having in them water closets, urinals, foot tubs, bidets and other fixtures." Washington was the first city in the nation to issue regulations regarding plumbing and house drainage, which it did in 1881.[18] With water and sewer service available for almost all new houses in the city, bathrooms became standard features in late nineteenth-century row houses (see fig. 66).

Germs and Conveniences

The germ theory, taking hold in the late nineteenth century, redefined what was healthy. Once diseases were linked to specific bacteria, or germs, the focus shifted to eliminating those occasions for transmission. Much attention dwelt on the individual—isolating the sick, not sharing utensils and cups, and observing basic personal cleanliness such as handwashing and bathing. Location was also important. One ad for a row house assured potential purchasers that "a gentleman prominently connected with the Smithsonian Institution" had just bought a house in the neighborhood, "influenced largely by the purity of the air, and that he feels there is no malaria or microbes." For the home, eliminating places where germs might dwell became important, and germ theorists initially believed that dust and dirt harbored germs. A stripped-down aesthetic, removing heavy draperies, carpets, and dark wallpapers, took hold. In the early twentieth century, germ theorists also believed that sunlight could kill germs and that fresh air was essential. As engineer Jonathan K. Allen asserted in 1907, "Fresh air and sunshine are such effective destroyers of bacteria whose presence is inimical to the family health, that plenty of both are to be sought always."[19]

This new interest in air and sunshine as disinfectants had ramifications for the row house, seen in a more open plan and the addition of porches. As noted in chapter 2, regulations restricted the size of the courts created by back buildings to the point where developers no longer found them practical on narrow lots, and the row-house form shifted from bay fronts with back buildings to quadrant plans. In 1905 the District's building inspector, Snowdon Ashford, invoked public health concerns when he explained that the preservation of open space on a lot "makes good use of [property] by affording health and comfort for future generations and preventing the spread of deadly diseases by imposing a safe distance for the play of sunlight between the bed room of a scarlet fever or diphtheria sufferer and the windows of his neighbors." In articles and editorials with titles such as "Ventilation Discussed" and "More Air," the *Evening Star* stated that "one of the most important factors in the preservation of the public health is a free circulation of air."[20] Detached houses in new forms, such as bungalows and foursquares, employed a more open plan than in the late nineteenth century, with special-purpose rooms such as pantries being discarded in favor of built-in kitchen cabinets. Larger openings between rooms, instead of doors, were enabled by central heating, which did not need closed-up rooms to be effective.

To facilitate air flow in the row house, the quadrant plan, such as that of Edna Perry's house, had wide openings between the living room and dining room, and between the front hall and the living room, and the number of rooms on the first floor was reduced to a compact three: living room, dining room, and kitchen, plus a front hall (see fig. 19). The attic, which without operable windows was negligibly efficient at promoting air circulation, was advertised as promoting ventilation. The *Evening Star* quoted an unnamed real estate agent as saying that the "attic effect . . . affords better ventilation by taking the heat away from the sleeping rooms." The quadrant-plan house also benefited from a broad front porch, which provided a space for leisure and socializing, and a sleeping porch, which brought the bedroom outdoors (see figs. 67 and 68). Sleeping outdoors was a common part of the treatment for tuberculous patients, but by 1909 advocates heralded it for the healthy. Drafts and dampness, the commonly perceived drawbacks to night air, were "infinitely less dangerous than foul air and house dust." Sleeping outside became a deterrent to all sorts of ailments. "Sleep outdoors and be well" was the rallying cry.[21]

"The compact, convenient arrangement of rooms with ABUNDANT FRESH AIR AND SUNLIGHT (TWO INVALUABLE ASSETS IN ANY HOME) PROVIDE DELIGHTFUL FACILITIES FOR HOUSEKEEPING IN THESE HOMES," loudly proclaimed a Shannon and Luchs ad for row houses at 14th and Parkwood Streets built by developer Harry Wardman in 1910. Rather than touting the physical assets of the houses, which appeared in the last paragraph—"six rooms, reception hall and bath, comfortable kitchen and pantry, hot-water heat, electric lighting, double floors, double back porches and steel construction"—the ad argued that sunlight and ventilation were among the elements that assisted the housekeeper in her duties. "The housewife's comfort has been considered in every detail. Every feature has been designed to lighten the task of housework. The advantage of the upstairs

Figure 67. Row houses. The front porch of the quadrant-plan row house provided a space for gathering, socializing, and dining. (National Photo Company, 1924, Library of Congress)

Figure 68. Row houses, rear view. Sleeping porches were another feature of the quadrant-plan house. The backyards no longer had privies and high board fences, but more open landscapes with wire fences and lots of laundry. (David Myers, photographer, 1939, Library of Congress, Prints and Photographs Division, Farm Security Administration)

kitchen [i.e., not in the basement], the snug pantry, the easy ascent of the stairs, the light airy cellar and the unusual window capacity are values quickly recognizable by every woman. The whole dwelling . . . illustrates the importance of providing abundant light and air to contribute to the cheery, wholesomeness of the home."[22] The ad assumes that it is the housewife who is the home laborer, and her tasks are best accomplished with light and air.

In the early twentieth century, officials also saw the bathtub as increasingly necessary, because personal hygiene was an important part of combating germs. In 1907 building regulations required bathtubs in all new houses that rented for more than $10 per month, effectively ruling out houses for the poorest. Two years later, the plumbing code qualified this regulation in revealing ways: the rent minimum was removed, and multifamily buildings had to provide one bath for every four rooms; there had to be adequate space around and under the tub to clean the bathroom, reflecting the fear of germs lurking in dirt; and a minimum size for tubs was specified, because builders had been "endeavoring to cut down the size of bathrooms."[23]

There were limits to the benefits of ventilation, though, and as fears of sewer gas dissipated in the face of the germ theory, developers found a more efficient arrangement for the bathroom. In 1909, a change in the building regulations permitted ventilating shafts or skylights, rather than exterior windows, for bathrooms. In that year, Shannon and Luchs advertised Harry

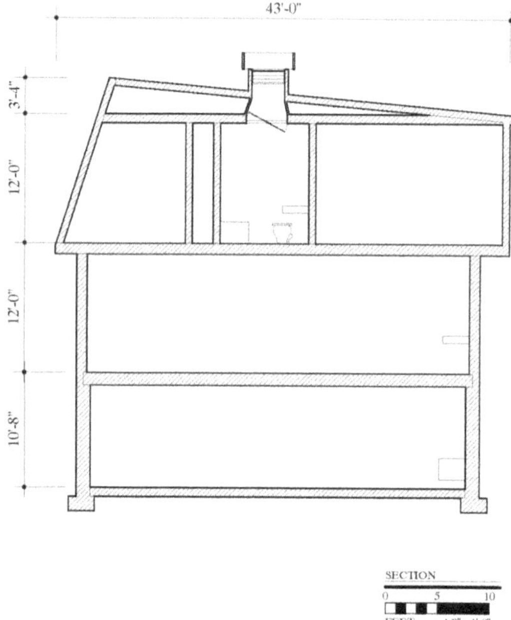

Figure 69. Row house, Third and Bryant Streets NE, sectional drawing. This section of a row house shows the skylight ventilating the interior bathroom. (W. W. Taylor, architect, 1926, Library of Congress, Heaton Architectural Drawing Archive, ADE unit 931, redrawn by Ruben Melendez and Onairis Perez)

Wardman's row houses at 14th and Buchanan Streets in an elaborate booklet that included this claim: "A new feature of construction is an air shaft in the bath room leading directly to the roof, insuring a perfect ventilation of the entire house."[24] With this, developers began to place the bathroom on the interior of the second floor, not on an exterior wall, freeing up an additional window for a bedroom. Within a decade, most row houses of the quadrant plan had an interior bathroom (see fig. 69). Edna Perry's house had two bathrooms, both interior, and both ventilated by skylights.

Electricity was another convenience that affected the plan of the row house. Electricity was available in the 1880s, but it did not become widespread for domestic use until the 1890s. Although electricity was inherently safer than gas, the new technology's reputation for shocking users meant that it did not meet with universal acceptance initially. In many neighborhoods, the appearance of electricity was tied to streetcars. George Truesdell, who developed a trolley system that drew electric power from overhead wires in conjunction with his development of the new suburb of Eckington, in Northeast Washington, was the pioneer of electric streetcars in the city. Electricity flowed freely in Eckington; as the newspaper enthused in 1890, "It is almost like a glimpse of fairyland to witness the illumination of Eckington by electricity every evening, the brilliant spectacle being heightened by the appearance of the streets and approaches." Houses could receive electricity too: "the interiors of the residences at Eckington are such as to satisfy the most exacting, and open fireplaces, hardwood floors, and all the appliances for electric light illumination are only a few of the factors which go to make life pleasant." Truesdell ran into opposition from city leaders who insisted that streetcar wires be placed underground, although satisfactory technology for that had not yet been developed. Truesdell's streetcar business went bankrupt in 1896, and the newly formed Potomac Electric Power Company acquired his streetcar power plant.[25]

The aesthetic appearance of the streets of Washington benefited from an early effort to discourage the proliferation of a jumble of wires overhead. Crosby Noyes, editor of the *Evening Star,* led the campaign to place all wires—electricity, telephone, and telegraph, as well as streetcar—underground. The effort took several decades, beginning in the mid-1880s, but was ultimately successful.[26] After finding a way to power their streetcars by underground wires and avoid the overhead clutter, existing streetcar companies shifted from horsecars and underground cables to electricity, and Potomac Electric acquired them as customers.

In 1897, the city issued its first regulations for electric wiring in buildings, indicating that electricity for domestic use was becoming a reality (see fig. 70). Progress was slow, though; in 1910 Washington had only 14,000 electrical meters, averaging one meter for every twenty-four residents. Just four years later, one of every fifteen people in Washington had electricity, and by the time Edna Perry bought her new house in 1922, electricity was a standard amenity. Lighting was the primary use for electricity in the home, and

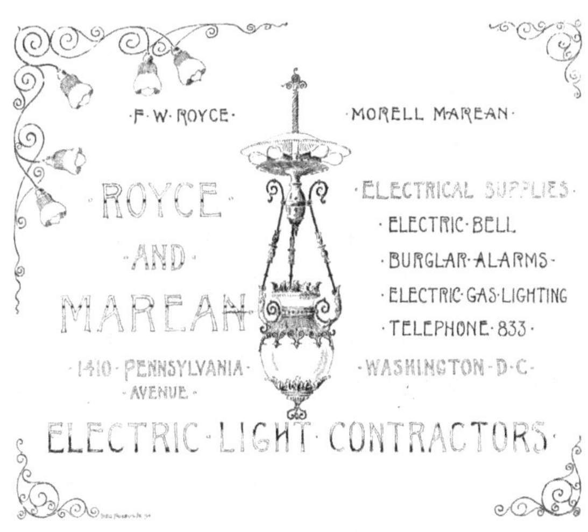

Figure 70. Advertisement, Royce and Marean, 1410 Pennsylvania Avenue NW. In the 1890s, electric fixtures often resembled gas ones. (From *Selections from the Work of T. F. Schneider, Architect* [Washington, DC, 1894], DC History Center, NA 712.S37)

although a wealth of appliances became available, large appliances such as refrigerators, ranges, and water heaters were too expensive for many. Small appliances such as toasters, irons, percolators, and waffle makers were more readily acquired.[27]

Installing electric wiring in an existing house was much easier than bringing in gas, because electric wires were flexible and gas pipes were not. By the 1910s electrical contractors saw retrofitting as an integral part of their business. Arthur F. Carroll, who specialized in "old house wiring," advertised in 1912 that his business had more than doubled in the previous three years. He employed a dozen electricians. In 1916 F. J. Lusby claimed to "make a specialty of wiring ready-built houses." He attempted to assuage homeowners' fears of dirt and disruption by promising, "Your hand-decorated or expensively-papered walls and your highly-polished floors and woodwork will not be injured." Eight years later Ralph P. Gibson advertised that he would wire any six-room house "including Bath, Halls and Basement" for $60.[28]

Central heating also became more popular in the early twentieth century. Enabling all the spaces of a house to be the same comfortable temperature, a furnace in the basement heated hot air, which rose passively through ducts, or hot water or steam, which circulated through radiators. Edna Perry's house had hot-water heat distributed through radiators. Central heat was a significant project, though, requiring both a furnace and a basement in which to put it. Ductwork or piping through the house added to the cost and effort, so central heat was most often installed in newly built houses, where it added minimally to the ultimate cost. In contrast, retrofitting a row house with central heat was prohibitively expensive for most owners, so the city's older row houses tended to lag behind.[29]

In 1905 home economics pioneer Ellen H. Richards examined the sharp rise in the cost of dwellings nationwide. "The cost of construction has doubled, and the sanitary requirements have again doubled the cost, so that it is easy to see why the family with a stationary income has quartered its dwelling-space." The overall size of row houses in the twentieth century did not seem to shrink—Edna Perry's quadrant-plan house was just 250 square feet smaller than Grace Smith's bay-front house—but the quadrant plan was simpler, with fewer rooms, and cheaper to build, while economies of scale further reduced the cost. In 1911 the Zepp Brothers built twenty-one quadrant-plan houses on Sherman Avenue NW, each with central heating, electricity and gas, and a front porch, "colonial in design." The Zepps estimated the cost of construction for these standard houses, 17½ feet wide, at just $1,800 each, which was cheap by any measure. Seven years later, they sold for $4,000 each.[30]

Advertisements for houses often mentioned these latest improvements.

An ad from 1892 touted the latest amenities: "For Sale—218 11th St. SE. Near Lincoln Park; new house; 6 rooms and bath; electricity; speaking tubes, all mod. imps.; only requires $300 cash." One of a row of sixteen bay-front houses, this 16-foot-wide house cost $3,000 to construct, putting it in the middle range of speculative row houses. Another ad from 1892 hails the central heating and electrically assisted gas lighting: "For Sale—507 Florida Ave., NW. New two-story six-room brick, with all mod. imps.; heated by furnace; handsomely papered; electric gas lighting; speaking tubes, tiled vestibule and cabinet mantels; price only $5,500; house in same row sold for $6,500. This is a rare bargain." In 1914 a house on Staples Street NE claimed electricity, gas appliances, and a fully equipped bathroom: "stucco front [house] containing six well-ventilated, bright rooms, having electric lights, parquet flooring on the first floor, gas stove, gas hot-water heater, large concrete cellar, long back [yard], Colonial front porch, back porch, modern bath with lavatory, low down tank, full-size enamel tub." The ad specified that the unfurnished house was for rent to white tenants for $22.50 a month.[31]

The advertisements also point to a shift in labor brought by changing technologies. The 1892 ads mention "speaking tubes," a device for communicating with servants—and Grace Smith's modest rental house had this feature (see fig. 71). In contrast, a 1926 Potomac Electric ad shows that the burden of the household work, with the added convenience of "labor-saving" devices, had shifted to the housewife: "home comfort lies in the number and location of convenience outlets for electricity, for by these magic loadstones drudgery in home work is banished and women's time is put to uses that in reality makes the home 'Sweet.'" In the late nineteenth century, live-in servants were rare in the middle-class households that occupied speculative row houses, and Grace Smith would have been an exception. Living with her, her husband, and their two-year-old son was Emma Harris, an African American servant who doubled as a cook. More common were day workers. As a report from the Census Office noted about Washington in 1887, "The great majority of household servants do not sleep at their places of service, but return to their homes at night." Laundry was a particularly onerous task, and if a middle-class housewife did not have a laundress come in to do the laundry, she was likely to send it out (see fig. 72). Grace Smith's basement contained a large soapstone laundry tub, while Edna Perry's basement contained a toilet, probably designated for domestic workers (see fig. 73). After the turn of the century, and especially after World War I, servants became rarer. In 1920 there were half as many domestic servants, per capita, in Washington as there had been in 1880. On the one hand, other types of jobs, such as factory work, opened up for working-class women; and as the Potomac Electric ad implied, once the "drudgery" was "banished," servants were no longer nec-

Figure 71. Row house, 1524 T Street NW. Speaking tubes in the second-floor hallway allowed the homeowner to give instructions to a domestic servant in the kitchen. (Justin Scalera, photographer, 2018, Library of Congress, Prints and Photographs Division, HABS)

essary for middle-class households. No longer the supervisor, the housewife became the worker.[32]

The introduction of central heat and electricity affected the plan of the row house. The closed-off rooms of Grace Smith's bay-windowed L-shaped plan, desirable for containing heat from stoves and for airing out rooms that had been lit by gas, gave way to the more open plan of Edna Perry's quadrant plan with its wide openings between the public rooms on the first floor. With central heat, all of the rooms were heated equally, and with electricity, concerns about drafts extinguishing gas flames were alleviated.[33] The new open plan, which satisfied a desire for ventilation and light, easily accommodated central heat and electric lights.

Air continued to be a concern after the mid-twentieth century, still affecting the plan of the row house. The electric ventilating fan had been developed

Figure 72. Unidentified alley. When homeowners sent their laundry out, it was usually laundresses living in alleys who took on this task. (Photographer unknown, 1930s, DC History Center, General Photograph Collection, CHS 04507)

Figure 73. Row house, 1524 T Street NW. If laundry was done in the home, it was in laundry tubs in the basement, such as this. (Justin Scalera, photographer, 2018, Library of Congress, Prints and Photographs Division, HABS)

in the 1930s, but building regulations, and the Federal Housing Administration, did not approve it as a sufficient replacement for a window or ventilating skylight until the 1950s. In 1957 one Washington official warned of "unhealthful conditions" if the bathroom were not properly ventilated, hearkening back to sanitarians' concern for sewer gas, but that year Washington's plumbing code allowed "windowless bathrooms" in houses, if they were equipped with a ventilation fan.[34] This permitted interior bathrooms not only on the second floor, but also on the first, which had been difficult to equip with skylights.

The concern for adequate ventilation also haunted the debate over the windowless kitchen. First proposed in 1952, the interior kitchen brought out well-organized opposition described under the headline "Housewives Oppose Windowless Kitchens." The "housewives," representing several citizens' associations and women's clubs, argued that homemakers wanted daylight, resented confinement, and feared "a malodorous situation." Further, they cited "the Health Department's belief that sunshine, even through windows, is more healthful than artificial light." Or, as one woman wrote in a letter to the editor, "in Heaven's name, grant us respite from these men who endeavor in the name of efficiency to drive their wives, mothers and sisters quite mad, as I assure you they will if windowless kitchens become a national custom." One male member of the D.C. Building Code Advisory Committee also opposed windowless kitchens, associating them inexplicably with a wide range of evils—"unhealthful housing, slums and slum problems, including increased rates of disease, mental illness, family instability and other attendant social and community problems." The protesters prevailed, and the building code banned windowless kitchens, but a few years later, in 1956, real estate interests raised the issue again. This time the housewives were overruled, and regulations permitted windowless kitchens with mechanical ventilation.[35]

The windowless kitchen and bathroom had been pioneered in apartments, but they soon found great utility in row houses. In the urban renewal area of Southwest Washington, Chloethiel Woodard Smith's Capitol Park row houses incorporated the windowless kitchen into the designs. Smith's former partner in an architectural firm, Nicholas Satterlee, wrote a letter to the *Washington Post* in which he explained, in effect, the situation that she would be facing—how to put a kitchen in a small row house. He wrote, "with the exterior kitchen, the living space becomes tunnel-like, with the wider most unhealthy allocation of space at the corridor end . . . with the interior kitchen the wider living area occurs at the exterior wall and benefits psychologically from extended view and natural light."[36] With the changes in regulations, Smith's plans for the smaller town houses at Capitol Park included, on the first floor, an 8-by-8-foot interior kitchen and, on the second floor, a 5-by-7-foot interior bathroom (see fig. 21). By bringing the kitchen forward—

Figure 74. Capitol Park, Southwest Washington. In this redevelopment area, the backyards accommodated leisure, not laundry. Each row house's patio was defined by shrubbery. Photographer unknown, ca. 1960s. (Library of Congress, Prints and Photographs Division, PR13 CN2010: 100 C. W. Smith container 211, folder 37)

and in some variations, not just to the middle of the house but all the way to the front—she reoriented the house to the backyard, which was no longer a place of utility, but a space for recreation and entertainment (see fig. 74).

The backyard had undergone severe changes as the facilities within the house had changed. Among the various sheds that a backyard might acquire was a summer kitchen. In 1882, just as he completed construction of four row houses on Twenty-Fifth Street NW, R. A. Tilton added 10-by-12-foot summer kitchens behind them. Other buildings in the yard might include a fuel shed, such as the 12-by-20-foot one built by Noah Price, or the 8-by-8-foot bathroom that C. C. Walker added to a summer kitchen. All of these functions were gradually absorbed into houses, but it was the elimination of the privy that created the biggest transformation. Besides making the sleeping porch more feasible, the removal of this smelly and offensive shed was the first step toward the creation of the ornamental yard. With it gone, no longer were high board fences desirable, and officials moved to eliminate them in 1915. Echoing the precepts of the New Public Health, a Chamber of Commerce report called these fences not only "unsightly" but also "a menace to public health," because they "exclude much of the sunlight, God's given germicide, and prevent a free circulation of air in the yards, which is so necessary for the elimination of dampness." Dampness bred filth, which attracted vermin; "disease-producing germs are carried from such into our dwellings by flies and rats." The chamber favored low picket or wire fences, and noted that speculative builders were already building these, because their houses had bathrooms instead of privies, as well as sleeping porches. Residents who valued light and air, and therefore health, preferred low fences, the chamber implied.[37]

In the late twentieth century, health and comfort inside the row house increasingly depended on air-conditioning. In 1960 a little more than 20 percent of Washington households had air-conditioning, following the introduction of the window unit in 1951.[38] In the second phase of Capitol Park, completed in 1963, a central source—not just central to the house, but to the 241-house development—piped in cold air. Windows were large, and hallways were mostly nonexistent, so that the small space (about 500 square feet on a floor) seemed light and airy. The air did not come from the 4-foot-wide windows and, in fact, windows weren't necessary for ventilation at all. But at the moment of their obsolescence, the desire for the appearance of air was stronger than ever.

By 1991 almost 90 percent of Washington households had air-conditioning, which found acceptance in row houses with their inherent constraints on providing cross-ventilation. Central air has been accompanied by a new sense of airiness, a visual openness, resulting in ever more open plans, larger windows and glass doors, and visual connections. The hall has virtually disappeared. Concerns about air continue to plague homeowners, though, because air is now seen as potentially inimical to good health for different reasons. Radon, Legionnaires' disease, sick building syndrome, and house dust mites are all threats potentially borne by bad air.[39] The pendulum has swung back to a concern about environmental health, as Americans identify threats not just from other people, but from the home itself.

The provision of utilities not only enhanced the health and comfort of the city's residents, but it also affected the design of the row house. In the years around 1890–1920, electricity replaced gas as the preferred method of lighting, stoves gave way to various forms of central heat, and the bathroom, consolidated into an efficient three-fixture space, reflected new ideas about health and sanitation. Concurrently with these changes, and to some degree due to them, the plan of the row house underwent a dramatic transformation, from the L-shaped plan with back building to the quadrant plan. Both of these plans evince a concern for air; the bay-windowed L-shaped plan for the movement of air, through bay windows, bathrooms with windows, and tall ceilings, and the quadrant plan for the quality of air, by eliminating the court, taking advantage of a privy-less backyard, and moving the family onto porches to obtain fresh air. Changing ideas about air and ventilation facilitated the open plan of today's forward-kitchen row house as well, with the acceptance of mechanically moved and treated air.

Not all houses were new, though; the new, well-equipped row houses coexisted with older ones whose amenities were soon perceived as inadequate. By 1922, when Edna Perry's quadrant-plan house with electricity and central heat was built, Grace Smith had long moved away from her L-shaped rental house, which had neither amenity. The older house presented an opportunity, though, to Susie Thomas, who bought a well-built, centrally located row house and lived there for the next fifty years. The next two chapters look at the people who interacted with health and comfort in row houses—the builders who constructed and equipped the houses and the consumers who bought and rented them: the Grace Smiths, the Edna Perrys, and the Susie Thomases.

5

Building and Selling

Washington's row houses underwent a shift in scale from the nineteenth century to the twentieth, from rows of four or six to whole frontages of squares, or even whole squares of identical buildings. One reason for this was the evolution from the speculative builder to the operative builder, who instituted a more vertical management structure and cultivated a larger business. With land acquisition, design, construction, and sales all under one roof, the operative builder benefited from economies of scale, offering cheaper dwellings. Another reason for the shift was geographic, as new construction moved from the old city, where available land was interspersed among lots already built on, to the area beyond, where farmland was being subdivided into lots and squares. Marketing their developments aggressively, operative builders promoted explicit racial segregation to attract white buyers. In early twentieth-century Washington, home building became a big business, and row houses were the first product.

Speculative builders have such a shady reputation that it is worth exploring the term. Associated with cheap construction and a disregard for the homeowner or neighborhood, speculative builders view the market for their product as a primary concern. Therefore, their buildings have to have a broad appeal and sell for the price at which they would make a profit. For some builders, their reputation for fair deals and high-end construction were selling points, so "speculative" does not necessarily mean "cheap." For the purposes of this discussion, a speculative builder is anyone who builds houses in quantity, counting on a market for them emerging, rather than building for specific clients. With their eye on the market, speculative builders developed row houses equipped with common features, allowing for insight into the dwellings occupied by most people—neither the highest nor lowest end, but the broad middle market.

Building

Washington has always had speculative builders, beginning with James Greenleaf and his partners John Nicholson and Robert Morris. After their

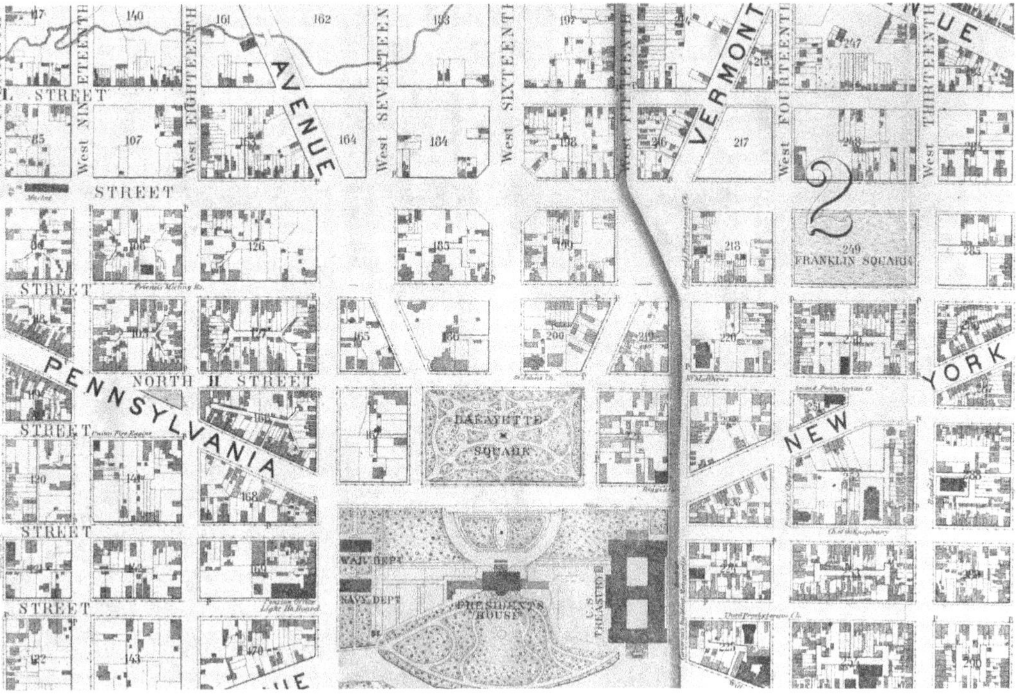

Figure 75. Boschke map, detail. In this portion of an 1857 map showing the area north of the White House, settlement is dense to the east, which was the main commercial area, and to the west, along Pennsylvania Avenue on the way to Georgetown, but the area directly north was sparsely settled, with few row houses. (A. Boschke and Julius Bien, *Map of Washington City, District of Columbia, seat of the federal government: respectfully dedicated to the Senate and the House of Representatives of the United States of North America* [Washington DC: A. Boschke, 1857], Library of Congress, Geography and Map Division)

disastrous attempts to provide row houses in the 1790s, though, no significant speculative builders arose. The city developed slowly with little demand for great numbers of houses. Most builders built a few row houses at a time, singly or in pairs.[1] The 1857 Boschke map, which locates buildings, shows the situation (see fig. 75). Aside from the densely packed squares between the White House and the Capitol, few other squares are completely built out. Just north of the White House and east of the Capitol, only a handful of buildings occupy the squares.

The influx of population during the Civil War, though, created a demand for housing. With many of those newcomers staying after the war, and benefiting from the public improvements initiated by Alexander Shepherd's Board of Public Works, Washington real estate became a safer investment. By the 1880s, Washington's real estate industry was booming. Social scientist John Hitz observed in 1882 that "whole squares have literally been built up with two, three, and four-story dwellings, many being provided with all the so called 'modern improvements.'" Construction-related firms, which numbered 251 in 1880, grew to 744 by 1900, while the value of buildings they produced grew from nearly $2 million to almost $14 million in those same years.[2]

Builders entered the speculative market. Whereas before the Civil War master builders would do the work themselves, and maybe subcontract to masons and other specialties, after the war master builders tended to employ journeymen, who did the actual work. The master builders became speculative entrepreneurs, taking on the financial risk of constructing a row of houses and hiring all of the craftsmen necessary to complete the task. They were not always successful, and most of these builder-entrepreneurs undertook only one venture, but they participated fully in the expanding real estate market.[3]

One example of a successful builder is Charles Gessford, who came to Washington from Baltimore in 1850 and began working as a carpenter's apprentice. Although not much is known of his early career, he was doing well enough by 1864 that he advertised to hire carpenters. By the 1880s he had a flourishing career that involved building houses for himself more often than for others. In that decade, he undertook thirty-two projects for a total of 149 row houses. Half of them were only 12 or 13 feet wide, and one row's houses were only 11 feet wide, so he apparently saw his market as the working class. He did not build in great quantity at one time, with the average project being four or five houses. He usually built without an architect, designing the houses himself with some hallmark features, at least among the larger row houses: corbeled cornices, molded brick ornamentation, and chamfered polygonal bays topped by ornamented gables, interspersed with rounded bays with conical roofs. As the decade went on, he moved from building workers' houses and alley dwellings to larger, L-plan row houses, concentrating most of his work on Capitol Hill.[4]

African American entrepreneurs also participated in the industry as owners, architects, and builders. For example, William A. Stewart, an African American real estate broker, commissioned nine row houses at the corner of Fourth and E Streets NE, in 1889. He hired the prominent African American architect Calvin T. S. Brent, who was also listed as the builder on the permit. Brent, whose oeuvre as an architect included seven churches, served as the builder on several other projects. In 1893, for a pair of row houses at 116–18 Fifth Street SE, he was listed as owner, architect, and builder.[5]

By the late 1880s, "builders" were more often men who had never learned a construction trade but instead were real estate professionals, skilled at raising the financing and subcontracting the work. In the 1880s, builders constructed row houses in small groupings; the output of only a few builders exceeded a couple dozen in a year. After the 1893 depression, Ray E. Middaugh was the most prominent row-house builder, but his production remained small until the end of the decade.[6] By 1900, the effect on the streetscape of this small-scale building was clear. For the most part, the squares in the L'Enfant city were all or partly built up, with few large expanses of undeveloped land. Even where land was available, mostly north of Massachusetts Avenue, builders chose to develop row houses in small projects of six or eight.

The construction of row houses involved many materials, workers, and skills, but the structure itself was fairly simple; brick bearing walls supported the interior wood frame. Building regulations dictated the thickness of the party walls and prohibited any structural members from running continuously through them. While joists and beams could be notched into the party walls from both sides, at least four inches of wall thickness had to be left intact. In row houses, an interior bearing wall often ran from front to back, separating the stair hall from the main rooms. Here, a large timber beam supported on a masonry pier would provide for openings and support the wall on the floor above. In the early twentieth century, row-house builders began using a steel beam supported on a steel column for this purpose, a fact they heralded in their advertisements (see fig. 48).[7]

The building trades began organizing in 1866, when two thousand workmen went on strike, resulting in an agreement on the nine-hour-day. By the 1880s, factory production of windows, doors, and other parts of buildings had made it easier to introduce piecework, in which workers were paid by the product instead of the time. For example, in the carpentry trade, "the bosses would offer but 30 cents per square (100 square feet) for laying flooring, and three squares were considered a fair day's work if properly laid," compared to a day wage of $2.50, according to an 1888 union report. Union activity and job actions persisted among the building trades, with piecework continuing to be a sore point. Piecework enabled speculative builders to drive down prices, but it was also associated with cheap construction, in contrast to day work, as evidenced by this 1889 ad for "the prettiest Queen Anne Home; in best improved location northeast, on two car lines; two-story and back building; bay window and balcony; 7 rooms; hot and cold water; oak finish; oak mantels; built by day-work."[8]

African American craftsmen were not usually welcomed in the white trade unions, despite their long history in Washington's building industry. The construction of the Capitol and White House relied on slaves hired out for the purpose. By the mid-nineteenth century, African Americans worked in all the building trades, but their efforts to gain security and prominence were stymied by white unions and the specialization of the building trades in the late nineteenth century. A 1901 directory of Black "mechanics, business, and professional men and women" listed 29 carpenters, 16 contractors (some of whom overlapped with carpenters), 23 painters, 2 plumbers, and 7 tinning, heating, and roofing workers in the city. Only three of the building-oriented crafts had formed unions, the largest by far being the Hod Carriers' Society, affiliated with the Federation of Labor, with 450 members.[9]

A snapshot of the building industry is provided by the discussion surrounding a strike of the building trades in 1906–8. At that time, an employer such as a master plumber dealt with five unions: journeymen; apprentices, who could handle tools; helpers, who could not handle tools; skilled laborers; and unskilled laborers. By an agreement reached after a previous strike, four years earlier, only two apprentices were allowed to work in each shop, no matter how large an operation, and only two helpers were allowed for each three journeymen. The unionized journeymen were concerned with limiting the labor pool so as to enhance their opportunities, while the employers preferred to hire cheaper labor, such as apprentices and helpers. The seasonal nature of construction amplified both the need for labor, during the building season, and the excess of labor, during the winter. During the strike, the master plumbers threatened to do the work themselves: "We will don the overalls and jumpers . . . and go to work with the tools."[10]

The strike, which began with a lockout by the Master Plumbers Association in March 1906, spread to the other building trades in the spring of 1907. The issue was the open shop—whether unionized workers should be forced to work at a site alongside nonunion workers. Initially the unionists avoided actions at the congressional office buildings then under construction and targeted the Municipal Building (now called the District Building), the Metropolitan Club, and a row of houses in Park View, in Northwest Washington. By June 1907, two thousand workmen were on strike, affecting $2 million worth of building operations. But also in 1907 the economy was descending into a recession. The newspaper noted "a falling off in the amount of private building, but in that particular Washington does not stand alone among the cities of the country. The shrinkage in the building activities has been general," which counteracted an oversupply, giving time for what had been recently built to be absorbed.[11] In May 1908 the bricklayers and masons went back to work, and the strike ended with no gains for the workers.

A 1912 newspaper article discussed the specialization that had occurred in the building industry, naming a number of different building trades: architect; construction engineer, "a profession unknown a generation ago"; excavator; stone man, "who erects the retaining walls and sets the anchors and foundations on which the building will rest its weight"; steel construction man to erect the skeleton; then "the concrete men and the terra cotta men and the elevator men, all putting the skin on this skeleton"; plasterer; electrical man; plumber; concrete man, "a product of the age," who "lays floor and facings alike: puts in cellar supports and parlor mantelpieces" and in some cases builds the whole structure; heating man; and gas man (see fig. 76). Curiously, the list omitted several trades included in the Building Trades Mechanics' Alliance: bricklayer, carpenter, sheet-metal worker, hoisting engineer, painter, interior marble worker, stone cutter, wood, wire, and metal lather, tile setter, and sheet and tile roofer. The product of the work

Figure 76. J. T. Walker Sons, 204 Tenth Street NW. Building materials, such as the lime, cement, plaster, pitch, and felt sold here, suggest the kinds of expertise necessary to use them in building a house. (Photographer unknown, early twentieth century, DC History Center, General Photograph Collection, CHS 03115)

of all these craftsmen, a row house, could be completed in as little as three months.[12] And the person putting all this together, the speculative owner-builder, undertook significant risks but reaped considerable profits.

Builders

Just as there were shifts in the building trades in the early twentieth century, so were there changes among the builders who hired them. By 1906, the *Evening Star* asserted, "the individual builder of houses has disappeared, and the large builder, the man who puts up rows of houses, has taken his place." In 1899 Ray E. Middaugh built 56 row houses, an annual total that was not exceeded until Harry Wardman built 74 five years later. In the first decade of the new century, Wardman dominated the industry, routinely building more than twice as many in a year as Middaugh, who usually had the second-greatest output. Between 1900 and 1910, Harry Wardman built a total of 925 row houses, while Middaugh and Shannon built 323. For the next decade, Wardman also led, with 665, but close behind was Harry Kite, with 658, as Wardman's production dropped off before the war, and he moved into other forms of housing afterward.[13] A closer examination of some of the more prominent builders illustrates the growth of the industry of speculative row-house construction.

Trained as a lawyer, Ray Middaugh entered the real estate field with no background in building. Born in 1870 in Upstate New York, he attended Cornell Law School and came to Washington after graduating in 1892. Middaugh worked in the law office of George Kern, who had a practice in patents and pensions. Kern's brother, Edward, was a builder who designed and built a house for George at 51 R Street NW. Both the profession (builder) and the location (near Bloomingdale) likely influenced Ray Middaugh's foray into real estate.[14]

Middaugh began building row houses in Bloomingdale, listing himself as "builder" and at least once as "architect." He found a partner in William E. Shannon, who apparently handled sales, and in 1900 they formed the firm Middaugh and Shannon. They later claimed to have built more than 500 houses in Bloomingdale, "and every one of these 500 residences was sold before its completion." In 1906 the firm shifted its attention to Park View, where Middaugh and Shannon advertised themselves as "the people who built Bloomingdale." They continued on to other neighborhoods, building hundreds of row houses. Middaugh died in 1910 at the age of forty; the firm's primary architect, Joseph Bohn Jr., also died that year, at the age of thirty-three.[15] The firm continued until Shannon's death in 1930, but its output of row houses diminished after 1910.

Besides sheer numbers, the firm of Middaugh and Shannon is significant for its innovations in the plan of the row house, as noted in the discussion of the three-room plan in chapter 1 (see figs. 11 and 12). The introduction of angled, windowed walls into the dining room and back building and the innovation of a glass-roofed conservatory at one end of the dining room attempted to bring natural light to the dark spaces of the three-room-plan row house. This concern for light and air in the court predated the change in building regulations, but these builders clearly saw the limitations of the L-shaped plan. In 1905, two weeks before the building regulation was changed but after it had been announced, Middaugh and Shannon applied for a building permit for a new plan of row house on Adams Street NW. These 20-foot-wide two-story buildings with two-story bay windows did not look different from the standard bay-front design, but they were perhaps the first in Washington with the quadrant plan. The newspaper described the innovations: "The arrangements provide for six rooms and each one has direct light and plenty of it, for there is no back building. On the first floor, the space in front is given up to the entrance hall and the parlor, and the rear with windows looking into the back yard to the dining room and the kitchen. On the second floor there are two bedrooms in the front and a bed room and bath room in the rear. It can be readily understood from the arrangement that there are no dark or insufficiently lighted rooms in the houses. All of them have direct light and plenty of it."[16]

Once the building regulations were changed, on December 1, 1905, Middaugh and Shannon produced row houses in several plans, seeking a viable alternative to the court and back building. One option was to build the wings back-to-back, so that the court was wider, but this meant that windows and doors that faced onto the court were uncomfortably close to the neighbor's windows and doors, which faced onto the same court. Another option was semi-detached houses, which required wider lots and produced more expensive houses. Middaugh and Shannon built twelve pairs of semi-detached houses in Park View early in 1906. As with their "copyrighted" row houses on First Street, they employed architect B. Stanley Simmons for the first set, then turned to Joseph Bohn for the remainder. They hailed these houses as being in "a style of building which is an innovation in the city," in that "there will be no houses in rows" and they intended to alternate architectural styles—"Old English, Spanish mission, Colonial, and Italian renaissance type." They also intended the houses and lots to be wider than they were but, as built, the houses were all in a Colonial Revival mode, 20 feet wide on a 32-foot-wide lot. Two-story bay windows projected into the generous side yards. A few years later, Middaugh and Shannon concluded that "the public does not want that type of house, or, at least, is not willing to pay the increased cost," which they estimated at about $2,000.[17]

Finally, by July 1906, Middaugh and Shannon returned to the quadrant plan, adding a front porch—the solution that was to change the character of Washington's residential streetscapes. The quadrant plan had four rooms on the first floor in a squarish arrangement, with the kitchen behind the hallway. As the ad described it, "No dark, unsanitary areaways, but each room an outside room." Middaugh and Shannon built 6 of these houses on Warder Street, just around the corner from their semi-detached houses. Concentrating their efforts in Park View, a few months later they built 17 of these on Manor Place and 6 more on Warder Street, and added 40 more on adjacent streets by 1907 (see fig. 77). Bohn was the architect of all of these row houses, each of which had a porch covering part of the front, leaving a door to the basement exposed. The houses were a generously sized 20 by 32 feet, with 10-foot ceilings on both floors. A fireplace with mirrored overmantel was the focus of the living room, and the kitchen had a built-in cabinet and swinging doors to the

Figure 77. Row houses, 400 block (north side) Manor Place NW. In the fall of 1906, Joseph Bohn Jr. designed some of the first quadrant-plan row houses for Middaugh and Shannon, who built these in the neighborhood of Park View. (Photograph by the author, 2022)

dining room and hall. On the second floor, the bathroom was in the rear and the three bedrooms took the rest of the windows, with a linen closet in the hallway. By the end of November, Middaugh and Shannon claimed "22 houses sold before they are under roof, and 24 houses sold before they are started."[18]

Harry Wardman built so many of this quadrant plan of row house that his name became identified with them. Born in England in 1872, Wardman came to the United States as a young man and took up the trade of carpentry, first in Philadelphia and then, in 1895, in Washington. After a few modest projects, in 1901 Wardman built 36 row-house flats for the Washington Sanitary Improvement Company, a philanthropic organization that provided alternatives to alley dwellings for the poor. The two-story row-house flats had an apartment on each floor, each equipped with a bathroom and running water. Wardman then went on to build row-house flats for profit. At the same time, he undertook construction of bay-fronted, L-plan row houses, such as those in Columbia Heights in 1903 and 1905, Capitol Hill in 1903, and Shaw in 1905. In 1905 he built a row of houses opposite the Simmons-designed Middaugh and Shannon row houses on First Street in Bloomingdale. Like Simmons's row, these were "pretentious Roman brick dwellings." Wardman's ad emphasized the interior fittings: "The artistic excellence of these modern residences is much enhanced by the rare judgment exercised in the selection of mantels and mirrors, and the ornamental character of the china closets . . . the rooms being elaborately decorated with fresco and mural paintings." All 18 houses sold within eight weeks of their completion. In 1906 Wardman built 116 row houses, 154 in 1907, 179 in 1908, and 254 in 1909, dwarfing his competition. In 1909 the next-largest producer of row houses was H. R. Howenstein, who built 53.[19]

The change in building regulations in late 1905 demanded a change in row-house form. Like Middaugh and Shannon, Wardman first turned to doubled-back buildings and then to semi-detached houses, such as those at Columbia Road and Biltmore Street NW, which he constructed in 1906. His first usage of the front porch and quadrant plan occurred in Eckington, in Northeast Washington, in November 1906, just months after Middaugh and Shannon. For Wardman, Albert Beers designed 9 houses on Quincy Place and 4 more around the corner on Eckington Place, then 16 more on Quincy Place a few months later. And from then on, that was the type that became associated with Wardman (see fig. 78). He embraced the new building form in a full-page ad in the real estate section of the *Evening Star* in 1908. "A Master Production . . . The only home of its kind ever built in America . . . Steel-girded reinforced construction," the Shannon & Luchs ad blared. The ad included a

Figure 78. Row houses, 1404–22 Buchanan Street NW. Wardman built hundreds of quadrant-plan row houses such as these, designed by Frank Russell White in 1912. They measured 20 by 30 feet and cost an estimated $4,000 each to construct. (Photograph by the author, 2022)

photograph of the houses at 14th and Newton NW, as well as two floor plans, which showed the quadrant plan and front porch. The three-story houses had "unusual width [22½ feet], massive colonial porches and Spanish tiled roofs" and sold for $7,350. The ad also proclaimed that "Modernizing home building is the great accomplishment attained by MR. HARRY WARDMAN in the completion of this beautiful row of homes."[20]

One innovation that Wardman claimed was the skylit bathroom, as described in the previous chapter. After the regulation change in 1909 that permitted operable skylights in the bathroom, Wardman and his architect Albert Beers built 16 row houses at 14th and Buchanan. At 24 feet wide, these row houses were wider than most, permitting the second floor to have four bedrooms and an interior bathroom.[21] This bathroom placement was gradually adapted to narrower row houses, and the interior bathroom became a standard feature of quadrant plans.

At one point in 1910, Wardman claimed to have 485 houses under construction, which would sell for prices ranging from $3,750 to $8,250. In 1913 a flattering article in the newspaper noted that in the previous four years, Wardman had built and sold more than 1,000 houses and 39 apartment buildings, reaping $6.5 million. The houses were "for the most part" occupied by the people who owned them. He also ventured "into localities where there were no improvements and created new centers of population." An article a few weeks later noted that he had sold 15 buildings that week. About to go on the market were 14 row houses on Perry Place NW, containing "six rooms and a bath," and "houses that Mr. Wardman considers the best he ever built" on the 1500 block of Buchanan Street NW.[22] All of these had front porches and quadrant plans.

Wardman built 1,682 row houses between 1901 and 1923. Increasingly, though, he turned to apartment buildings and other large complexes, constantly taking his business into ever more luxurious buildings. In a 1928 ad he claimed, "We house one-tenth of Washington's population," and few doubted him.[23]

Wardman was not the only prolific developer of row houses. Close on his heels in the 1910s was Harry Kite. Born in 1881 in Virginia, Kite began working for a real estate company, Moore and Hill, and then started his own development firm in 1909. Before the war he built economical row houses, such as those in the squares surrounded by Constitution, Thirteenth, Fourteenth, and D Streets NE. Over five years, from 1911 to 1916, Kite built 162 row houses, filing 20 different building permits, in these two squares. The houses ranged from 12½ feet wide on Warren Street to 18 feet wide on Tennessee Avenue. Most of the earlier houses had back buildings, abutting each other so that the court was wide enough to satisfy the regulations, but from 1912 on, Kite's basic type was the front-porch, quadrant plan. For most of this development,

Figure 79. Advertisement, Phillips and Sager. Between 1911 and 1916, builder Harry Kite constructed 162 quadrant-plan row houses just north of Lincoln Park. He promised the potential homeowner that owning a house would cost no more than renting one. (*Evening Star*, November 22, 1913, pt. 2, p. 1, reprinted with permission from the DC Public Library, Star Collection, © Washington Post)

Albert E. Landvoigt was the architect. In 1916 Kite turned to George Santmyers, but the basic design did not change, and the houses all sold rapidly. In November 1913 Kite's ad boasted of his developments in these two squares that "Operation No. 1 Sold—No. 2 Sold—No. 3 Sold" and this was Operation No. 4. He priced these "homes of the $4,000 kind" at $3,675 with "terms as easy as rent" (see fig. 79). When he was selling houses on Corbin Place, they looked so much like ones he had already built that he used a photograph of one on C Street and the same written description.[24] After World War I, Kite shifted his practice into apartment buildings and fancier addresses in Northwest, as well as more modest houses in Northeast, before his death in 1931.

The third-most prolific builder in the 1910s was D. J. Dunigan, who produced 461 row houses in that decade. In the 1920s, Dunigan built more row houses than anyone else, totaling 1,047. A native Washingtonian, Dunigan was born in 1880 and apprenticed as a plumber. By 1907 he headed his own firm, which the newspaper called the largest single contractor in plumbing, sewer, steam, and waterworks in the District. A year or two later, though, he moved into building. In Petworth and the area to its north known as Fourteenth Street Heights, he developed block after block of row houses with the quadrant plan and front porch. In 1926 he advertised "42 brand-new, all-brick Dunigan-built homes" on Farragut Street, noting that "the same type of homes we built on Emerson Street were sold on sight—without being advertised." The six-room houses sold for $8,950. Like the other builders, he also developed grander houses in Northwest, many of them, like his own home at 1915 Biltmore Street NW, of the "English basement type." By the time Dunigan died in 1928, he had built more than 2,000 buildings and was worth more than one million dollars.[25]

The final builder who constructed a striking number of row houses was Morris Cafritz. Born in Russia in 1888, Cafritz immigrated to the United States as a child. In 1921 he partnered with Harris Shapero in constructing 11 row houses, discussed in the next chapter. In 1922 he built 11 more houses with Shapero and 73 on his own; in 1925 he built 252 row houses. In 1926 the newspaper called his "a phenomenal rise . . . to a position of leadership in the real estate field within the last four years." Cafritz bought the land of the former Columbia Golf Club and developed 38 squares as part of Petworth. The row houses were "of tapestry brick of six rooms and bath with deep yards and thoroughly modern in every detail of construction and equipment." By 1926 Petworth had "thousands of new homes with broad streets and avenues, its own churches and schools, splendid transportation facilities and a commercial artery supplying its needs." Cafritz's business slumped in the late 1920s, as it did for all; in 1929 he developed the most row houses, 53, compared to Wardman's 33. But Cafritz persisted in the business through the 1930s, building a dozen or two row houses a year. By 1939 the newspaper concluded that he had built "upward of 5,000 homes, from two-story dwellings to mansions," and more than 100 apartment houses. Cafritz also built commercial and industrial buildings, and his business continued to flourish after World War II. When he died in 1964, Cafritz left an estate worth $66 million.[26]

The Operative Building Industry

These builders—stretching from Middaugh and Shannon in the first decade of the twentieth century to Harry Kite in the 1910s, D. J. Dunigan in the 1920s, and Morris Cafritz in the 1920s and 1930s, all of them overshadowed by the formidable Harry Wardman—signaled a new kind of speculative builder, one who dealt in quantities of row houses not conceived of in the nineteenth century (see fig. 80). "Operative builder" was the new term for this twentieth-century developer, a term that shed the negative connotations of "speculative builder." The term first appeared around 1910, and in 1925 developers fully embraced it by forming the Operative Builders Association. In 1931 realtor

Figure 80. Row houses, 5500 block of Thirteenth Street NW. Operative builders, constructing on a large scale, developed raw pieces of land with long rows of quadrant-plan row houses. D. J. Dunigan built this row in 1919. (National Photo Company, undated, Library of Congress)

William C. Miller estimated that "about 85 percent of the homes constructed in Washington are effected by operative builders."[27]

In 1928 Waverly Taylor of the Washington Real Estate Board explained to a class at the YMCA that, formerly, the home builder would go to the banker for financing, the architect for plans, and the builder to construct, but now, all of these experts were within one organization. The operative builder had departments "dealing in finance, brokerage and the handling of the technical phases of home planning and construction." In another interview, Morris Cafritz emphasized the economies of scale available to the operative builder, mentioning the cost of land, the savings in labor and materials, and better design. William C. Miller articulated even more economies in operative building. Besides buying land in raw acreage, he listed "employment of an architect in annual salary instead of commission, purchase of building materials on large-scale basis, by continuing employment of mechanics from year to year, by the cumulative force of continued advertising and employment of a sales force by the developer."[28] Several aspects of the operative builder's undertaking bear more examination in relation to row houses.

A critical factor in the operative builder's scale of construction was the availability of land. As early as 1887, builders such as C. C. Martin complained that available land had been bought up by speculators: "Why they've tied the builders hand and foot. They have bought up everything. Builders today can't buy any land in this city for a price that would warrant them to build a decent house upon it." Builder John Henderson Jr. also found exorbitant prices outside the old city: "When it was proposed to extend the streets into the suburbs, real estate men got up syndicates of speculators, and they bought up every bit of land they could on the line of the extensions with the expectation of making a big thing of it." After several attempts to have the street layout in subdivisions north of the old city accord with the L'Enfant Plan, finally the 1898 Highway Act insured that this would happen, adding more certainty to potential subdivisions. Also aiding development of this area was the extension of streetcar lines. In 1888 the Brightwood Railway Company extended the streetcar line on Seventh Street north to the District line, and the Eckington and Soldiers' Home Railway was chartered to run out New York Avenue to Fourth and T Streets NE. By 1925 there were five lines that extended northwest, north, and northeast from downtown to the edge of the District, and several more lines in between, opening up vast swaths of undeveloped land. In 1906 the newspaper observed that the northwest section of the city was the most desirable, and that "it is probably true that at present there is no more ground left in the northwest section that can be bought by the acre."[29]

In fact, there were tracts awaiting purchase and subdivision, but after 1920 they were often closed to row-house construction. The zoning law of that year insured that few row houses would be built west of Rock Creek Park or in the northern part of the city. By 1925, in complaining that the Zoning Commission refused to rezone a parcel of land in Northeast to accommodate row houses, the Operative Builders Association argued that there was not enough land zoned for row houses in the city, and would-be residents would be forced to live outside the District or in apartments.[30]

Another factor in the booming development of outlying areas was the perceived obsolescence of the older neighborhoods. A 1934 report observed: "Nowadays a building suffers obsolescence long before its structural usefulness is over. . . . In Washington few dwellings are now built more than two stories in height. Incomes and standards of living frown upon houses with three or four stories, and down town is filled with such. Nor do old dwellings have modern improvements."[31] Without servants, a three-story house involved additional labor for the housewife. And many of the old row houses still lacked central heating, electrical appliances, and modern bathroom fixtures.

The scale on which operative builders were undertaking business called for new sources of financing. Speculative builders in the early nineteenth century relied on personal networks of friends, families, and social organizations to raise money. In the late nineteenth century, they turned to local banks, building and loan associations, and formal partnerships.[32] For the building surge in the early twentieth century, speculative builders relied on those sources as well as national institutions and offered installment purchasing to their homebuyers. What they did not have available to draw on was the power of ground rents.

In both Philadelphia and Baltimore, ground rents encouraged the development of row houses and enabled homeownership. With the land being conveyed separately from the building, houses were more affordable. Rather than acquiring land, builders could simply rent it, build a row of houses, then sell the house, turning the obligation for the ground rent over to the new homeowner. Thus a barrier to entry for homebuilders and homeowners—the need for capital—was mitigated. Historians of both Baltimore and Philadelphia link ground rents to those cities' plethora of row houses, enabling their construction by a speculator and their purchase by a homeowner. Homeownership rates in those cities in 1920 were some of the highest in the country.[33]

Washington did benefit from building and loan associations, which enabled homeownership as well as small-scale speculative development. The purpose of these institutions, which arose after the Civil War, was "to take the savings of their investing members and loan them to their borrowing members." Members paid monthly into savings, which garnered dividends of 5 percent, and the capital was lent out to borrowers at 6 percent interest. In 1887 the newspaper interviewed a building association member, by way of illustrating how the institution worked. The member, a police officer who earned $90 a month, said that he paid $12.50 into the association and $18 in rent. He was intending to borrow money to buy a house, for which he could pay $30.50 a month "without making any more effort than I am making now." Building and loan associations prioritized lending to members who had saved money, such as this policeman; then people who had previously borrowed money from them and had paid off the loans; and lastly to "a speculator who wanted aid in building three or four houses or a row of houses." In 1882 a sociologist found "any number of excellent building associations" in Washington, but only one savings bank.[34]

In 1910 Washington had the highest per capita investment in building and loan associations in the United States, with assets of $15 million in nineteen associations that had almost thirty thousand members. Although the comparison was to other states, not cities, accounting for Washington's impressive standing, building and loans were still a booming business; by 1920 the investment had doubled to $30 million. A rosy view of homeownership arose around building and loan associations, which were credited with enabling "so many houses in Washington [to] have been purchased by people of moderate means." They educated people "in habits of economy and thrift," causing them to "become industrious, reliable, and in every way good citizens."[35] Aside from the rhetoric around these associations, they did enable some moderate income earners to buy their own homes. They also helped create a ready market for row houses, which tended to be more modestly priced than freestanding houses.

Borrowing from other lending institutions was less viable for the homeowner, because in the nineteenth and early twentieth centuries, mortgages tended to be short-term and not amortized, meaning that the entire amount of the mortgage would come due and need to be refinanced. This was better suited to speculative builders, who could sell off the houses before the mortgage needed to be repaid. In the early twentieth century, commercial banks, mutual savings banks, life insurance companies, and savings and loan associations (as building and loan associations became known) granted multiple mortgages to property owners. The real estate investment business fluctuated wildly, with economic downturns in the 1890s, 1907, and the late 1910s temporarily halting the flow of cash to speculative builders, but the market always bounced back. In the early 1920s, more than thirty mortgage investment companies, specializing in the purchase of second and third mortgages at large discounts, operated in the District and were capitalized at more than $10 million. The operative builders could take advantage of this capital; as a congressional committee found in 1924, "Builders and operators doing building on a large scale and affiliated with the large financial institutions are able to secure sufficient money to carry on their operations without any difficulty."[36]

Speculative builders offered installment purchasing to homebuyers. In 1887 one observer noted that purchasing real estate on the installment plan had been "in vogue" for the previous ten years in Washington, "which have done a great deal to make it a city of homes owned by those who live in them." During the depression of 1893, though, "there were too many examples of homes being lost through failure to make the payments. . . . This frightened off any one who might have bought a home on time." By the end of the decade the marketing of houses though installment purchasing had picked up again, and the large-scale operative builders seized on it. Middaugh and Shannon advertised a row house in 1907: "Price, $3,850. $500 cash and $27.50 a month will pay for one of these homes, including every dollar of interest." By keeping the financing in-house, an operative builder had a steady stream of income. For the homeowner, the purchase seemed straightforward because the interest was built in. Actual ownership was not effected until the final payment, which might be ten or twelve years down the road, though, and protections for buyers were minimal. But realtors found it a beneficial system; as one realtor exulted, "The prompt payment of these monthly installments is indeed remarkable. There isn't one case out of 500 where the trustees under a trust ever have to sell out for non-payment."[37]

Figure 81. Row houses, Petworth. The efficiencies inherent in constructing identical row houses resulted in a cohesive, even overpowering, neighborhood. (Theodor Horydczak, photographer, ca. 1920–50, Library of Congress, Prints and Photographs Division, Theodor Horydczak Collection)

The construction of multiple buildings to the same plan had many advantages to the seller (see fig. 81). One was that a builder could use one house as a model to sell the rest of the houses in the row, which might be in various stages of completion. Even in 1897 a real estate agent, looking back, said "Formerly rows of these [new] houses were constructed in Washington and practically sold before the ground was broken." The market only heated up from there. As one 1911 ad for houses in Park View proclaimed, "Some people are always too late . . . to take advantage of a good home offering. In the last week we have sold five houses in this row of seven new homes, and yet they have not been entirely completed." Or, as Morris Cafritz advertised in 1925, "We are building 121 homes . . . 68 will be completed in 60 days . . . We have sold 69 of our wonderful home values in less than 60 days."[38]

Part of selling was, of course, marketing, and this also changed in the early twentieth century. Four daily newspapers were the primary medium for getting a builder's message to the public. The buildings were never described as "row houses"; usually a reference to an "inside house" was the best indication it was a row house. In the nineteenth century, ads tended to be short and textual, but by 1900 ads were larger, headlines bigger, and line drawings of houses appeared, as the market became more competitive. By 1906 photographs accompanied the ads. In the early twentieth century, the ad copy took several approaches. It often promoted the location, especially the proximity to streetcar lines; for example, "very convenient—3 minutes car schedule—NO NEED FOR HORSE AND CARRIAGE—splendid car service transferring at 11th; 10 minutes' ride to Treasury Department; 15 minutes to Center Market and depots." The ad sometimes claimed an association between the builder and quality, such as "The reputation of the builders and architects, KENNEDY & DAVIS, is sufficient guarantee as to construction" or "STERLING silver, DRESDEN china, houses by MR. C. H. SMALL—all convey the same idea in their respective classes." They usually mentioned some aspect of the interior fittings, including "large tiled bath; porcelain tub; nickel plumbing; cellar under entire house; hot-water heat." The affordability of installment purchasing, with the assurance that buying a house cost no more than renting—"BUY a home with the money you are wasting in rent"—was another selling point. The ads encouraged people to come look at the model home, furnished from local department stores such as the Hecht Company.[39] They mentioned what streetcar to take to get there and kept the model home open on weekday evenings.

In the late nineteenth century, real estate agents tended to handle sales for speculative builders. Labor Commissioner Carroll D. Wright even joked in 1899 that "the population of Washington is divided into two classes—real estate agents and those who are not." In the spring of 1900, houses "Built by Middaugh" were advertised by Wm. E. Shannon, who claimed, "I Sell Houses." Later that year, Middaugh and Shannon entered into a partnership and a few years later hired Shannon & Luchs, a real estate firm founded in 1906 by Herbert T. Shannon, William's younger brother, and Morton J. Luchs, who had been working for Stone and Fairfax, a prominent real estate firm. Shannon and Luchs became one of the prominent real estate firms of the twentieth century, lasting until 1993. For several years they sold houses for Harry Wardman, until Wardman brought sales into his firm in 1913. In the 1920s Shannon and Luchs undertook development of their own row-house subdivisions.[40]

As operative builders folded the sales function into their firms, they used their own names and reputations as selling points. By the end of the 1920s, identifying the builder was part of the sales pitch, such as Wardman—"we house over one-tenth of Washington's population"; Cafritz—"owners and builders of communities"; and Shapiro—"beyond comparison." Real estate agents continued to thrive, nonetheless, in the overheated Washington market. A 1925 help-wanted ad for real estate salesmen called it "An Unexcelled Opportunity to Make Money."[41]

Whether the row houses were priced fairly is another issue. In 1924 Wardman said that he got out of the house-building business, discouraged at the small profits. He testified before Congress that "the last 300 houses that I built—that was about 1912 to 1914—those 300 houses I sold to the Washington public at less than $100 a house profit. I took notes on those houses, some of them running 10 years, and I still have some of those notes." He said that "when I was building houses, when I was turning out houses at the rate of one a day . . . there was really no housing in Washington that would pay 6 per cent net on the money invested. It almost broke me under." After the war he got back into house building but was frustrated at the profits that homeowners were getting from reselling them. "I built and sold those houses for $7,500 at a very small profit, and took long time payments, and . . . I do not believe there is a house in the block that now belongs to the same owner that I sold them to and those houses that I sold for $7,500 have sold for as high as $12,000. They have got the profit and I didn't."[42]

But in 1924, in the midst of a seller's market, a Senate committee investigating housing and rental conditions in Washington found falsely inflated prices for houses, with profits of 25 to 75 percent. The specific operator the committee cited was Joseph Shapiro, Inc., which was building 32 row houses on the 2700 block of Woodley Place NW, just a block west of Rock Creek (see fig. 82). Designed by George Santmyers, the houses had the standard quadrant plans: "the six-room box type, with sleeping and breakfast porches," as well as front porches. Amenities included "double French doors connecting the bedrooms with the sleeping porch, tiled bath and shower, servants' bath in the basement, French beveled drop ceilings in the living and dining room, lower floor furnished with polychrome side lamps and center fixtures, and

Figure 82. Row houses, 2700 block of Woodley Place NW. In 1924 Joseph Shapiro came under investigation by a congressional committee for price gouging in the development of row houses designed by George Santmyers on Woodley Place NW. The committee concluded that Shapiro was reaping a profit of 47.5 percent, but he proceeded undeterred. (Photograph by the author, 2022)

Pittsburgh instantaneous water heater."[43] Although the newspaper heralded "five distinct styles," the differences were subtle and the plans identical. These 32, on the west side of the street, were the first of 100 houses that Shapiro intended to build in this area.

The houses raised the suspicion of the Senate committee because of their cost. On the building permit, J. B. Shapiro estimated the cost of construction at a little more than $20,000 apiece. This was so outrageous that the building inspector called Shapiro in and had him change the estimate to $9,200. Shapiro was selling the houses for $12,950. The committee estimated the cost of land at $800 per lot, making the total cost of each house $10,000, for which Shapiro was getting a 29.2 percent profit. The committee then deducted the financing and selling costs and determined that the true cost of the house and lot was $8,753, which meant that Shapiro was making 47.5 percent profit. Most of the committee's ire was directed at overpriced apartment buildings resulting in excess rents and worthless mortgages, and Shapiro proceeded undeterred. By the time of the committee's hearing, he had sold 23 of the 32 houses. Two months later he had sold most of them and started construction on 36 more.[44]

Another aspect of the vertical organization of operative builders was the ability to have a large staff providing technical expertise, from professionals in financing and advertising to land acquisition and engineering. Operative builders continued to subcontract the work of construction, maintaining flexibility, yet they also had some craftsmen on staff, as evidenced by this classified ad: "Help wanted: Painter—Live young man experienced in operative builder's painting; references required; permanent position and good future for right man." When they subcontracted, the builders chose between union or nonunion workers, with the unionized workers perceived as more professional and capable. But unionized workers were a thorn in the side of operative builders; the Operative Builders Association was formed, in part, to deter unions from demanding increased wages. An article in *Architects and Builders Journal,* advocating an open shop and quoted extensively in the *Evening Star* in 1907, stated, "For years Mr. Wardman's firm had temporized with the unions, granted concessions, yielded to demands until the power of reasonable endurance had been passed, employing every means to avoid antagonism, all to no purpose, and finally it cast the irksome burden from its shoulders, threw off the shackles and was free." Wardman "has boldly declared that in the future he will have nothing to do with organized labor in the building trades, and that he will conduct his business on the principle of the open shop. Mr. Wardman has found no difficulty in securing competent workmen. There is not a union man employed on any of his contracts, yet he is getting satisfactory results, his work is progressing, harmony prevails and the men are content." That same year, the construction of Middaugh and Shannon's row houses at Park View was disrupted by unionized strikers, who refused to work alongside nonunion workers in other trades.[45]

The builders also retained some flexibility in dealing with architects. While they undoubtedly had some on staff, they also had ongoing relationships with other architects. They might turn to more-renowned ones on occasion, as Middaugh and Shannon had used B. Stanley Simmons for new ventures, but used Joseph Bohn for the bulk of their dwellings. Harry Wardman had relationships with several well-regarded architects. Working for him on row houses were Nicholas Grimm (from about 1897 to 1905), Albert H. Beers (from 1905 until 1911), Frank Russell White (from 1911 to 1917), Eugene Waggaman (from 1920 to 1924), and Mirhan Mesrobian (from 1923 to 1928).[46]

The architect who designed the most row houses was not associated with a single builder, but instead ranged widely. George Santmyers designed more than 8,000 row houses in his career; the second-most prolific was Albert Beers, with fewer than 2,000. Santmyers, born in Virginia in 1889, had little education beyond high school and, like many Washington architects, learned his trade by apprenticing in the offices of others. He opened his own office in 1914, at the age of twenty-five. When he died, his obituary was a mere four paragraphs long and did not mention his incredible output. Santmyers achieved his astonishing amount of work by associating with many builders; in 1925, Santmyers designed more than 1,000 row houses for thirty-five different speculative builders. In his career he also designed more than 400 apartment buildings and more than 15,000 buildings in total. Santmyers's stock in trade was the quadrant-plan, front-porch row house, of which he probably designed thousands. Despite architects such as Santmyers developing a recognized expertise in row houses, specific architects were apparently not a selling point, because they were rarely mentioned in ads.[47]

Racial Segregation

A less savory aspect of marketing row houses involved racial discrimination. Operative builders believed that excluding African Americans from certain neighborhoods would enhance those neighborhoods in the eyes of white purchasers, so they deployed a variety of methods to ensure this. Deed restrictions excluding African Americans, and in some cases Jews, were the most direct method. With these restrictions, and others, segregation of African Americans went from segregation by building quality—placing Black people in inferior housing, although geographically intermixed with whites—to one of geography, in which Blacks were excluded from blocks or whole neighborhoods. But while the quality or the location of the row house might have varied according to the race of the occupant, the row houses themselves did not; plans, facades, and fittings corresponded to the socioeconomic class of the occupant, regardless of race. To understand the shift that African American housing experienced, from segregation by building quality to one dictated by geography, a brief overview of housing for Washington's African Americans in the nineteenth century is necessary.

Before the Civil War, the proportion of African Americans in Washington who were free steadily increased. In 1830, the population in the District was roughly divided between free and enslaved, with about 2,000 of each, but by 1860, 78 percent of the African American population of 14,316 was free. Economic opportunities and movement through the city were restricted by laws that applied to these Black people, and they generally lived in housing of lesser quality than whites in trade and service occupations. As a 1929 study noted, "These early Negro inhabitants of pre–Civil War days lived in the little huts, hovels, and shacks which were stuck here and there among the shadows of the finer and more pretentious homes of the white population." Between 1824 and 1845, 307 of them owned property in Washington City, most likely including the houses they lived in. Free Blacks lived throughout the city, clustering, like the rest of the population, around the White House, Capitol, and Navy Yard.[48]

Enslaved persons were restricted, by law, to living with their owners or the people to whom they were hired out. Their accommodations were often in incidental spaces, such as attics and basements, not specifically built or designated for them. Some lived in separate outbuildings on the backs of lots, such as on the second floor above a stable or wash house.[49] Industrial and commercial buildings such as ropewalks or livery stables might have their own living quarters for enslaved people. Like the free Blacks, these African Americans resided all over the city, not in separate areas.

The influx of impoverished African Americans during and after the Civil War complicated the housing situation. While the poor newcomers lived in shacks and shanties and other found spaces, as the impoverished had always done, they increasingly congregated in alley dwellings (see fig. 83). This building type, which became identified in Washington with slums, had arisen earlier in the nineteenth century as housing for workers. Unlike buildings constructed at the back of lots that faced the street, these were usually on lots that were separated from the street lots by an alley, so that they had no connection, in either contiguity or ownership, to the street-facing lots. The alleys accommodated buildings for other purposes as well—industrial uses, stables and carriage houses, warehouses and workshops, and, later, garages.[50] The large size of Washington's squares enabled this lot rearrangement, and

Figure 83. Alley dwellings, Schotts Court NE (between First, Second, B, and C Streets). Located on lots separated from those facing the street, alley dwellings were small and crowded. Usually owned by absentee landlords, they were deteriorated and lacked basic amenities. (Marion Post Wolcott, photographer, 1941, Library of Congress, Prints and Photographs Division, Farm Security Administration)

the design of alleys—often in H or I shapes—meant that the alley dwellings were not visible from the street. Although the police were frustrated by their inability to see activity in these alleys and thought that they fostered crime, the secluded alleys also permitted communities to develop.

The usual form of the alley dwelling was a row house: long rows of attached buildings with separate entrances. Alley dwellings built in the mid-nineteenth century tended to be wood frame and more likely to be inhabited by whites than by Blacks. But beginning in 1872, building regulations applied equally to alley dwellings as to other buildings, and frame houses were not permitted in the old city after 1877. Their width was also prescribed after 1887—12 feet minimum—and they generally ranged in depth from 24 to 30 feet (see fig. 84). Regulations also specified a window in every room, so given the small interior lots, alley dwellings tended to be only two rooms deep. Beginning in 1877 a privy or toilet was required for every dwelling, so their small yards usually had a privy on the back fence, sometimes replaced by a toilet, and a hydrant for water.[51] Alley dwellings adhered so closely to the minimums specified in the building regulations that they appeared to use a standard plan: brick, 12 feet wide, two stories tall, two rooms deep, each room lit by a window, small yard with hydrant and privy.

Construction of new alley dwellings was effectively prohibited by an 1892 law that focused on the physical dimensions of the alley itself. First, dwellings could not be built on alleys that were less than 30 feet wide and not supplied with sewerage, water mains, and lights. Second, dwellings had to be set back

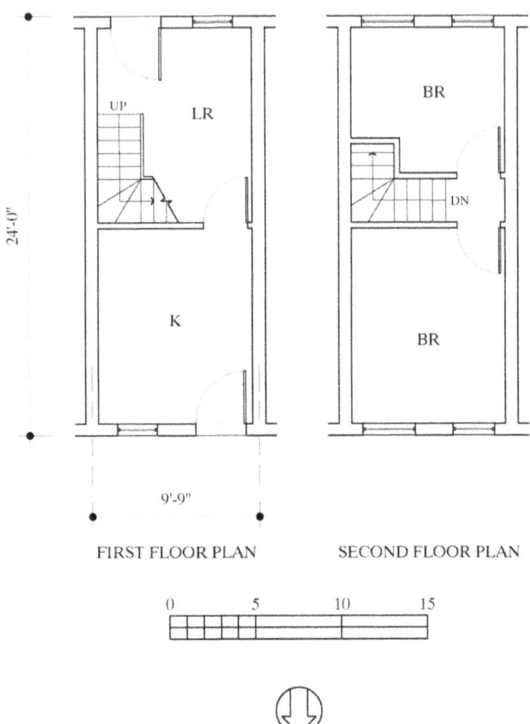

Figure 84. Alley dwelling, 17 Snow's Court NW, plans. The 1884 building permit provided for a row of two-story alley dwellings, 10½ wide by 24 feet long. As measured, though, this house was only 9 feet wide on the interior. Stoves would have provided any heat, a hydrant in the yard was probably the source of water, and a water closet probably stood in the yard as well. Three years later regulations required that buildings be at least 12 feet wide. (Conjectural original plans, Ruben Melendez, Onairis Perez, and Mark Schara, delineators, 2020)

20 feet from the center line of the alley to allow for a 5-foot-wide footpath on either side of the 30-foot-wide alley, which would have pushed already small dwellings back on very small lots. Third, alleys had to run straight and open at right angles to the streets, ruling out the H- and I-shaped alleys that characterized Washington's alley system. The law applied only to new construction, though, so existing alleys continued to flourish as places for the poor to live.[52]

Between 1877 and 1892, building permits were issued for 2,549 houses in alleys. A 1913 survey counted 2,528 alley dwellings, which probably included most of these post-1877 brick ones. Frame ones became increasingly rare, particularly once efforts to remove alley dwellings became effective. In the first decade of the twentieth century, progressive reformers surveyed alley dwellings and exposed the inadequate living conditions. Finally, in 1914, at the deathbed urging of First Lady Ellen Wilson, Congress enacted legislation to remove alley dwellings, an effort that took decades and was ultimately abandoned. Housing shortages during World War I delayed implementation of the Alley Dwelling Act of 1914, and lack of alternative housing slowed its implementation in the 1920s and 1930s. The Alley Dwelling Act of 1934 ordered the abolition of alley dwellings in ten years, but due to World War II it was extended to 1954. By then new interest in these small buildings, as quaint buildings worthy of rehabilitation, worked against their complete erasure.[53]

The failing of alley dwellings was not so much in their design as in their execution—they were shoddily built with minimal amenities. As one reformer noted in 1913, "The fundamental idea of the four-room one-family house is excellent." The problem was overcrowding, deterioration, and shoddy construction, she alleged. Reformers' descriptions and photographs depicted dark rooms with holes in walls and broken windows. Cooking occurred over coal stoves in kitchens without running water or electricity. The lack of amenities became increasingly shocking as the twentieth century wore on, and photographs of outdoor hydrants and privies, with the Capitol looming in the background, drove the point home.[54]

Someone stood to gain from this, of course, and that was the building's owner. Very few of the alley dwellings were owner-occupied; nearly all of them were owned by landlords who lived elsewhere in the city or even out of town. The profits were considerable for minimal buildings minimally maintained; the cost of construction for a brick house was as little as $500. The ads explained the economics: "Two new brick houses, Union Court, nw, will rent for $10.50 per month. Price $1,100 each"; "For Sale—we have some choice alley houses in Southeast, which will pay about 11 per cent"; or "For Sale—we have a lot of alley houses for investment 10 and 12 per cent." In 1913 Edith Elmer Wood investigated ownership of 88 four-room dwellings in four alleys and found that the average gross return was 16 percent—"about twice what is considered a fair return in street property." The 47 owners were mostly professionals and included 20 women. A more comprehensive survey of owners in 1913 showed hundreds of owners of multiple properties, rarely living on the same block as their alley dwellings.[55]

By 1897, 93 percent of the 17,244 occupants of alley dwellings were Black. As sociologist William Henry Jones observed in 1929, "So closely have the terms *Alleys* and *Negroes* been associated, that in the minds of most of the older citizens they are inseparable." But the alley dwellings were located in squares that were otherwise occupied by whites. For example, in 1897 the square in Foggy Bottom that included Snow's Court housed 242 whites, none of them living in the alley, and 420 Blacks, 249 of them living in alley dwellings.[56] Because habitable alleys were spread throughout the old city, the African American population was as well.

When living in houses on streets, not alleys, working-class African Americans often inhabited poorer-quality dwellings than their white neighbors—a segregation of quality, not space (see fig. 85). Their houses tended to be wood-frame row houses, older, smaller, and valued less than those of their neighbors. For example, on one square on Capitol Hill, discussed in more

544 HARPER'S NEW MONTHLY MAGAZINE.

court. Black men and women are numerous, and laugh very loud on the streets with refreshing freedom. There is everywhere about the city a slight but racy touch of Southern characteristics, interfused with the vigor of other portions of the Union; and for the sake of this you are willing to forgive the copious tobacco stains—those blots on the national escutcheon—which disfigure the sidewalks, and around which you see an English tourist and his wife making their way with a pardonably imperial disdain.

One local improvement in particular deserves our praise. From the park east of the Capitol to the President's House and Lafayette Square there is a long stretch of government land, within which stand the Capitol itself and the Congressional Greenhouse (which is *not* intended for forcing green members), the Smithsonian Institution and new National Museum, the Department of Agriculture, the Washington Monument, the Departments of State, War, and the Navy, the Treasury and White House, and the superb building dedicated to official printing and engraving, together with a large but still unfinished parade-ground by the Potomac. This territory, several miles long, and from a half-mile to a mile wide, has been hitherto short-sightedly broken up by fences and walls, and a railroad even yet scars it with a cindery track; but it has nevertheless almost taken shape as the continuous public park it is intended to be. One President gets this fence taken down, and another President demolishes that wall; and so the process goes on of making the tract a noble pleasure-ground, containing the central offices of a great nation's popular government. A carriage and pair can thus be driven through our political system from one end to the other without disturbing it in the least. In this domain ought to be included the romantic old Van Ness mansion, near the Potomac, and close to the parade-ground. This spot, which is owned by a millionaire, and is threatened by him with ruin to make room for a railroad station, is closely united with the history of the capital and its illustrious founder. It was owned by David Burns, who sold to the government most of the ground on which the city stands, and here are the trees under which Washington sat negotiating with him; here, too, the poor old tottering house in which the famous beauty, Marcia Burns, received the most distinguished company. She married Governor Van Ness, of New York, who built a prouder abode, in style a diminutive White House, within

NEGRO SHANTIES.

Figure 85. "Negro Shanties." The accompanying text reads: "Here and there you see a relic of the village era—some little whitewashed hut sticking pertinaciously to the side of a fine modern brick structure of comfortable and tasteful style, like a wasps' nest attached to a real human habitation." In illustrating the proximity in which Blacks and whites lived, this drawing casts poverty as picturesque. (A. B. Frost, delineator, illustrating George Lathrop, "A Nation in a Nutshell," *Harper's New Monthly Magazine* 62 (March 1881): 544, courtesy of University of Virginia Library)

depth in the next chapter, the 1900 census showed just one African American household out of thirty-five; Henry Brent, a laborer, his wife, a laundress, and his son, a tailor, were living in one of the three frame buildings on the square. In 1910, that house was gone, but non-whites occupied the two other small frame houses on the square.[57] All other residents on the block were white.

In the late nineteenth century, Washington had a solid population of middle-class Black residents who were able to own their own homes. Government jobs offered good, steady wages, and Howard University attracted an educated elite, some of whose graduates taught in the segregated school system, producing first-class educations for African Americans. In 1883 a rosy article in the *Evening Star* on "Washington's Colored People" identified a "second rank" of a hierarchical Black society composed of "government clerks and people in comfortable circumstances. . . . Many of them own comfortable little houses, and one of the finest streets in the city is occupied by them. This is 16th street, between the Scott statue and the White House. It is a splendid avenue, broad, well paved, and in the heart of the most fashionable part of the city. Nearly all of these colored residents own their houses, and refuse to sell." By 1913, some 2,500 African Americans worked for the federal government, about 300 of them in white-collar positions, and dwelled in the District. They lived in most neighborhoods but by then had begun to concentrate north of downtown in a neighborhood later called Shaw, and specifically around U Street. Prominent African Americans such as historian Carter G. Woodson and activist Mary McLeod Bethune bought row houses near Logan Circle in the 1920s. Although the houses, at 1538 Ninth Street NW and 1318 Vermont Avenue NW, respectively, had been built half a century before their famous owners acquired them, they still retained the grace and elegance of substantial row houses (see figs. 7, 8, and 45). As late as 1929, sociologist William Henry Jones noted that "there are scattered communities which distribute the Negro population throughout practically the entire city. Negroes live 'all over Washington.' . . . It would not be serious exaggeration to state that Negroes live in every residential block in Washington, either as residents or as servants in somebody else's household."[58]

But change was already underway, as spatial segregation began to take hold. In the early twentieth century, racial restrictions limited job opportunities for African Americans, even in the federal government; Jim Crow laws restricted daily life; and the real estate industry attempted to exclude Black people from specific areas. The most direct way to prevent African Americans from living in certain neighborhoods was to put covenants on deeds. Some of these were added when the neighborhood was first divided into lots and developed, but this occurred only outside of the old city, where the land had not yet been subdivided. For example, Middaugh and Shannon, prolific row-house developers of Bloomingdale and other neighborhoods, frequently attached covenants to their deeds. In 1899 they added one to the deeds for the houses designed by B. Stanley Simmons on First Street, which specified that the house on the property "shall not be rented, leased, sold, transferred or conveyed, to any negro or colored person under a penalty of $2,000.00."[59]

For areas that had already been developed and sold, a property owner could add a covenant onto an existing deed. Commonly, a group of neighbors did this en masse, in order to keep a block occupied only by whites. Across the street from the Middaugh and Shannon covenant-protected houses, the row houses that Wardman developed on the 2200 block of First Street did not initially carry a deed restriction, but by petition of the homeowners one was added in 1925, to extend for twenty-one years. Similarly, in 1927 the Petworth Citizens Association distributed contracts that they urged residents to sign, pledging "not to sell their home property to persons of any other race."[60]

Several factors drove the addition of covenants in the early twentieth century. In some cases, African Americans were acquiring property nearby and developers and homeowners wanted to stop the trend. The sense of a racial shift in real estate was exacerbated after World War I, which saw an influx of both Blacks and whites into the city, creating a housing shortage. The razing of alley dwellings and downtown areas, such as the Federal Triangle, contributed to the housing crisis. As one article noted, "Demand by colored families for modern homes and all conveniences has been heavy for some time . . . the conversion of alley streets and courts into interior parks and consequent demolition of many alley houses being largely responsible for the increasing demand." It is unlikely that alley dwellers, who were mostly renters, immediately became purchasers of new houses, but they did put pressure on the market. Repeatedly, articles in the newspaper highlighted the lack of options for Black people in the 1920s. "Homes for the Colored Reported in Big Demand," one 1923 article proclaimed, reporting on the activity of African American real estate broker Victor R. Daly.[61] As Blacks sought housing in fewer available neighborhoods, whites in those neighborhoods added covenants to keep them out.

White homeowners usually claimed that their interests were economic, not racist. Housing values would decline, they argued, if African Americans lived in the neighborhood. Usually, covenants added to deeds were directed at maintaining the physical quality of the buildings of a block or neighborhood in the time before zoning. The covenant for the Middaugh and Shannon houses on First Street included two provisions other than the racial restriction. One attempted to keep out undesirable businesses: "spirituous liquors shall never be sold upon said lot nor in any building erected thereon." The second was aimed at maintaining the value of the neighboring row houses: "no building shall be erected upon said lot which shall cost less than $2,500.00, and that no building shall be erected on First Street in said square of less than three stories, exclusive of cellars."[62] Racial restrictions, though, took what might have been an attempt at insuring economic stability into the realm of social engineering.

In some neighborhoods, Jews were seen as equally detrimental to property values. W. C. and A. N. Miller developed two subdivisions of detached houses, Spring Valley and Wesley Heights, in Northwest Washington, in 1923 and 1929, respectively. Their racial restrictions prohibited sale or transfer to "negroes, or any person or persons, of negro blood or extraction, or to any person of the Semitic Race, blood or origin, which racial description shall be deemed to include Armenians, Jews, Hebrews, Persians and Syrians," with the exception of domestic servants. It was a limitation the Millers were proud to feature, as their advertisements explained it in coded language: "Spring Valley has restrictions to protect its residents against unfortunate changes." Similarly, in Columbia Heights, where much of the property was restricted from sales to African Americans, a 1904 brochure advertised, "Nowhere within the District of Columbia can be found a community freer from the objectionable classes than that on the 'Heights'; and there is every assurance that present conditions in this regard will continue in the future development and building up of the section."[63]

Racial covenants were repeatedly upheld by the courts from the 1920s until the 1940s, and some of the nationally significant cases originated in Washington. In 1921, residents of the 1700 block of S Street NW, near Dupont Circle, placed a restrictive covenant on their deeds. Later that year, Irene Hand Corrigan attempted to sell her row house at 1727 S Street, which had been built ten years earlier at an estimated cost of $8,000. The would-be purchaser was Helen Curtis, an African American and wife of a prominent ophthalmologist, Arthur Curtis. John J. Buckley, a neighboring homeowner, sued. In deciding the case of *Corrigan v. Buckley,* the Supreme Court of the District of Columbia upheld the covenant, and on appeal, the U.S. Supreme Court declined to hear it in 1926.[64]

With that, white homeowners' associations considered covenants legal and implemented them citywide. The Bloomingdale and North Capitol citizens' associations advertised, "Attention White Home Buyers! The largest restricted White Community in Washington Invites your attention—the decision of the U.S. Supreme Court—that negroes cannot buy in a restricted white section. Buy or Rent in the section known as Eckington, Bloomingdale, High View, Edgewood" (see fig. 86). By 1948 the Federation of Citizens' Associations estimated that about half of the residences in the city had racial covenants. Areas without covenants included "the greater part of 'old Washington,' the area roughly south of Florida avenue and including Georgetown." But "covenants blanket most other sections, particularly the Northwest, and most subdivisions developed in the last twenty years."[65]

The issue was hardly settled by the 1926 Supreme Court decision, though; African Americans continued to try to buy restricted houses, and white homeowners continued to try to sell to them, stopped by their neighbors. In the 1940s, two cases in Bloomingdale were again ruled to uphold the covenant, but the U.S. Supreme Court heard their appeals along with *Shelley v. Kraemer,* a case regarding racial covenants that originated in St. Louis. In declaring racial covenants unenforceable by states in 1948, the court also decided *Hurd v. Hodge* and *Urciolo v. Hodge* so that covenants could not be enforced by District law either.[66]

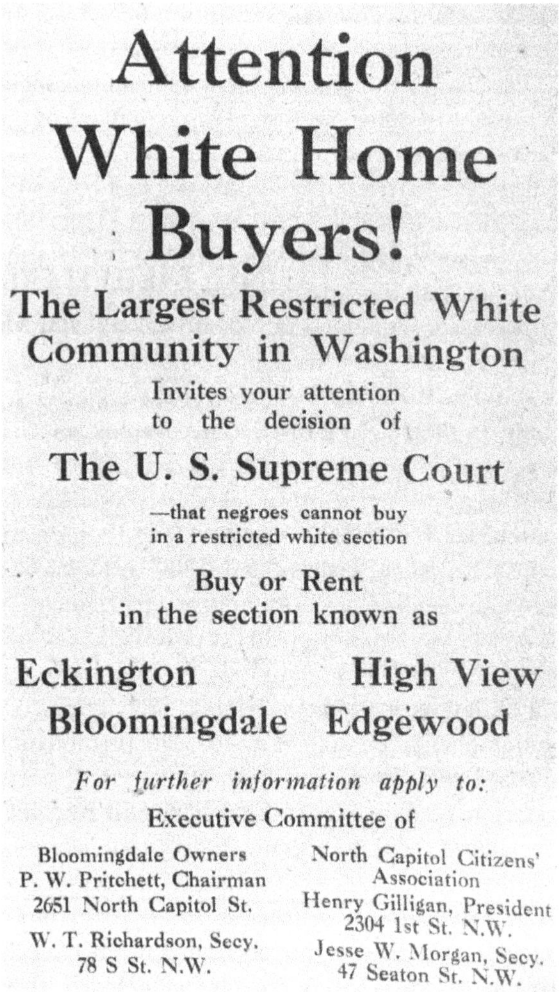

Attention
White Home
Buyers!

The Largest Restricted White
Community in Washington

Invites your attention
to the decision of

The U. S. Supreme Court

—that negroes cannot buy
in a restricted white section

Buy or Rent
in the section known as

Eckington High View
Bloomingdale Edgewood

For further information apply to:

Executive Committee of

Bloomingdale Owners
P. W. Pritchett, Chairman
2651 North Capitol St.
W. T. Richardson, Secy.
78 S St. N.W.

North Capitol Citizens' Association
Henry Gilligan, President
2304 1st St. N.W.
Jesse W. Morgan, Secy.
47 Seaton St. N.W.

Figure 86. Advertisement for four neighborhoods. Once the Supreme Court upheld racial covenants in 1926, neighborhood associations touted racial exclusion as a desirable feature. (*Sunday Star,* May 30, 1926, p. 3, reprinted with permission from the DC Public Library, Star Collection, © Washington Post)

Racial covenants were not entirely effective. Some people moved in anyway, either through straw purchasers or willful ignorance on the part of the sellers. Even on the 1700 block of S Street, where white homeowners had adopted a covenant in 1921, Black people bought houses and moved in; one house on the block was even advertised "FOR SALE TO COLORED" in 1923. And as neighborhoods changed, neighbors had less incentive to bring suit. Further, in a neighborhood such as Bloomingdale, which became less fashionable through the 1930s and 1940s as whites moved to neighborhoods farther out, the remaining white homeowners, unable to sell to Blacks, filled their houses with tenants and boarders or left them empty. After enforcement of the covenants ended, the change was, in some places, nearly absolute; by 1960 Bloomingdale was 99 percent Black.[67]

Perhaps even more effective than legal instruments, though, was a tacit enforcement of systemic racism. Mary Church Terrell, an educator and civil rights activist, and her husband, Robert Terrell, a prominent lawyer and jurist, sought a house in Washington in the late 1890s (see fig. 87). Mary described their difficulties: "We looked with longing eyes upon many a dear little house which was exactly what we wanted in every respect, but we were frankly told we could not buy it, because we were colored." Finally, they purchased one through a straw purchaser. Several decades later when seeking another house, they ran into similar problems. In the end they paid $2,000 more than a white purchaser would have. Terrell concluded bitterly, "African blood is truly a luxury in the United States, for which those who show it or acknowledge it pay dearly indeed."[68]

Real estate agents understood which neighborhoods were to be white-only and steered their clients accordingly. As Ernest Eiland, an African American real estate agent recalled, "Those of us in the real estate industry were not permitted by [covenant], by custom, by operation of the Board of Realtors, to get out of the areas that were 'designated' for non-whites." By 1924, the Board

Figure 87. Mary Church Terrell. The African American civil rights activist encountered systemic racism when she attempted to buy a house in Washington. She also charged that Blacks paid more than whites for the same quality of house. (Photographer unknown, ca. 1880–90, Library of Congress, Prints and Photographs Division)

of Realtors' code of ethics included this directive: "No property in a white section should ever be sold, rented, advertised, or offered to colored people." White neighborhood associations encouraged the complicity of realtors; in 1912 members of the North Washington Citizens Association pledged to boycott real estate agents "placing or endeavoring to place colored people in this neighborhood," which was Bloomingdale and Reservoir Heights. The *Evening Star* recognized the ramifications, headlining the article "Citizens Plan Race Segregation in City."[69]

Until 1960, newspapers included ads explicitly directed at Blacks, implying that all the unlabeled ads were for whites. As one ad proclaimed in 1910, "FOR SALE TO GOOD COLORED PERSON, A good home near 15th and Q sts.; 10 rooms and bath; bay-window brick; semi-detached. Easy terms. Price reduced." Washington's major developers—among them, Harry Kite, Harry Wardman, and Morris Cafritz—constructed row-house developments specifically marketed to African Americans. For example, Harry Kite built a row of houses at Irving Street and Georgia Avenue NW in 1920. B. B. Pinn, a prominent Black real estate agent, advertised them: "YOU'LL BE MORE THAN PLEASED With these new Homes just completing for Colored People at 711–31 Irving St., NW . . . They will appeal to you for what they are—the most completely appointed Homes in this desirable section. Six rooms and tiled bath; hot-water heat; electricity; gas range; sleeping porch; kitchen porch; front porch; deep lot—and every detail of superior construction."[70] White developers often used Black real estate agents; B. B. Pinn, of whom little is known, was one of the more prominent ones in the 1920s.

Sociologist William Henry Jones documented a trend of developers overcharging Black purchasers, as Mary Church Terrell had suggested. According to his study, for 15 six-room houses, Blacks paid $7,250 on average, while whites paid $750 less. For 20 eight-room houses, Blacks paid an average of $12,500, while whites paid $2,000 less. Developers claimed that the financial risk justified the differential, but Jones found this not to be true. African Americans charged that these new dwellings were shoddily built: "Most of them contain an inferior grade of brick, cheap fixtures and floorings, and ceilings and walls that crack within a few months after the houses are completed." Although these new houses "display a rather attractive appearance, because of their extreme modernity and their improvement in facilities over the old houses, equipped with oil lamps and built-in stoves," the better-built older houses were, according to Jones, "generally preferred by Negroes who desire durable homes." Mary Church Terrell disagreed, arguing that African Americans wanted to live in white neighborhoods "because the houses there are modern, as a rule, and better in every way than those which have been discarded and turned over to their own group." According to Jones's 1929 study, more than half of the African American population lived in two-story six-room row houses, which would include the newly built types, and which were "characterized by a uniformity of structure, which, even though tiresome and inartistic, give to the community a certain physical characterization."[71]

African American builders and buyers had less access to capital in a racist society. Capital Savings Bank of Washington, founded in 1888, was the first Black-owned bank in the city, as well as in the country, joining the building and loan association Industrial Building and Savings Company, founded three years earlier, as sources of financing for Black homeowning and construction in Washington. But these institutions lacked the resources to finance construction on the scale of white operative builders, and for the most part, home purchasers relied on Black as well as white financing, including that offered by operative builders. In 1900, 11 percent of Black residences were owned by their occupants, compared to 29 percent of white residences. By 1930, that had grown to 24 percent of Black households, while a little more than 40 percent of white households were owner-occupied. In some neighborhoods, Black homeownership was quite high; in his 1929 survey of more than five thousand houses occupied by African Americans in Northwest and Southwest Washington, sociologist William Henry Jones found that 46.5 percent of them were owned by their occupants. He noted that homeownership varied by area, with little of it in Southwest or Georgetown, but most of it in Northwest "in the newer sections of the city, chiefly those sections into which the Negro population is expanding."[72] Those places, too, had higher property values, while the renters lived in deteriorating, ill-equipped housing.

Residential segregation was further reinforced by the federal government through the policies of the Federal Housing Administration, established in 1934 to insure mortgages. The FHA effectively institutionalized segregation by evaluating risk based in part on the racial composition of the neighborhood. In Washington, all of the highest-graded area was west of Rock Creek Park, while most of the L'Enfant city, as well as part of Anacostia, was described as follows: "These areas have lived their span of life as residential areas and are now declining rapidly into very undesirable sections." The FHA further noted, "these areas house over three-fourths of the negroes in the metropolitan district and are showing effects of negro occupancy."[73] Without insured mortgages in the areas to which Blacks were restricted, investment in the older building stock was actively discouraged.

The result of these efforts, both explicit and tacit, was a spatial segregation of the city. The 1940 census showed that, at a time when Black people formed only 28 percent of the total population, twenty of the ninety-six census tracts had a majority-Black population. Half of the city's African American population at the time lived in Shaw and Southwest. As whites moved to new row-house neighborhoods, Blacks moved into the older ones. As whites moved into detached houses in far Northwest or beyond the city, Blacks moved into neighborhoods of detached houses in Northeast and Southeast.[74] By midcentury, the row-house neighborhoods were overwhelmingly Black, and desegregation efforts after World War II focused on single-family neighborhoods far from the city's core.

The spatial segregation of Black residents into inner-city row-house neighborhoods was accompanied by an economic segregation. With Blacks unable to access funding to purchase or reinvest in inner-city housing, they were unable to acquire the kind of intergenerational wealth that real estate investment permits. In 2010, Black homeownership rates still lagged behind rates for whites, 38 percent to 48, leaving them less able to compete in, and profit from, an expensive housing market.[75]

Segregation was just one of many tools that operative builders employed to achieve marketable row houses. The sheer numbers of row houses constructed with cost-saving efficiency made them appealing to many homeowners and renters. The appearance of Washington changed dramatically as the city burst its bounds, and hundreds of near-identical row houses sprang up on newly paved streets in a newly segregated city.

Builders may have played the major role in how these row houses looked, but the occupants determined how they worked. Owning or renting a house is often a personal decision, and one that changes through a lifetime, as a resident's financial and family situation change. The next chapter examines occupants through close study of a handful of squares to determine who was living in what kind of house, how big or small their households were, and how their housing situation related to their neighbors.

6

Owning and Renting

Compared to freestanding houses, the row house was small, affordable, and therefore conducive to homeownership. Several observers have credited the drive toward homeownership in Washington to the city's federal employees. Once a modicum of job security was guaranteed by the Pendleton Civil Service Reform Act of 1883, the theory went, federal employees were inclined to buy houses. In 1887 Joseph West Moore claimed that government clerks were homeowners: "Many are householders, over 5,000, it is estimated, owning comfortable homes of their own, paid for out of their savings." He credited building and loan associations as well as installment purchasing for having made Washington "a city of homes owned by those who live in them, like Philadelphia." In 1899 statistician and Labor Commissioner Carroll D. Wright said that since the civil service act, "governmental employees have felt warranted in purchasing their homes rather than in living in rented houses."[1]

Government employment might have contributed to the slightly higher rate of homeownership in Washington, but the city's rate was not dramatically higher than the average. In 1890, the first year that the census collected data on homeownership, 25.2 percent of Washington homes were owned by the occupant, compared to a 22.8 percent average among the twenty-six largest cities. Thirty years later, Washington's homeownership rate was 30.3 percent, compared to 26.9 percent among large cities.[2]

Speculative row houses were built not only to sell, but also for the rental market; some developers held onto the houses they built for years. Renting and boarding played a large part in the city's residential history, from its first years when congressmen congregated in boardinghouses. By 1887, a government report found, renting was popular for government employees. "On every hand are rooms to rent, furnished and unfurnished, with or without board. The price paid for furnished rooms usually includes their care, fuel, and lights. Furnaces, heating- and cooking-stoves, and ranges are to an unusual extent a part of the fixed equipment of rented houses."[3] Washington's row houses accommodated a variety of rental, boarding (with meals), and lodging (without meals) arrangements.

For the broad middle class, row houses also provided a comfortable home for a family. For those at the lower end of the scale, row houses might shrink in size or be located in unhealthy alleys; they might also be crowded with extended family members and unrelated boarders. For those on the high end, their large houses provided room not only for entertaining but also for servants. For many, homeownership was a method of wealth accumulation, enabling families to gain a financial foothold, to live in their dream house, or to use the row house to move up to a more desirable dwelling.

This chapter examines how owning and renting played out on a micro-level scale. Four squares are studied to determine who was buying or renting what kind of houses. Referring to the typical plans outlined in chapter 1, and with close attention to the houses' sizes, the number of people and their relationships can be placed in specific kinds of houses. Each square's statistics are framed by the experience of one or two homeowners, in order to bring the numbers to life and the buildings to three dimensions. And in order to consider these row houses through time, some of the focal families are not the first owners, but rather from later in the house's history.

The selection of the squares is, of course, idiosyncratic; to find truly representational squares would be impossible. The use of these squares is not to challenge the statistics, but only to show how they played out in various situations. Thus, the homeownership rate might be very low on a square in working-class Foggy Bottom, but it is possible to see certain residents using their small dwellings to gain a foothold in the housing market. Row houses in upper-class Dupont Circle might have some of the highest population densities, but they were also some of the largest houses, well suited to boarding-houses and multiple units. The development of a square on Capitol Hill might have been undertaken by investors, but the construction of row houses in twos and threes made them affordable to their developers. And the overwhelming sameness of a square in Petworth, with nearly identical row houses all built within three years, and boasting a high rate of homeownership, is also evidence of racial exclusion, because for the first several decades of its existence the square was entirely white.

For each square, the discussion concentrates on the row houses that were speculatively built, which are related to the basic floor plans outlined in chapter 1.[4] In some squares, row houses were demolished and apartment houses erected but, because the three older squares have been protected by historic district designation for the last forty years or so, they maintain most of their original row houses (and, in fact, a large number of original buildings was a criterion for selection). By selecting squares in different neighborhoods, the character of those neighborhoods is implied, but no neighborhood is without both pretentious and humble row houses. Each square has an internal hierarchy, too, that of the roadways. Avenues attract the grandest houses, wide streets were more prized than narrow ones, and alleys were valued least of all. This chapter offers a biography of each square, relating the row houses to their residents generally, and to one or two families in particular.

Workers' Row Houses and Alley Dwellings: Square 28

On March 9, 1866, the *Evening Star* advertised the sale of some real estate: "Two frame buildings, situate on west half of Lot 6, in Square 28, on I street north, near the [Washington] Circle, each house containing two rooms."[5] John Leonard, an immigrant recently arrived from Ireland, bought them and moved his family into the house at the corner of Twenty-Fifth and I Streets. He worked as a watchman in the 1870s, but by 1880 he and his wife, Margaret, ran a grocery store out of the corner building, which they had expanded to house their six children as well. In the 1860s they also built a two-story, wood-frame house facing onto Twenty-Fifth Street, which they rented out; in 1880 it was occupied by fellow Irish immigrants Michael Clancy, his wife, and two children, and Patrick Welch and his wife (see fig. 88). By 1900, though, John Leonard's son, also named John, lived there with his wife and two chil-

Figure 88. Row house, 909 Twenty-Fifth Street NW. Irish immigrants John and Margaret Leonard built this row house in the 1860s. They lived next door, above their since-demolished grocery store, and their son and his family were living here by 1900. (Photograph by the author, 2021)

dren. The son had died by 1910, but his widow continued to live here with her then-grown children and her daughter's husband and two children. Beginning with a two-room house, John Leonard expanded his modest real estate holdings to provide a home for his family for fifty years and four generations.

Similarly, on the other side of the block, Noah Price, an African American coachman, owned his own home at 928 Twenty-Fourth Street, where he lived with his wife and eight children, while operating a stable on the alley. The frame house, 14 feet wide, was probably built in the 1850s. Price bought the house in about 1892, and nearly fifty years later it was still in the family, housing his widowed daughter-in-law.[6]

The physical distance between these two family homes was not great, but several gulfs separated them. One was that of time; John Leonard had died by the time Noah Price moved to the block, so their paths did not cross. Another was race; the experiences of Blacks and whites in Washington were very different, even while inhabiting virtually the same space. Both Leonard and Price were working-class men, providing for their families and using real estate to do so. They lived on a square that was full of people like them, whether renting, boarding, or owning, living in different family arrangements. And while we do not know much about Leonard's and Price's initial houses—Leonard's was demolished in the 1920s, Price's in the 1950s—we know that they were modest houses in a square that was full of them.[7]

Bounded by New Hampshire Avenue and Twenty-Fourth, K, Twenty-Fifth, and I Streets, Square 28 is located in the Foggy Bottom neighborhood in Northwest (see fig. 89).[8] Today this area adjacent to George Washington University and Hospital, just off Washington Circle, has several apartment houses and other large buildings that have replaced original building fabric. But a few row houses survive to tell the story of a working-class row-house neighborhood, and the square contains one of the largest collections of surviving nineteenth-century alley dwellings in the city. The history of the square is also one of racial change. From 1880 to 1950, although the alley residents were nearly all African American, the residents of the street-facing buildings were mixed. In 1880 whites constituted 51 percent of the population of the square; in 1900, 37 percent. The trend toward an increasingly African American population continued, so that in 1920 the square's population was 87 percent African American, and in 1940 and 1950, 97 percent. Then a dramatic shift occurred, so that in 1960 whites were nearly 80 percent of the square's population, as they were in 2010.

While the proximity to New Hampshire Avenue and Washington Circle might have suggested that this would be an upscale neighborhood, the development of industries to the south and west meant that Foggy Bottom would be the home of working-class residents. In the nineteenth century, a gas

Figure 89. Square 28 in 1913, showing construction of the speculatively built row houses. Located just off Washington Circle in the Foggy Bottom neighborhood, Square 28 had both working- and middle-class speculatively built row houses, along with a number of alley dwellings. (Ruben Melendez and Onairis Perez, delineators, adapted from 1913 Baist map, building permit, and tax assessment data)

works and two breweries populated the neighborhood, while industries located on Rock Creek, which was just three blocks away from this square, and the slightly farther Potomac River included a paving company, a coal dealer, a glass factory, and lime kilns.[9] By the time of the Civil War, there were about twenty houses on this square, but none survive. Except for one fairly grand house on K Street, valued at $2,400, the rest were modest in value, and because of the sparse development, few were row houses.

After John Leonard bought his two two-room houses on I Street at the corner of Twenty-Fifth Street, three more houses were added to this row along

I Street. Two of these survive, later encased in brick, at 2433 and 2435 I Street. Two stories tall with side-gable roofs and a two-room plan, these are characteristic of the type of small row houses that would have dotted the square after the Civil War (see fig. 90). A few doors down at 2429, John Scanlon, a contractor, built a house with a two-story bay window for his family in 1885.[10] Twenty-five years later, Scanlon's son Daniel, an electrician for the Potomac Electric Company, owned it, living there with his wife and six children. The four houses in between the Leonards and the Scanlons were rented; in 1900 all but one of the tenants were, like Scanlon and Leonard, Irish immigrants. Not surprisingly for a working-class neighborhood at the end of the nineteenth century, these seven 16-foot-wide lots accommodated row houses for Irish workers, both tenants and homeowners.

Three foursomes of row houses filled in the I Street frontage and were also intended for rental to working-class residents. Duvall and Marr, an insurance and real estate firm, built four small row houses at 2413–19 I Street in 1885, renting them to African American workers. In 1889 an investor for the Tayloe family built four small row houses at 2421–27 I Street and rented them to white workers (see fig. 91). And in 1909 Simon Oppenheimer built four row houses at 2407–11 I Street and rented them to African Americans.[11] The

Figure 90. Row houses, 2433–35 I Street NW. An investor built these gable-roofed houses in the 1860s and rented them to Irish immigrants. Restoration in the 1950s included facing the houses with brick. (Photograph by the author, 2022)

Figure 91. Row houses, 2423–27 I Street NW. Built in 1889, these row houses were an investment for the Tayloe family, which held onto them for sixty years. Initially they were rented to white workers. (Photograph by the author, 2022)

row houses were all small, 12½ feet wide for Duvall and Marr's houses, which had no back building, and 14 feet wide for the others. The Tayloe houses, designed by Charles Burden, who had designed the English-basement houses discussed in chapter 1, had an unusual appearance for modest dwellings, with slate-covered mansard roofs facing the street. For the Oppenheimer houses, built twenty years after their neighbors, architect Albert Beers designed flat-fronted buildings, three bays wide, with rough-faced lintels, modillioned cornices, and brick facades laid in Flemish bond to give them a slightly Colonial Revival appearance.

On Twenty-Fourth Street, near Noah Price's house, in 1884 A. D. Elliot built four brick dwellings, each 12½ feet wide with back buildings, at 936–42 Twenty-Fourth Street (see fig. 92).[12] The small dwellings have corbelled cornices and segmental-arched windows. They were clearly intended for investment; Elliott sold two of them to Jacob H. Reisinger and two to Henry Luckel, who in turn rented them to African American tenants. In 1900 all of the houses on the Twenty-Fourth Street side of this square were occupied by African Americans, although Noah Price was the only homeowner.

The houses on the K Street side of the square had a different character, including two costly houses and two pairs of speculative row houses. K Street, one of Washington's broader, more elegant streets at 148 feet wide, attracted grand houses. George Lowry, a Georgetown grocer and occupant of a house at 2408 K Street, apparently became wealthy in the mid-1860s; his house, which no longer survives, was valued at $15,000 in 1869. Nearby, at 2422 K Street, Joseph Brown built an Italianate mansion with an elegant oriel in the early 1870s. The K Street frontage also had speculative row houses built in the late nineteenth century, which were more appropriate for the working-class neighborhood that this had become. The two-story brick bay-fronts built in 1885 at 2424–26 K Street and the three-story brick bay-fronts built five years later at 2418–20 K Street were all rental properties. In 1920 a Black family at 2426 headed by John Hutchinson, a stock laborer at the government printing office, lived next door to a white family headed by Martin Smith, a steward at a hotel.[13]

The Twenty-Fifth Street side of the square also saw a mixture of house types and races. Like John Leonard's rental house at 909, some property owners built single houses for rent. At 947 Twenty-Fifth Street, in 1879 J. Leonard McGraw built a two-story house that was a generous 20 feet wide, but only 17 feet deep, with a back building (see fig. 93). McGraw rented the house to white families, first to laborer George Nichols and his wife and two children. Next door to the south, set back on the lot, was a small brick building that may have been related to a greenhouse that once stood nearby.[14] In 1900 Lucy Payne, an African American charwoman who worked for the government, lived with her four children in this small building.

Some landlords lived next door to their rental properties, as John Leonard did. Scottish-born James Gowans built a two-story brick bay-front house at

Figure 92. Row houses, 936–42 Twenty-Fourth Street NW. Built in 1884, these houses, not much bigger than alley dwellings, were rented to African American workers. (Photograph by the author, 2022)

Figure 93. Row houses, 947–53 Twenty-Fifth Street NW. J. Leonard McGraw built the house at 947, on the right, in 1879 and rented it out. Scottish immigrant James Gowans built the house at 951, two doors down, in 1883, lived there for a few years, then built the taller house next door at 949, and moved in, renting out 951. George W. Ray built the house on the left at 953 for rental in 1909. (Photograph by the author, 2022)

951 Twenty-Fifth Street for $3,500 in 1883. Gowans, a plate printer, moved in with his wife and six children. Just seven years later, he built an even grander building next door at 949 and moved into the new house with his family, renting out his previous home to a white family, government worker Milton Ailes and his wife and two children.[15] Also living with the Ailes family was an African American servant, Florence Page, the only live-in domestic help on this square in 1900.

Next door to the north, a small wood-frame building at 953, rented by an African American woman, Ella Jones, a nurse, and her dressmaker daughter, was replaced in 1909 by George W. Ray, a Georgetown grocer. Classical Revival in appearance, with garlands applied to the Flemish-bond brick facade below the plain cornice, the house had a traditional L-shaped plan, with living room and dining room in the main block and the pantry and kitchen in the back building (see fig. 94). On the second floor were two bedrooms, with the bathroom and another bedroom in the back building.[16] At 15 feet wide, the house was too narrow for a side hall.

Two other early twentieth-century groupings on Twenty-Fifth Street were constructed by Harry Kite, the prolific developer of row houses, and his architect, Albert H. Beers; one was for rental, the other was sold to homeowners. In 1909 Kite built three row houses at 915–19; the new owner rented them to African American tenants. At 955–63, at the corner of K Street, Kite built five small row houses in 1911 (see fig. 95).[17] In 1920, four of these were owned by the occupants (the fifth was not recorded in the census). Samuel Longo, an Italian shoemaker, lived in 963, on the corner. His neighbors were all African

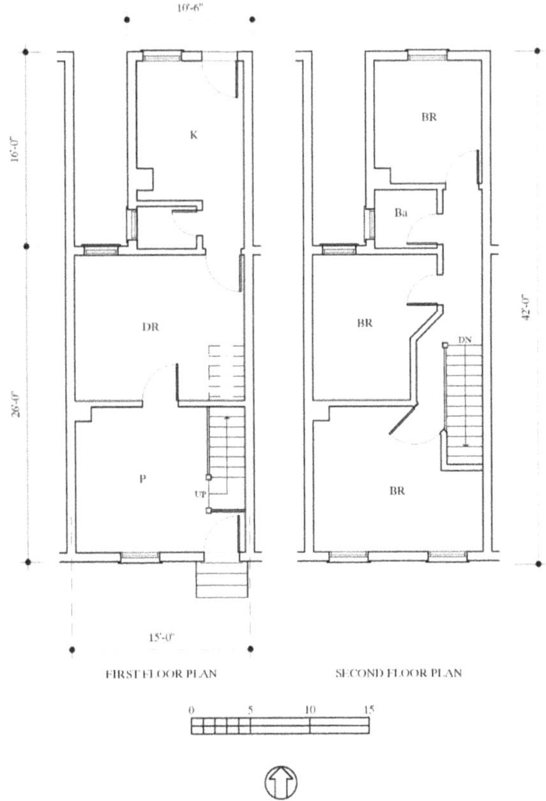

Figure 94. Row house, 953 Twenty-Fifth Street NW, plans. Built in 1909 for grocer George W. Ray, this row house with a Classical Revival front has a standard L-shaped plan. The first floor has living and dining rooms in the main block and a pantry and kitchen in the back building, while the second floor has three bedrooms and a bathroom. The 15-foot width made it too small for a side hall. (Plans from Permit #1000, August 4, 1909, redrawn by Ruben Melendez, Onairis Perez, and Mark Schara, delineators)

American: Joseph Dickens, a post office employee, at 961; Isaac Brown, a laborer at the Navy Yard, at 957; and Alice Tatum, a charwoman for the Pullman Company, at 955.

In the late nineteenth century, the residents of the street-facing buildings on this square were racially mixed. In 1880, 79 percent of the residents were white, and twenty years later, 59 percent. Whites were as apt to live next door to African Americans as to cluster in groupings, such as the Irish immigrants on I Street near Twenty-Fifth. Substantial, middle-class houses sat next to minimal dwellings, and the square seemed to express the full range of houses and people found in the larger neighborhood.

But one part of the square housed overwhelmingly African American residents, and that was the alley. Snow's Court was shaped like the letter *I*, with an access road from the middle of the *I* to the middle of the Twenty-Fifth Street frontage, and a 6-foot-wide footpath from I Street. This alley housed, at times, more than 200 African Americans; in the 1880, 1900, and 1920

Figure 95. Row houses, 955–63 Twenty-Fifth Street NW. Built in 1911 by developer Harry Kite, these modest houses were owner-occupied by 1920. Three of the homeowners were African American. (Photograph by the author, 2022)

censuses, no whites were recorded as living there. Although the alley accommodated stables and workshops, mostly the alley provided space for housing built and owned by absentee landlords. In 1872, Thomas Martin subdivided a lot on Twenty-Fourth Street to create four alley lots, and John W. Fitzhugh created five alley lots behind his property on Twenty-Fifth Street. They built frame alley dwellings that do not survive but were probably among the seventeen houses on Snow's Alley, occupied by 109 African Americans, recorded in the 1880 census.[18]

Determining how many people and even how many houses were on Snow's Court at any given time is difficult. The residents—poor, disenfranchised, and African American—were likely to view census takers with suspicion. Reformers who undertook counts of buildings and inhabitants while depicting squalid conditions perhaps overestimated the numbers in order to build their case. The police survey of 1897 found 249 African Americans in Snow's Court, the 1900 U.S. census found 208, the police found 286 in 1905 and 261 in 1908, and the 1910 U.S. census found 183. Similarly, the number of houses varied widely, with the census showing 41 in 1900 and 37 in 1910, while reformer Wilbur Vincent Mallalieu found 47 in 1912. An 1891 newspaper article asserted that there were 69 houses, "each containing at least two families."[19]

After 1880, until construction of new alley dwellings was effectively prohibited in 1892, absentee landlords built brick alley buildings on this square several at a time. In 1884 Edwin Greer built thirteen alley dwellings, the largest grouping in the alley (see fig. 96). Constructed at a cost of less than $540 each, the two-story brick buildings measured just 10½ feet by 24, for a total

Figure 96. Alley dwellings, Snow's Court. On the left are some of the thirteen built by Edwin Greer in 1884, while on the right are the pair built by James H. Grant in 1890 and the threesome built by Louise Veerhoff in 1885. The latter two groupings do not survive. (Photographer unknown, ca. 1935, Alley Dwelling Authority, National Capital Housing Authority)

of 504 square feet in each.[20] Like many alley dwellings, they had modest brick corbeling at the cornice, flat roofs, and segmental-arched windows. Greer soon sold four of these to Eliza W. Lippitt and the rest to Rebecca G. Dodge, who held onto them for three decades.

When the same developer built modest housing on both street and alley, the alley housing was always smaller. Behind the working-class dwellings on I Street, developers Duvall and Marr and Tayloe built even smaller alley dwellings, and on K Street developers Louise Veerhoff and James H. Grant built smaller alley dwellings behind their brick bay-fronts. Others, like Edwin Greer, built only alley dwellings. In 1890 Samuel Norment built a row of seven 13-by-28-foot alley dwellings, which remained in his family into the 1920s.[21]

In 1888 Eugene Bettes, who owned frame double houses on I Street near Twenty-Fourth, subdivided the lot and built three alley dwellings unlike the others, with back buildings attached to their 12 by 30-foot main block. These 846-square-foot dwellings cost just $575 apiece to build. Reformer Frederick Weller described them in 1908 as being arranged as three-room flats, with separate entrances for the upper rooms. There were no backyards, and no rear windows on the upper story (today they have both). The absence of a rear window meant that the tenants could not look at the backs of the houses on the street, securing both of them some privacy. The absence of a backyard meant that the toilet was indoors, but, according to Weller, it was in a room that measured a little more than 5 by 8 feet that also was used for food storage. That room counted as one of the three.[22]

All of these brick alley dwellings were constructed in groups of two or three or more, owned by landlords who usually held onto them for decades and clearly saw them as an investment. None of the landlords lived on this square. Although only twenty-three alley dwellings survive in an alley that once contained forty or more, and the survivors are all brick whereas historically about half of them would have been wood fame, it is still possible to generalize about them. Most were two stories; there may have been some one-story wood-frame ones early in the development of the block, but two stories became the norm by about 1880. In appearance, they were minimally decorated, with flat roofs; their width did not permit more than a window and door at the first level and two windows in the second-floor front. Most of them had two rooms on each floor, echoing a plan that dated to the eighteenth century. They were small, ranging between 10½ to 13 feet in width. Only three of them had back buildings. Their size ranged from 500 to 850 square feet.

The houses were certainly crowded: the average number of people per house was 6.4 in 1880, 5 in 1900, and down to 3.6 in 1920. As sociologist Daniel Swinney noted, "where there are more persons than rooms, death and illness rates begin to rise," and most of these were four-room houses. In 1905 Frederick Weller found a family of eight living in two rooms; they all apparently slept in the rear room. Upstairs, one room accommodated a family of three, while the other had a lodger. The crowded conditions also reflect an impoverished population struggling to get by. The intricate family relationships suggested by the census—with households including in-laws, nieces and nephews, stepchildren, adopted children, and so on—point to a community with an expansive notion of family. Lodgers—presumably people without families that they could rely on—provided welcome income to pinched households.[23]

Besides privacy, sanitation also suffered in Snow's Court. Water and sewer service was available in the alley, but landlords supplied most dwellings only with a hydrant from which to obtain water and a flush toilet in the yard. Reformers found the filth shocking. Frederick Weller mentioned in his 1905 assessment of one of these alley dwellings the "smoke-stained, grimy walls; the poorly lighted rooms; the falling plaster; broken stairs and sagging, leaky ceiling." Similarly, Wilbur Vincent Mallalieu deplored the conditions, describing a mother who moved into a house in Snow's Court in 1911 "with her four children ranging from a girl of eleven to a boy three weeks of age. They have two wretched rooms for which they pay six dollars. The back room is used for a kitchen and dining room and the front room as a bed room for the entire family, including an aunt who is a confirmed drunkard." He described the appearance of the house: "The kitchen was piled up with cinders, ashes and pans of garbage from which food was being picked for the children. There was one bed and a couch which opened out to a half-bed, a small stove, a broken chair and a cupboard for food, all in the most filthy condition imaginable." As late as 1938, thirty-three of the forty-six dwelling units were without inside water; those with inside water had cold water only. Forty did not have inside toilets, and none had gas or electricity.[24]

As might be expected, the crowded conditions and lack of sanitation fostered disease. In Washington in 1910, the death rate per 1,000 was 30.09 in the alleys, compared to 17.56 in street-facing dwellings. In the Health Department district that included Snow's Court, the death rate was 34.14. Tuberculosis, pneumonia, and diarrhea in babies struck alley dwellers particularly hard. Weller recounted a case of typhoid fever stemming from the one remaining privy in Snow's Court. The privy had no lid and stood in a shed with no door.[25]

Crime too was rampant, with Mallalieu asserting that a police officer called Snow's Court "the worst place in the United States . . . there is no crime unknown to it." In the year beginning in March 1911, police arrested 114 Snow's Court residents, out of a population of 204. The charges were "drunkenness, disorderly conduct, assault, unlawful assembly, larceny, cruelty to animals and accusations relating to sexual crimes." With the onset of Prohibition, Snow's Court also became a place to make and buy illegal alcohol. But, somehow, the crime situation improved; in the first six months of 1936, police made only 28 arrests in Snow's Court, mostly for minor offenses.[26]

Snow's Court had a reputation as a dangerous place. Alaveta Mitchell, an African American who moved to Washington from South Carolina in the early twentieth century, described her interaction with "Snowy Court, in the Bottom," when she first moved to the city. "A bad place, I'm here to tell. Now, I saw a dog run down there and then run out—scared by just the looks of the people who lived in there. And they told me to not even look down there 'cause them was some rough people—just too rough. And not a one from South Carolina, so I wasn't never to go in there to see for myself. But a time or two I went in, just to see it. A small place, dirty like I can't tell you. Small houses, but people who looked out for one another. I took up with a girl who took me in there and into where she lived. So I seen the place inside to out. But I shouldn't been in there. See if I had no people to be seeing in there I wasn't to go there or anywhere else."[27]

Unlike the street-facing buildings, the forty or so houses on the alley were racially cohesive, creating an isolated community where African Americans did not have to interact with the white world. The structure of "blind" alleys such as this one might have prevented the police from surveilling them, but it also fostered an intimate community, safe from prying outsiders. One observer noted, "the strong community spirit in the alleys is their most notable attribute. They feed their own hungry, house their own homeless, lend to their own penniless, and shelter their own refugees from the law." Swinney noted that "the generosity of the alley inhabitants is remarkable," opening their homes to those in need.[28]

Houses are more than shelter; they can also be an important financial investment. The residents of Snow's Court, all African American, were all renters and therefore reaped no long-term financial benefit from their living arrangement. A congressional report compiled in 1913 to determine alley dwelling ownership found that the 36 dwellings in Snow's Court were owned by six different people. Not only did they reside elsewhere, but most of the owners' addresses were given in care of agents or banks, indicating the business-like aspect of absentee ownership. Newspaper ads from the late 1880s give an idea of the range of rents. For "two-story frames of five rooms each" on the alley, the rent was just $6 per month, while frame dwellings at the corner of Twenty-Fourth and K Streets rented for $33 per month. The profits to landlords, though, were much higher on the alley dwellings. In 1938, Swinney calculated, 29 of the 37 dwellings brought in a gross profit of 20 percent or more, calling them "exorbitant profits." Furthermore, maintenance costs were negligible; 90 percent of the tenants alleged that their landlords refused to maintain the dwellings.[29]

For the street-facing houses, the homeownership rate was low but not nonexistent. Between 1900 and 1920, only ten to twelve people on the square owned their own homes, for a rate of 15–16 percent. For some of the homeowners, it is possible to infer that their houses brought them some prosperity or at least stability. John Leonard and Noah Price both managed to provide houses for generations of their families. By 1940, African Americans owned all but one of the fifteen owner-occupied houses; a Filipino owned the other. But for the most part, this was a square occupied by renters, and the profits went to the landlords. The renters were highly mobile, rarely appearing in two consecutive decennial censuses.[30] In this square, the speculative row houses provided short-term shelter to working-class families, both Black and white, often intermixed.

After World War II, the neighborhood's character changed. The construction of the State Department Building in 1941 at Twenty-First and E Streets, with a large addition in 1958, as well as the Potomac Plaza in 1954 on the site of the old gas works, began Foggy Bottom's turn to an office-oriented area rather than industrial. On Square 28, developers saw a market for Colonial Revival row houses, trading on Georgetown's popularity. A pair of row houses at 911–13 Twenty-Fifth Street, built in 1956, had brick fronts and gable roofs, along with pedimented doorways (see fig. 97). Up the street at 939–45 Twenty-Fifth Street, a block of four bow-fronted row houses, arranged in flats and built in 1959, was in a Federal mode. Also in 1959, a nine-story apartment house was built in the middle of the Twenty-Fifth Street frontage of the square, the first of six apartment buildings to disrupt the low profile of the single-family dwellings. Renovation of older houses occurred here as well. One of the houses featured in the 1956 house tour of Foggy Bottom was at 2423 I Street, a modest dwelling constructed in 1889 (see fig. 91). Homeowner Henry Kennard, an architect, gutted the house and installed a "suspension-

Figure 97. Row houses, 909–17 Twenty-Fifth Street NW. Next to the Leonards' house at 909 stand two Colonial Revival row houses built in 1956, illustrating the mid-twentieth-century reinvestment in this square. (Photograph by the author, 2022)

Figure 98. Alley dwellings, 1–7 Snow's Court. In 1890 Samuel Norment built these seven alley dwellings, renovated by Jonas and Jean Robitscher in 1953. (Photograph by the author, 2018)

type staircase that bisects the living room, and a decorating plan keyed to a color scheme of yellow, turquoise, and black."[31]

Alley dwellings also became the focus of renovation efforts. In 1953 Jean and Jonas Robitscher acquired the seven dwellings built by Samuel Norment and renovated them (see fig. 98). The Robitschers, who lived in Georgetown, were following the trend there, where alley dwellings were being refurbished. They hired Russell Eldridge, the builder who renovated Georgetown's Bell's

Court, to be their contractor in Snow's Court (see fig. 58). The work on the Snow's Court alley dwellings was extensive, as reported by the *Sunday Star:* "The 93-year-old dwellings [actually 63 years old], which had deteriorated into scarcely more than hovels . . . were stripped back to the bare brick walls. All interior partitions were removed, and new flooring was laid over the old. Gas, electricity and inside plumbing, none of which the houses had before, were installed. A brick fireplace was added to each, flanked on each side by shelves or cabinets or a combination of the two." Four of the dwellings were sold before the work was completed; the new homeowners, all white, were a woman who worked for the State Department and her widowed mother; a lawyer who planned to use the house as an investment; and two female reporters.[32]

By 1956 the Robitschers had renovated 15 more houses on Snow's Court, including the 13 built by Edwin Greer. For these, the Robitschers extended the 10-by-24-foot buildings by almost a third (see figs. 99 and 100; see also fig. 84).

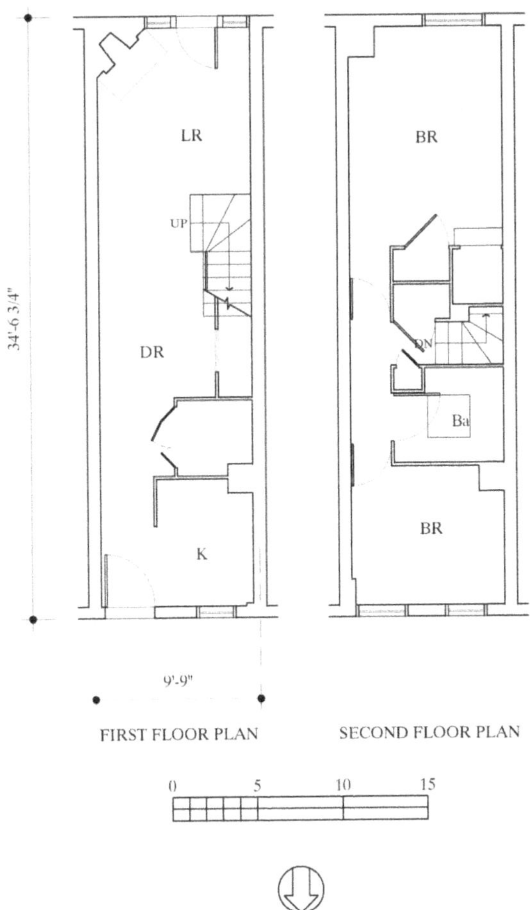

Figure 99. Alley dwelling, 17 Snow's Court, plans. Built in 1884, this is one of Edwin Greer's thirteen row houses, which were extensively remodeled by the Robitschers in 1956. Increasing their length by almost a half, the Robitschers moved the kitchen to the front, put a fireplace in the rear corner, and added a skylit bathroom on the second floor. See figs. 84 and 96. (Ruben Melendez, Onairis Perez, and Mark Schara, delineators, 2020)

Figure 100. Alley dwellings, 10–18 Snow's Court. Once remodeled by the Robitschers, the alley dwellings sold to individual homeowners. (Photograph by the author, 2022)

They moved the kitchen to the front of the house and added a corner fireplace in the rear of the living room, beside a door that led to a patio, enclosed with brick walls. On the second floor they added a skylit bathroom between the two bedrooms. Russell Eldridge was, again, the builder, and Eldred Mowery was the architect. A study of the economics of this rehabilitation found that for 9 of these alley dwellings, the Robitschers had paid $27,000 for acquisition and $80,000 for remodeling, then sold them for $135,000, for a 20 percent profit.[33]

The reinvestment on Square 28 has been considerable, with new row houses and apartment buildings crowding smaller nineteenth-century row houses and transforming the square from working class to middle class and from predominantly African American to mostly white. The houses with the two-room plan served not only as minimal rental accommodations, in the alley, but also, when located on the street, as the first opportunity for homeownership for Noah Price and John Leonard, and for other Blacks and whites. These small dwellings also fostered a mixture of races in the late nineteenth century, before Jim Crow segregation changed the housing landscape.

The Middle of the Middle Class: Square 965

"Everyone knew each other," reminisced Betty Sizer, who was born in 1927 in the row house at 131 Tenth Street NE (see fig. 101).[34] "When I grew up, none of

Figure 101. Row House, 131 10th Street NE. Built in 1885, this speculative row house is typical of the two-story dwellings that characterize this square on Capitol Hill. Here, Mary Sizer, a widow, took in boarders in the 1930s and 1940s to support herself and her four children. (Photograph by the author, 2021)

the houses were painted colors but all were natural brick red. Our front yard was mostly bricked but there was a small patch of about three foot square that grass was supposed to grow in but never seemed to do very well. There were always two benches in the front yard and people sat on the benches in the 'evening,' it was always called then. There was no air conditioning or television in those days. We visited with whoever went by and the kids played there or we would play baseball in the alley if we had enough kids to play." Betty's parents, Charles and Mary Sizer, had married and moved into the house in 1914, then had four children—Dorothy, Joseph, Georgette, and Betty.

During this fondly remembered childhood, Betty's parents took in lodgers. Her father, a proofreader at the government printing office, died in 1930 and, as Betty described it, "My mother had no other income so she did what she knew how. She made a kitchen in the basement and a bedroom and another smaller room that could [be] used for one and she took in roomers and boarders." Mary advertised in the newspaper: "Two nicely furnished rooms for light housekeeping; all modern improvements; near bath"; "Three large rooms furnished for light housekeeping; hot-water heat, gas, electricity, second floor, semi-private bath; reasonable"; and "Twin beds, suitable for two men; second floor, next [to] bath."[35]

The house, a brick bay-front built in 1885, proved its adaptability through its accommodation of lodgers. One of three two-story row houses, 19 feet wide with back buildings, the house had been built by W. C. Peake, a painter who lived down the street in another brick bay-front, at 121. The house at 131 remained a rental property until the Sizers acquired it. To accommodate lodgers, Mary Sizer added a kitchen in the small room in the front of the hallway on the second floor. The two main rooms on the second floor could use this kitchen and share the bathroom with the lodger who took the room in the second floor of the back building. Although Betty remembered the main kitchen as having been moved from the first floor to the basement, it was more likely that it was always there. The Sizer family squeezed into rooms in the basement and first floor, the first-floor dining room was converted to a bedroom, and all of the dining took place in the kitchen. The arrangement was flexible, though; Betty recalled having to give up her room for a lodger at one point and share her mother's bedroom.

Finally, in 1932, Mary Sizer was able to purchase the house she had been living in for eighteen years.[36] In 1940, Mary's house accommodated her son Joseph, age twenty-three, a concrete-mixer operator; her daughters Georgette, sixteen, and Betty, twelve; her daughter Dorothy, a dressmaker; Dorothy's husband, a maintenance man in a dry-cleaning plant; their one-year-old son; and three lodgers: a bus driver for Capital Transit, an auto salesman, and his wife.

Located catercorner from Lincoln Park in the Capitol Hill neighborhood, Square 965 is bounded by Tenth and Eleventh Streets and Constitution (originally B Street) and Massachusetts Avenues NE.[37] Real estate investments were characteristic of this square, in which a majority of the houses were speculatively built row houses constructed between 1882 and 1891 (see fig. 102). And like W. C. Peake, many of the investors were local, living either elsewhere on the square or a few blocks away. The uniform streetscapes of two-story brick bay-fronts housed residents who tended to be overwhelmingly white and middle class.

They also tended to be homeowners at a higher rate than those of Square 28. On Square 965, of the 37 houses that were recorded in the 1900 census, 13 of them, or 35 percent, were occupied by their owners. The homeownership rate increased in the next decade, with 24 occupants of the 40 houses in the square owning their houses, or 60 percent. The brick bay-front row houses were ideal for middle-class homeowners.

The speculatively built, bay-fronted row houses concentrated on Tenth and Eleventh Streets. The largest development was the group of eight identical row houses built in 1886 at 134–48 Eleventh Street (see fig. 103). These houses, a little less than 15 feet wide, two stories tall with two-story bay

① 128-30 11th, Hesler, 1860s
② 115-19 10th, Rothwell, 1882
③ 152-56 11th and 1013 B (Constitution), Donohue, 1883, 1885, 1890
④ 127-31 10th, Peake, 1885
⑤ 134-48 11th, Smithson and Richards, 1886
⑥ Alley dwellings, Getz, 1887
⑦ 112-16 11th, Warren, 1889
⑧ 121-25 10th, Carrico, 1889
⑨ 1004-06 Massachusetts, Wright and Stockett, 1890
⑩ 120-22 11th, Newton, 1900

Figure 102. Square 965 in 1913, showing construction of the speculatively built row houses. Located just off Lincoln Park in the Capitol Hill neighborhood, Square 965 had a solidly middle-class collection of row houses. Most of the more upscale, custom-built row houses were on Massachusetts Avenue. This portion of B Street was renamed Constitution Avenue in the 1960s. (Ruben Melendez and Onairis Perez, delineators, adapted from 1913 Baist, building permit, and tax assessment data)

windows, were ornamented with prominent corbeled brick cornices, brick hoodmolds over the segmental-arched windows, and other brick decoration. The developers were a partnership of Thomas E. Smithson, a contractor and brickmaker, and William H. Richards, who had a wood and coal business. More than likely, Smithson provided the brick and Richards the lumber for this row. They moved into their new houses. Smithson, who at his death in 1918 at the age of eighty-two, was "one of the oldest members of the Association of Oldest Inhabitants," lived out his life at 142.[38] By 1902 Richards owned

Figure 103. Row houses, 134–48 Eleventh Street NE. The largest development on this square, these eight row houses were built in 1886. (Jarob Ortiz, photographer, 2021, Library of Congress, Prints and Photographs Division, HABS)

Figure 104. Row houses, 100 block Tenth Street NE. The Tenth Street side of the block consists primarily of bay-front row houses built in groups of three by different developers in the 1880s. (Photograph by the author, 2022)

three of the houses they had built, including the one at 134 where he lived with his wife, Jane.

Twelve houses on the square were built in groups of threes between 1882 and 1889, including the house that became the Sizers'. The triples of row houses—115–19 Tenth Street, 121–25 Tenth, 127–31 Tenth, and 112–16 Eleventh Street—are similar in appearance, an effect of their tight time period (see fig. 104). All are brick, two stories tall with two-story bay windows. Some had back buildings, and others had kitchens in the basements, but the fronts that they presented to the street were remarkably similar. Variety stemmed from the width of the projecting bay and whether it could accommodate one or two windows, how the corners of the bays were articulated, and the brick ornamentation at the cornice. The buildings ranged in width from 17 to 20 feet.[39]

Another approach to building speculative houses was to do it gradually, as circumstances permitted. Eugenia E. and Daniel T. Donohue acquired a large lot at the corner of Eleventh and Constitution, on which there was a small frame dwelling, valued at only $50 in 1874. In 1883 they replaced it with a large brick dwelling and store, measuring 20 feet on Eleventh Street and stretching 71 feet along Constitution Avenue, where the three-story building had two bay windows, one square and one polygonal (see fig. 105).

Figure 105. Row houses and corner store, 152–56 Eleventh Street NE. Eugenia and Daniel Donohue built the corner building as their grocery store and residence in 1883, then added the two bay-front row houses to the left to serve as rental properties. (Jarob Ortiz, photographer, 2021, Library of Congress, Prints and Photographs Division, HABS)

The Eleventh Street storefront announced the Donohues' grocery store. Two years later they built a bay-front row house next door at 154 Eleventh Street. Five years after that, the Donohues added two more houses, one south of the previous one, at 152 Eleventh Street, and one around the corner on Constitution, along with a brick stable on the alley.[40] The three rental houses are distinct in appearance, but they share certain characteristics, such as raised basements, two-story bay windows, and elaborate corbeled brick cornices. Although the Donohues and their eight children originally lived above the store, by 1900 they had moved to a large, three-story row house about a block away at 1014 E. Capitol Street. While still operating the grocery, the Donohues rented out all three dwellings until around 1920.

Generally, the occupants of the speculative row houses on this square were nuclear families, including unmarried adult children. In-laws, grown siblings, and parents sometimes joined the household. Only seven of the thirty-seven households in 1900 had boarders, and only one had a live-in servant. By 1920, the houses were considerably more crowded, as the average number of people increased from 4.2 to 5.6. The occupations of the residents who worked ranged across middle-class professions, both white- and blue-collar, in 1900. As might be expected, there were a number of government clerks, as well as an architect (whose son was a draftsman), a stenographer, a physician, several teachers, a journalist, an engineer, a dentist, and an insurance agent. Blue-collar workers included printer, policeman, railroad conductor, and railroad motorman, as well as several in the building trades: painter, plumber, electrician, and cabinetmaker.

The parts of this square that did not fit the mold of speculative row houses were the corners and Massachusetts Avenue. At the corner of Tenth and Constitution, J. W. Boggs Jr. built a store and dwelling in 1882. At the corner of Eleventh and Massachusetts, diagonally across from Lincoln Park, an elegant four-story apartment house was built in 1906. The other houses on Massachusetts Avenue were similarly grand, and despite their individual construction, they form a cohesive whole. Erected between 1890 and 1915, most of them were built by individuals who intended to live in them.[41]

At the other end of the scale from the brick Massachusetts Avenue row houses were three frame dwellings. In 1900 William Henry Brent, an African American laborer, along with his wife and son, rented a frame house at Tenth and Massachusetts. By that time, the house was valued at only $100 and was probably about twenty years old. It was demolished a few years later.[42] In the 1860s, Laurence Hesler built frame houses at 128 and 130 Eleventh Street, valued at $600 (see fig. 106). Hesler, who farmed on this square, sold produce at Center Market and lived at 411 East Capitol Street, along with his son, Andrew, a gardener. By 1886 Andrew owned the house at 128 and held onto

Figure 106. Row houses, 128–30 Eleventh Street NE. These wood-frame dwellings, built in the 1860s, are the oldest buildings on the square. The tenants, both Blacks and whites over the years, were working class. (Photograph by the author, 2021)

it for the next twenty years or so. His father had sold 130 to Andrew Dorr, a butcher with stalls at Center and Northern Markets, by 1869. Dorr lived in this house only a few years. By 1886, August Getz, a builder who lived nearby, had acquired it and held it until after World War I.

The houses' history is hidden behind later additions. The house at 128 Eleventh Street has wide clapboard siding and a porch across the front, while the one at 130 has been covered in stucco. With flat roofs and a common bracketed cornice, these were some of the most modest dwellings on the square. Living at 128 in 1900 was Fannie Junghans, a baker, along with her grown son and a boarder. Ten years later, Emma Swann, an African American laundress, lived there, along with her adult son, daughter, and son-in-law. Next door at 130, in 1910 Nazzareno Chrieleiron lived with his wife and five children; all seven of them were identified as "octoroon" in the census, probably referring to their skin color more than their blood line. Having immigrated from Italy just two years earlier, Chrieleiron was a shoemaker with his own shop. In 1920 Anna Hughes, an African American domestic servant, lived at 130 with two lodgers.

Next to 130 is a rare side yard, adjacent to the alley; this portion of the lot was never built upon. Behind 130 and the vacant lot, August Getz added alley dwellings in 1887 (see fig. 107). Ornamented with corbelled brick cornices, the two-unit building measured 28 by 28 feet.[43] In 1910 an African American

Figure 107. Alley dwellings, Square 965. In 1887 August Getz, who owned the adjacent property on the street, built a pair of alley dwellings, since converted to garages. (Photograph by the author, 2020)

coachman, Mish Wilson, lived with his wife and five children in one unit, while next door Albert Holmes, also an African American coachman, lived with his wife, six children, and a lodger. The alley dwellings were converted to garages by 1928.

Segregation by building quality, in which African Americans lived in lesser-quality dwellings than whites but proximate to them, is illustrated by the housing on this square. Before World War II, the only African Americans to live on this square rented one of the three frame buildings or one of the two alley dwellings. That situation changed rapidly after the war, as spatial segregation became common. Once again, the Sizer family's experience is emblematic.

During the war, daughter Betty met a soldier at the Knights of Columbus USO. After he was discharged from the army, he rented one of the rooms at 131 Tenth Street until he and Betty were married in 1947 and moved to Iowa. In 1951 Betty's sister also married a lodger. At that time, Mary Sizer offered the house for sale: "Six rooms and 2 baths, row brick; conveniently arranged for 2 families. Priced for quick sale." The new owners, Meyer and Lillian Kushner, rented it to new residents, advertising, "Colored—131 10th St. NE. Furnished apartment, one room, kitchen, and semi-private bath; $57.50 month," and, a month later, "Colored—131 10th St. NE. Room and private kitchen, $12.50 per week," and, three weeks later, "Colored—131 10th St. NE. Studio room and kitchen; reasonable weekly rent."[44] These ads signal a change in population, but the use—as a multifamily dwelling—remained the same.

Like Square 28, the demographics of Square 965 shifted dramatically in the 1950s, but unlike Square 28, which went from Black to white, Square 965's population changed from white to Black. This square on Capitol Hill, which had been completely white in 1950, changed to 68 percent non-white in 1960 and 84 percent non-white in 1970. By 2010 the white population had risen again, to 80 percent.

As a whole, the architecture of Square 965 is remarkably consistent. Aside from the Massachusetts Avenue houses, the square was mostly two-story brick bay-fronts constructed for the speculative market. The relatively small size of the houses—averaging about 1,000 square feet spread over two floors—meant that they were affordable for middle-class families, both white-collar and blue-collar. They were also large enough to divide into apartments or to house lodgers, as circumstances demanded. As in Square 28, African Americans were initially segregated by building type, occupying the cheaper and smaller frame dwellings. These speculative bay-front row houses, whether sold or rented, supplied the housing market in a rapidly growing city with handsome, flexible dwellings.

Homes for the Professional and Genteel: Square 155

In 1929, sisters Josephine and Florence Patterson, two African American schoolteachers, bought a row house at 1728 Corcoran Street NW and moved in with their parents and siblings (see fig. 108). The family had been living in a row house at 1615 C Street SE that Josephine had bought in 1917. That house was small—two stories tall, 13 by 32 feet. Constructed at a cost of $1,500 in 1913, it had a flat front, porches front and back, and Latrobe stoves, not central heat. By contrast, the house on Corcoran Street must have seemed like a palace: three stories on a raised basement, two-story bay window topped with an open porch, 21 feet across by 40 feet deep, plus a small back building. The house had been built in 1890 at an estimated cost of $6,000.[45] The move was not only one of architectural quality, but also geography, as the Pattersons left the fringe of Capitol Hill for the heart of Dupont Circle. The Pattersons had arrived.

The accomplishment of Josephine and Florence, in buying such a large house, was intertwined with their family. James Patterson, born in Tennessee, and his wife, Ida, born in North Carolina, had come to Washington in the 1890s. James worked as a messenger for the government in 1900, then as a junk dealer by 1910. Ida stayed home and cared for their seven children. Their

Figure 108. Row house, 1728 Corcoran Street NW. Josephine Patterson, an African American kindergarten teacher, bought this house in 1929 and lived there with her parents and siblings. Along with the house to the left, this row house had been built in 1890. (Photograph by the author, 2021)

oldest daughter, Josephine, born in 1886, attended the prestigious M Street High School and then Miner Normal School, a teachers' college, both part of Washington's segregated public school system. Booker T. Washington, the apostle of African American self-help and hard work, spoke at her high school graduation. Josephine started teaching kindergarten in 1909 and retired forty-nine years later, having taught at seven different elementary schools. Florence, born in 1899, also attended M Street High and Miner Normal School; she taught in the public schools for forty-four years. When the family moved to the Corcoran Street house, their father was nearing sixty-five and no longer working. Their brother, James, a presser in a tailor shop, also lived with them. By 1940 their sister Evelyn Brown and her two children lived with them as well.[46]

Josephine and Florence seem to have been keenly aware of the financial opportunities that real estate provided. Josephine held onto the C Street house for thirty years, renting it out after she moved away. She and her sister borrowed against the Corcoran Street house nine times, whether to refinance it or for other purposes. Investing was not without pitfalls, however; in the early 1930s they were unable to pay their property taxes and lost the

Corcoran Street house at a tax sale, but they were able to buy it back the next year. In the end, they used the Corcoran Street house to advance as well; after Josephine married Lawrence Carrick in the early 1950s, she and Florence—not her husband—bought a semidetached house in Manor Park. Josephine and Florence sold the house on Corcoran in 1955 and moved to 301 Madison Street NW, along with Josephine's husband. That house, which had been built in 1930, measured 20 by 44 feet, was two stories tall, and sat across the street from Fort Slocum Park. In 1958, a few months before Josephine's husband died, Josephine and Florence gave part ownership in the house to their sister Evelyn. In 1963 the sisters sold the Madison Street house and bought a freestanding house at 6314 Sixteenth Street NW, in Brightwood. The new house, which had cost twice as much as the Madison Street house to build in 1924, backed up to Rock Creek Park. Once again, the Pattersons had arrived, although their pleasure was short-lived; Florence died in 1965 and Josephine in 1969.[47]

Josephine Patterson's story, as seen through real estate, shows a life of tangible achievement. On a teacher's salary she bought a row house to accommodate herself, her parents, and her siblings, and then, twelve years later, with the help of her sister's salary, she bought an even bigger one, more fashionably located. When she married late in life, she moved to a semidetached house, farther out from the city, and parlayed that into an even bigger, freestanding house toward the end of her life. Josephine seems never to have lived alone or just with her husband; she always shared a house with parents and siblings.

Her story was not only one of achievement and family support but also, inevitably, one of race. As aspirational as she was, she lived most of her life in the inner-city neighborhoods to which African American were confined. Just a few years before retirement she moved to an outer neighborhood. Although the properties she bought in Manor Park and Brightwood apparently had not had racial covenants, those two neighborhoods were blanketed with them, and she did not move there until after racial covenants were invalidated by the Supreme Court.[48] The segregation story plays out not only in the arc of her life, but also on the particular block of Corcoran Street where she lived the longest. In 1940, her block of Corcoran Street was inhabited entirely by African Americans, but the other side of the square, on Q Street, was entirely white. An examination of how this square developed shows that it too reflected broader trends, both in row-house architecture and in settlement patterns.

Located in the Northwest quadrant, Square 155 is bounded by Q, R, Seventeenth, and Eighteenth Streets and New Hampshire Avenue (see fig. 109). (For the purposes of this chapter, only the half south of Corcoran Street,

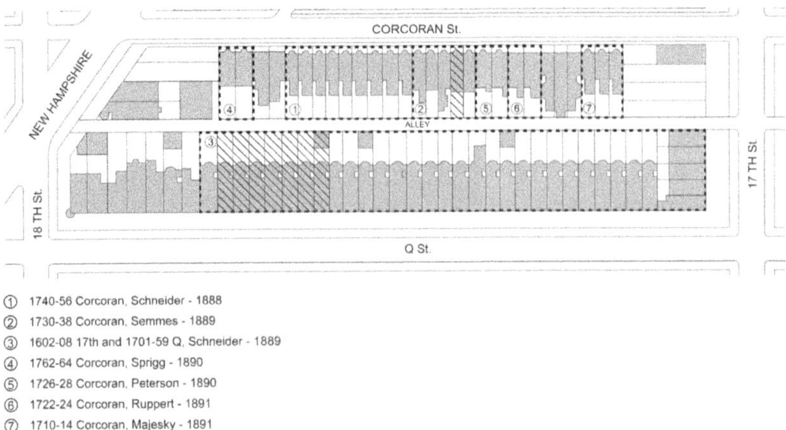

Figure 109. Square 155 in 1913, showing construction of the speculatively built row houses. Located near Dupont Circle, the southern half of Square 155, shown here, had a thirty-four-house development, mostly along Q Street, and the more typical construction of smaller groupings of row houses. (Ruben Melendez and Onairis Perez, delineators, adapted from 1913 Baist and building permit data)

which runs east–west through the square, is considered.[49]) The different characters of Q Street and Corcoran Street are striking, even though three-story row houses line them both. Q Street's twenty-nine-house cohesive row is one of the largest and most impressive developments of nineteenth-century speculative row houses in the city, while Corcoran Street was built in the twos and threes more common for development in the late nineteenth century.

In 1889 architect T. Franklin Schneider acquired much of the Q Street frontage and part of the Seventeenth Street frontage, re-subdividing it into thirty-four lots, each 20 feet wide. Here he built a spectacular row, twenty-nine bay-front houses facing south onto Q Street, all of them three stories tall and 20 feet wide, with the same three-room plan (see fig. 110). To enliven what could have been a monotonous streetscape, however, Schneider varied every element he could: walls were brownstone, serpentine stone, or brick, in various combinations; roofs were mansard or flat; bay windows were one, two, or three stories high, and square, polygonal, or round; oriel windows were at the second or third floor; windows were round-, flat-, or segmental-arched; and roofs of projections were gable, conical, or pyramidal (see fig. 111). The plan of the houses was a little unusual; to overcome the disadvantage of the three-room plan, Schneider included a light well, enclosed on four sides, to illuminate the middle room with a single window (see fig. 112). The front entrance led to a side hall, next to the front parlor, behind which was the large middle room, which had the stairway on the opposite wall. In back the dining room had a polygonal bay window facing onto the backyard. The kitchen was in the basement and a dumbwaiter brought food into the butler's pantry off of the dining room. The second and third floors each had three bedrooms and a bathroom. Above the first floor, the light well became a court, open on

the alley side, and this court ventilated the bathrooms and middle bedrooms. The interior was well appointed, with elaborate fireplaces, a skylight over the stairs, sliding doors between the main rooms, and 10½-foot ceilings.[50]

Thomas Franklin Schneider trained with the eminent Washington architectural firm Cluss and Schulze, headed by Adolph Cluss, and began his own practice in 1883, at the age of twenty-four. After a few years he began "building for himself," as the newspaper said, meaning that he developed property that he owned. He was not a developer in the usual sense, though; he contracted builders while playing the roles of owner and architect. On Square 155, he hired Darby and Davis to build "one of the most extensive building enterprises ever carried out in this city," as the newspaper described it. Beginning construction in February, 1889, Schneider started to sell the houses in

Figure 110. Schneider Row, 1700 block of Q Street NW. Schneider Row consisted of thirty-four brownstone and brick row houses stretching along Q Street and around the corner onto Seventeenth Street. (From *Selections from the Work of T. F. Schneider, Architect* [Washington, DC, 1894], DC History Center, General Photograph Collection, CHS 07066)

Figure 111. Schneider Row. Schneider varied every detail he could to add liveliness to what might have otherwise been a monotonous row. (Jack E. Boucher, photographer, 1974, Library of Congress, Prints and Photographs Division, HABS)

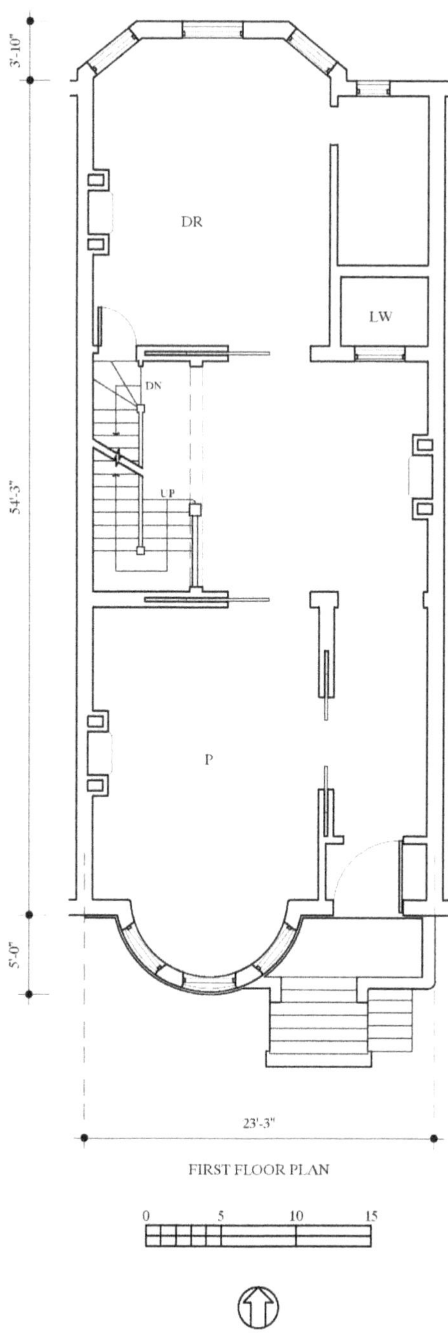

Figure 112. Row house, 1763 Q Street NW, first-floor plan. For a house designed for W. L. Spalding a few months after the large row, Schneider used the same three-room plan in slightly different dimensions. The dining room in the rear is served by the pantry to the right, which had a dumbwaiter in the corner. In front of the pantry is a light well (LW), open to the stair hall. (Plan from Building Permit #1798, April 20, 1889, redrawn by Ruben Melendez, Onairis Perez, and Mark Schara, delineators)

December, one on Q Street selling for $14,500 and one on Seventeenth Street for $9,000; they had cost, on average, $7,350 to build. Before those were sold, Schneider acquired the south side of Q Street for $175,000 and in 1891 built 28 row houses, as well as a mansion for himself. In 1889 Schneider had 150 houses under construction, including 6 on the 1800 block of R Street, 5 on the 1500 block of Twenty-First Street, and a row on the 1700 block of O Street. Schneider continued to expand his empire, shifting from row houses to apartment buildings (including the Cairo, just one block to the east) and totaling nearly 500 buildings in his career, about half of them row houses.[51]

The impressive row on Q and Seventeenth Streets was not Schneider's first development on the square. A year earlier, in 1888, he acquired eight lots on Corcoran Street and re-subdivided them so that he could built 9 row houses (1740–56 Corcoran), "which were purchased and occupied as soon as completed," according to the newspaper (see fig. 113). Compared to his Q Street row, his Corcoran Street row houses were modest but varied: all brick and 18½ feet wide, three stories tall with two- or three-story bay windows, back buildings, and a variety of dormers in the mansard roofs. The rest of Corcoran Street then developed in a familiar pattern, with speculative developers building a handful of row houses at a time. About a year after Schneider completed his Corcoran Street houses, A. H. Semmes built 5 row houses adjoining them on the east, at 1730–38 Corcoran. West of Schneider's row

Figure 113. Row houses, 1750–52 Corcoran Street NW. Before building his spectacular row on the Q Street side of the square, T. Franklin Schneider built a row of nine slightly more modest three-story houses on Corcoran Street. (Photograph by the author, 2020)

houses, developer J. C. Sprigg added a pair of row houses, 1762–64, in 1890 (see fig. 114). Abutting Semmes's row houses on the east was a pair of row houses, 1726–28, built by August Peterson in 1890, one of which Josephine Patterson would buy almost forty years later (see fig. 108). In 1891 Christian Ruppert hired architect J. G. Meyers to design a pair of row houses just to the east, at 1722–24. Three days later, Francis Mejasky applied for a building permit for 3 row houses closer to Seventeenth Street, numbered 1710–14 Corcoran (see fig. 115). Unlike the other row houses on Corcoran Street, one of these was occupied by its developer. Hungarian-born Mejasky, an artist, lived at 1710 with his Cuban-born wife.[52]

Within eight years, 1888 to 1896, twenty-five bay-front houses had been built on Corcoran Street, forming a block of row houses almost as harmonious as Schneider's row on Q Street. But here six developers took part, building groupings of nine, five, three, and three pairs, plus two houses built singly and an apartment house. While the Q Street frontage of this square might have been more impressive and more unified architecturally, the Corcoran Street side was more typical of the way row houses were built in late nineteenth-century Washington.[53]

Not all of the purchasers of Schneider's Q Street houses moved in or even held on to them, and by 1900 only 6 of Schneider's 15 Q Street houses listed

Figure 114. Row houses, 1762–64 Corcoran Street NW. Typical of the row houses on the Corcoran Street side of the square are these two on the right, built in 1890 for developer J. C. Sprigg. To the left, architect Glenn Brown designed the round-bayed house for Mary Wilcox in 1895. To the left of that is a house designed in 1896 by architect George S. Cooper. (Photograph by the author, 2020)

Figure 115. Row houses, 1710–14 Corcoran Street NW. Thomas J. King built these three row houses, varying the shapes of the bays and roofs, in 1891. The permit listed no architect. (Photograph by the author, 2022)

in the census were occupied by their owners, and 3 of his 4 on Seventeenth Street. The square as a whole attracted a well-to-do population, whether renters or owners. A little more than 60 percent of the houses were occupied by their owners, and two-thirds of them had live-in servants. Except for the servants, most of whom were African American, all of the residents were white. The legal profession was the most common occupation, with 8 of them among the 45 heads of households, along with 7 government clerks, 2 government officials, and 1 member of Congress.

After 1920, the population of the square began to change. That year, the owner-occupancy rate was still around 60 percent, and all the heads of household were white. Forty-four percent of them had live-in servants, of whom 15 were white, including one French governess, and 20 were African American, plus one Filipino. By 1930, though, fewer than one-third of the households on Corcoran Street were white; Josephine Patterson and her family were part of a wave of racial change. By 1940 all of the Corcoran Street residents were African American; the other sides of the square were all white, illustrating a stark divide. Owner occupancy slipped to 42 percent, with 26 percent (5 of 19 households recorded) among the African Americans on Corcoran Street and 45 percent (14 of 31) on Q Street. On the square, only 6 households had live-in servants. Boarders and lodgers were far more likely, with households of 10 or more residents not uncommon. Two houses had 21 occupants: at

1738 Corcoran all 21 occupants were Black, while at 1763 Q all 21 were white. The number of people per house on Corcoran Street averaged 9.2, while on Q Street the average was 6.5.[54]

Corcoran Street's shift to all African American residents reflected larger trends in the city as well as the neighborhood. With expanded transportation options and neighborhoods of new row houses and single-family houses—many of them restricted to white occupants—whites moved out of the old city to these newer, outer areas. In the 1920s and 1930s African Americans, their population swelled by migrants from the South as well as those dispossessed by neighborhood demolitions, moved into the older buildings. Just four blocks to the north, the area around the 1700 block of U Street was christened "Strivers' Section," as ambitious African Americans bought houses formerly occupied by whites.[55] By 1930 Corcoran Street was part of this movement.

Row houses served many situations.[56] The spacious three-story ones were well suited to multiple occupants, as illustrated by the numerous boardinghouses, both white and African American, in 1940. After 1960, the growing preference for small independent units over boarding arrangements accompanied another racial shift, as whites moved into the old city and African Americans moved farther out. To convert these large row houses into three or four apartments required capital, and such investment required higher-income buyers and renters. These new residents were white, with smaller households better suited to apartments. The non-white population, which had occupied 45 percent of the housing units on this square in 1960, dropped to 3 percent in 2010.

The reinvestment began on Corcoran Street in 1965, when Jon Gerstenfeld, a twenty-seven-year-old engineer, and Charlotte Levine, a design and planning consultant, acquired six row houses, gutted them, and created thirty-five apartments. One of these was 1728, which had been owned and occupied by Josephine Patterson and her family until 1955. At 1730 Corcoran, Gerstenfeld and Levine created one unit in the basement and first-floor levels, and a second one on the second and third floors. In the house that Levine and her husband occupied, they built "a 38-foot living room with conversation pit," and a bathroom with a Franklin stove and sunken tub. Some of the houses had "cathedral beamed ceilings, others have nine-foot glass doors leading to tree-covered 12 by 18 foot sun terraces, a few have wood-burning fireplaces and others have floor to ceiling 'Queen Anne' windows." On the alley in the rear, Gerstenfeld and Levine added "tiny Georgetown-style row-houses . . . that, in reality, are one-bedroom duplex apartments." Soon after this construction, Charles M. Schneider Jr. renovated several houses toward the west end of Corcoran, creating "two-floor town house living." The units had about 2,000 square feet of space and in one of them a completely open floor—a 53-by-20-foot room—as well as sunken bathtubs. Like Gerstenfeld and Levine, Schneider added units on the rear, calling them "Corcoran Mews" and adorning them with gaslights on poles.[57]

These investments spurred other renovations. John Cavanaugh and Philip Froeder bought the house at 1742 Corcoran in 1966 (see fig. 116). Like many whites who were moving into the neighborhood, they were artists—Cavanaugh was a noted sculptor, while Froeder was an architect and planner—and gay. Like their neighbors, Cavanaugh and Froeder converted the house into several units: the basement and first floor for their residence and Cavanaugh's studio, and three units on the two upper floors. At ground level, a glass-enclosed entrance opened into a two-story foyer where they displayed sculpture. The open floor plan accommodated the display of historic artifacts collected by Froeder as well as Cavanaugh's sculpture. Outside, metal hoods over the new entrance and windows were the work of Cavanaugh, who specialized in lead sculpture. In 1972 Cavanaugh and Froeder bought the

Figure 116. Row houses, 1740–42 Corcoran Street NW. Sculptor John Cavanaugh and his partner Philip Froeder renovated the house on the right in 1966, featuring Cavanaugh's sculptured lead hood molds. Robert and Susan Meehan renovated the house on the left two years later. (Photograph by the author, 2020)

row house at 1736 Corcoran, embedding some of Cavanaugh's sculptures in the exterior wall.[58]

Between these two developments, Robert and Susan Meehan bought the house at 1740 Corcoran in 1968. They were expecting to go overseas and rent their house, and they thought that a three-story 3,500-square-foot house would be hard to rent, so they remodeled it into three apartments, living on the lower two floors. The renovations were extensive, as described in the newspaper: "they put in all new plumbing; hot water baseboard heating and electric air conditioning, new floors, new doors. They tore out two fireplaces and put in three. They tore out interior walls. They rebuilt the stairs. They tore out four small windows on the front and replaced them with floor-to-ceiling glass doors onto a small balcony."[59]

On Q Street, several remodelings also signaled reinvestment in the row houses. After 1940, some African Americans moved into this row, and these large, six-bedroom houses functioned as boardinghouses for both Blacks and whites. A sign on the house at 1709 Q Street read, "Above Average Rooms. Kitchen Privileges. Colored Adults Only." Reinvestment in the 1960s involved conversion of these boardinghouses back to single-family homes, usually for white families. The renovations could be drastic; in his house at 1715 Q Street, photographer Robert Lautman created a two-story living room.[60]

In other cases, reinvestment meant providing smaller units. Raised nearly a half story above the street, these row houses permitted conversion of the basement to a separate rental unit, called an English basement in recent terminology, once the main kitchen had been moved to the first floor. In 1962–63, at the west end of the block, Cyrus Katzen acquired seven Schneider row houses, 1745–57 Q Street, and demolished them. He initially planned to construct a hotel, but neighbors' objections led to the construction of what appeared to be seven neo-Colonial row houses in 1977 (see fig. 117). Here, developer Barrett Linde created buildings with four units: one in the basement, one on the first floor, and two two-story units on the second and third floors. The units sold as condos and cost up to $60,500. The market for one-bedroom units was strong; by the time construction was nearing completion, only five of the twenty-eight units remained unsold. The next year, an ad for one of the units, whose owner was renting it, explains the attraction: "DUPONT ROW. 1751 Q Street, NW. Elegant one-bedroom and terrace apartment in new townhouse with small den, fireplace, hardwood floors, deluxe kitchen with self-cleaning oven, dishwasher/disposal, washer/dryer, central air conditioning, off-street parking available, patio. Fantastic location. $495 plus electricity."[61] While these condominiums resembled row houses and shared some characteristics of smaller neo-Colonial ones, such as a kitchen-forward plan, light-colored brick, pedimented doorways, keystones in concrete lintels, and

Figure 117. Dupont Row, 1749–59 Q Street NW. In 1975 Barrett Linde built four-unit condos designed to resemble row houses. While the scale may have been compatible with the row houses in this block near Dupont Circle, the neo-Colonial styling was not. (Photograph by the author, 2020)

shutters, the Q Street buildings were three stories tall on raised basements, compatible with the scale of the streetscape.

The three-story row houses on Square 155 attracted an upper-middle-class population. Schneider's Q Street row represents the high end of speculative row houses, but even the Corcoran Street row houses were large for speculative housing. As these row houses grew older and other neighborhoods became more fashionable, African Americans moved into the Corcoran Street houses. Josephine Patterson and her family were able to own a large, elegant row house, which may have been aging but still served their needs. In neighboring row houses, taking in boarders offered an affordable solution for homeowners and investors. When the market demanded small units, these row houses could be divided to accommodate several households, and the owners and renters shifted back to majority white. Through all these changes, these row houses remain an impressive and elegant collection of speculatively developed housing.

Subdivision Living: Square 3013

In 1923 Emil and Ella Himmighoefer bought a quadrant-plan row house from its builder, Morris Cafritz (see fig. 118). The house at 814 Decatur Street NW was located in the rapidly developing subdivision of Petworth. The

Figure 118. Row house, 814 Decatur Street NW. Morris Cafritz, who built this house in 1922, sold it to Emil and Ella Himmighoefer. Emil was a painter in the Government Printing Office's carpenter shop. (Photograph by the author, 2021)

Himmighoefers moved from a bay-window brick row house in Bloomingdale, and although their new house was not much bigger than their previous one, it offered a more modern arrangement, access to the outdoors in the form of porches, and the appeal of a less urban neighborhood. The Himmighoefers had three children. A veteran of the Spanish-American War, Emil Himmighoefer, who had been born in St. Louis, worked as a painter in the carpenter shop of the Government Printing Office; he died in 1939. Two of Ella's grown children continued to live with her: Walter, who was thirty years old in 1940, worked as a clerk at the A&P grocery store, and Evelyn, age twenty, who was a stenographer in a lawyer's office. Walter's five-year-old son, also named Walter, lived with them as well. Two years after Emil's death Ella sold the row house. By the later 1950s she was living in a small freestanding house in Bethesda and working as a saleswoman at the Woodward and Lothrop department store.[62] As with the history of the Pattersons and Square 155, the Himmighoefers' trajectory was one of leveraging row houses for a freestanding house farther out.

As Washington's population burgeoned in the late nineteenth century, the city burst the bounds of the L'Enfant city and spread into the outlying areas. By the early twentieth century, and even more so after World War I, developers realized that there was a market for row houses in these new subdivisions. The six-room, quadrant-plan row house with electricity and central heat suited this market, promising a modern, sunny, and outward-looking house, in contrast to the dark Victorian row houses of the L'Enfant city. With the strength of the housing market and the expertise and drive of the operative builders, these quadrant-plan row houses were built by the hundreds in Northwest DC east of Fourteenth Street, where permitted by zoning.

The Himmighoefers' house was one of eleven identical houses on the north side of Square 3013, which, like much of Petworth, experienced rapid and overwhelming development of remarkably similar quadrant-plan row houses (see fig. 119).[63] More than three miles north of the White House, Petworth is roughly located west of the Soldiers' Home and east of Fourteenth Street, north of Park View and south of Brightwood. Bounded by Eighth, Ninth, Crittenden, and Decatur Streets, Square 3013 was one block west of Sherman Circle and one block east of the commercial spine of Georgia Avenue. In fewer than three years, three developers constructed fifty-four row houses, all of which still stand.

Square 3013's few developers, rapid construction, and lack of any buildings but row houses resulted in extremely uniform streetscapes. The quadrant-plan row houses, light brown brick with front and rear porches and a little more than 1,000 square feet on the two floors combined, was the standard here, as it was throughout the neighborhood (see fig. 120). The mansard

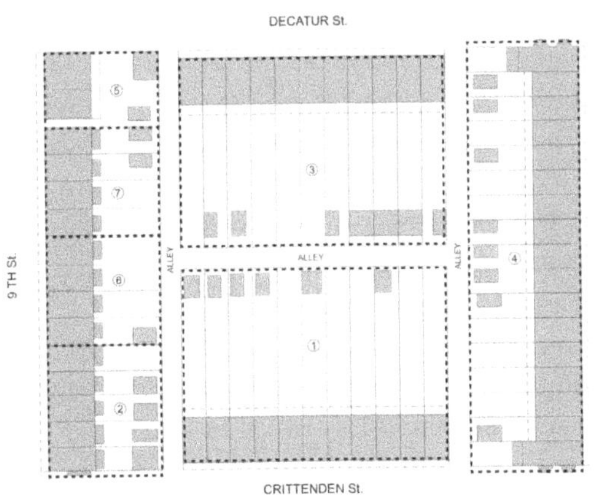

① 811-31 Crittenden, Cafritz and Shapero, November 21, 1921
② 4701-09 9th, Shapero, March 31, 1922
③ 800-20 Decatur, Cafritz, May 1, 1922
④ 4702-30 8th, 800 Decatur, 801 Crittenden, Cafritz, July 31, 1922
⑤ 4731-33 9th, Shapero, August 7, 1922
⑥ 4711-17 9th, Sanford, March 24, 1924
⑦ 4719-25 9th, Sanford, July 24, 1924

Figure 119. Square 3013 in 1927, showing construction of the speculatively built row houses. The fifty-four row houses on this square in Petworth, not far from Sherman Circle, were built in fewer than three years by three developers. (Ruben Melendez and Onairis Perez, delineators, adapted from the 1927 Sanborn map and building permit data)

Figure 120. Row houses, 811–19 Crittenden Street NW. On the first side of the square to be developed, beginning in the fall of 1921, the Crittenden Street houses resulted from a partnership of Morris Cafritz and Harris Shapero. Separately, Cafritz and Shapero built most of the rest of the houses on the square. (Jarob Ortiz, photographer, 2021, Library of Congress, Prints and Photographs Division, HABS)

roofs, while prominent in front, sheltered only very shallow attics, despite the dormer windows that promised a usable space.

The first construction on the square was in the fall of 1921, when Morris Cafritz and Harris Shapero built 11 row houses on Crittenden Street. Architect George Santmyers designed quadrant-plan row houses with 18-foot fronts, front porches, shed-roofed dormers, paired windows at the first floor, and varied cornices. These were completed and sold by April 1922, so Cafritz and Shapero continued building on the square, but separately, not in partnership. In the spring of 1922, Harris Shapero hired Santmyers to design 5 row houses with 20-foot fronts on Ninth Street at the corner of Crittenden. A month later, Morris Cafritz again used Santmyers to design 11 houses on Decatur Street. These row houses had 18-foot fronts and slightly pyramidal dormers but were otherwise similar to the Ninth Street houses, although, at 30 feet deep, they were 2 feet shorter than Shapero's.[64] In December 1922, Cafritz sold the house at 814 Decatur to Salvatore and Rosalia Bufalino. It is uncertain if the Bufalinos even moved into the house, because in March 1923 they sold it back to Cafritz, who immediately sold it to the Himmighoefers.

In July 1922 Cafritz hired Santmyers once again, this time for the entire frontage of Eighth Street, composed of seventeen houses. Also 18 feet wide and 30 feet deep, these appear to be identical to the Decatur Street houses. At the ends of the row, Cafritz built 15-foot-wide houses, but these were 43 feet long and had the advantage of the third exposure. Back on Ninth Street, Shapero hired architect W. R. Lamar to design a pair of houses at the corner of Decatur. The generous 22-foot fronts permitted four windows on the second-floor front, indicating two bedrooms.[65]

By the end of one year, 1922, the only vacant space on this square was on Ninth Street, between Shapero's two constructions. Robert H. Sanford, a contractor, filled this void in 1924, building four houses in the spring with 18½-foot fronts and four more in the summer with fronts that were just under 19 feet. Sanford listed himself as owner, builder, and architect, but by then the architectural form was set. On Sanford's houses the first-floor windows were not paired and the three second-floor windows were evenly spaced, but his houses were otherwise indistinguishable from the others on the square.[66]

When Morris Cafritz began construction on his Eighth Street houses at the end of July 1922, he declared that they would be "completed in time for the fall demand in homes." He described them as "of modern construction throughout" and promised that they would "have fronts of special architecture," although what he meant by that is unclear. "They will contain six rooms and bath each, with front, breakfast and sleeping porches."[67] And unlike the row houses that Cafritz would build in Petworth a year later, they did not have racial restrictions placed on their deeds.

Along with D. J. Dunigan, Cafritz was a major developer of Petworth. Like Dunigan, Cafritz placed racial deed restrictions on the houses he built after 1923. In 1924 Cafritz developed the north side of Decatur Street from Seventh Street almost to Georgia Avenue, and all of those properties excluded African Americans from ownership. In advertising these houses, Cafritz offered 835 Decatur Street, across the street from the Himmighoefers, as an "exhibit home," and noted that this was a "Restricted N.W. Neighborhood." North of Decatur, almost to Kennedy, from Third Street to Georgia Avenue, much of the row-house neighborhood was restricted. And south of Crittenden, east of Sherman Circle, much was also restricted. But these few blocks between Crittenden and Decatur, built in 1922, were not.[68] Nonetheless, all of the purchasers and residents of houses in Square 3013 were white.

As homeowners, the Himmighoefers were typical on this square. In 1930, a remarkable 81 percent of the houses were occupied by their owners; in 1940, at the end of the Depression, this had dropped only to 77 percent. This was the promise of these houses built en masse by operative builders: they were affordable. The owners were salesmen and cabinetmakers, draftsmen and meat cutters, streetcar motormen and taxi drivers. In 1930 ten of them worked for the U.S. government, as clerk, printer, painter, auditor, attorney, and efficiency expert. As appropriate for six-room houses with three bedrooms, their households were small, especially in comparison to those in the three-story houses on Square 155. These quadrant-plan houses averaged 4.6 people per house; that slipped to an even 4 in 1940. In 1930 more than 60 percent of the houses accommodated nuclear families of just parents and children, although many of the children were employed adults. Thirteen percent of the houses had extended families, with parents, in-laws, grandchildren, and so on, while nearly a quarter took in boarders or rented a room, and some did both. In 1940 the percentage of houses with lodgers had dropped to 19 percent, while those with extended families rose to 30 percent.

No African Americans lived on this square in either 1930 or 1940, but there was a high number of foreign-born residents. In 1930, 26 percent of the heads of households had been born outside the United States. The greatest number, 5, were from Russia and were identifiable as Jewish, 3 of them on Decatur Street and 2 on Ninth. Three household heads were born in Italy, and one each from Greece, Hungary, the Irish Free State, England, Scotland, Romania, and Spain. In 1940 there were even more foreign-born households, despite the previous decade's restrictions on immigration, for a total of 18, or a third of the square's houses. Again, the most were from Russia, then numbering 7, and the second-most from Italy, at 6. The same immigrants from Greece, the Irish Free State, England, Scotland, and Romania were present, and Poland was added to the mix. The number of immigrants is striking because city-wide, the foreign-born population in 1930 was just 6.3 percent of the total population, dropping to 5.3 in 1940.[69]

In 1950 the residents of this square remained white, but by 1960 only 17 percent of the housing units—ten—were occupied by whites. In 2010 the population had achieved a mix: of the 160 people living on the square, 100 were African American, 40 were white, and the rest were Hispanic, Asian, or a mix of races.

The quadrant-plan row house enabled many to attain homeownership. Cheaply built, in quantities not seen before, in repetitive rows that merged into long streetscapes of identical designs, the row house might have lacked individuality, but it was affordable. The kitchen, though small, was close to the rest of the house, not isolated in the rear. Three bedrooms permitted one for the parents and one for each gender of children. Electricity, central heat, and porches were standard. The house worked.

In looking at homeowners, renters, sizes of households, and types of houses, it becomes apparent that houses go through life cycles. Initially, when a house is new, for the developer of the houses examined in this chapter, this target family was usually white. But as the house aged and ceased to offer the kinds of amenities (central heat, electricity, bathrooms) or kinds of spaces (convenient kitchen, separate bedrooms for the children) that middle-class families wanted, the houses became more crowded and, in several of the squares, more likely to house African Americans. The slip in the status of the house was not explicitly racial; houses continued to be owned or rented at the same rates, by both Blacks and whites, and both Blacks and whites took in boarders.[70] But by 1960, when Washington was a majority-Black city, three of the case study squares had significant populations of African Americans. The exception, Square 28 in Foggy Bottom, had become majority Black by 1900 and by 1960 had shifted back to majority white.

The third stage for many of these houses was reinvestment and renovation, resulting in a marked increase of the white population. In the 1950s residents sought small units, but more independence than a room in a boardinghouse, so significant investment was required to transform each house. Beginning with the renovated alley dwellings in Square 28 in 1952, the construction of flats that resembled row houses in both Squares 28 and 155 and the division of row houses into several units in Square 155 indicate a market for singles and small families. By the mid-1960s, renovations of row houses for one family, with maybe a separate unit in the basement, show a market for larger houses. In the last fifty years, increased space has become even more important, with additions on rears and roofs of row houses to expand the livable area.

Through these changes, the various types of row houses have shown a remarkable resilience. The early nineteenth-century two-room plan reappeared as the ill-equipped alley dwellings of the late nineteenth century. As the home of Washington's poorest, these were the slums of the city. But when renovated with electricity and plumbing, they became desirable homes for in-town living. The L-plans and brick bay-fronts of the nineteenth century served as single-family homes, then as boardinghouses, their halls permitting easy private access to different rooms. Once renovated with additional bathrooms and updated kitchens, they serve single families once again. The quadrant-plan row house was perhaps least adaptable but also closest to modern needs, with a more open plan and convenient kitchen. As these building types went through their life cycles, they continued to adapt to new circumstances.

This chapter has looked not only at the changes that houses underwent, but also what the change of houses meant to specific families. John Leonard, Noah Price, Mary Sizer, Josephine Patterson, and Ella Himmighoefer all owned row houses. They used row houses to shelter their families and sometimes to provide for them. They used row houses to express status and sometimes to achieve a freestanding house in the suburbs. Mostly, they used row houses to create a home.

Epilogue

Just as row houses were constrained by their neighbors, so were they connected. The shared party walls may have restricted the row house, but they also provided tangible connections to the houses next door. Rows of houses framed the streets, defining them just as much as pavements and sidewalks did, connecting them to the larger, physical city. Row houses were also connected to the city in less indelible ways. People circulated in and out of them, delivering and taking away, traveling to shops and stores, and putting row houses at the center of activity and motion.

Before there were utilities providing for the automatic delivery and removal of essential items, there were deliverymen, shoppers, and servants. The volume of goods and people going in and out of a house in the nineteenth century is striking and also enables a view of the row house as a kinetic entity. Movement characterized these row houses; not the house itself, obviously, but the people in and out of it and the neighborhood around it. Frank A. Taylor, who was born in 1903 at First and C Streets NE, remembered his neighborhood as full of energy: "The dominant character of the place and time was the continuous movement of the people and conveyances in the streets from early morning to late at night. Heads of families went by at daybreak headed for the Center Market returning an hour or two later pulling boys' wagons filled with food. After breakfast the same men went by dressed for work. . . . Children walked and biked to school." People came into the neighborhood during the day: "The early milk and bakery wagons were followed by the ice man, coal and wood wagons and the hucksters who brought produce and game from the truck farms east of the Eastern Branch. The housewives and their cooks came out to buy and gossip, others met on the way to notion stores and grocers. At any moment one or more wagons, pushcarts, or a peddler with a basket on his head would be passing by. . . . The handsome green and gold Standard Oil wagon came once a week to peddle 'coal oil'—actually kerosene—for lamps and stoves" and so on throughout the day.[1]

Much of this activity concerned the procurement of food, which would have been done on a daily basis before reliable electrical refrigeration. Housewives or their servants obtained food several ways: through shopping for it at neighborhood stores or municipal markets; through delivery of it, once ordered; or through peddlers, who hawked food items in the street. Not all people ate at home, however. Boarders might stay at one house and eat at another. As described in a government report in 1887, "Many people prepare coffee or tea and the simpler dishes at their rooms for breakfast, under the name of 'light housekeeping,' taking a full meal once a day at a boarding-house." The report went on: "An individual or a family may find comfortable, neat quarters for a day, for a week, or for a month, securing lodgings and board under the same roof or separate roofs." Helen Au's reminiscence of growing up on Capitol Hill in the 1910s and 1920s noted a sign in a neighbor's window for "Table Board." Au described it: "This was done by ladies who were good cooks. It wasn't drop in; it was always pre-arranged. It was regular people who came every morning for breakfast; she'd pack them a lunch and then they came for their evening meal. It was almost all men, rarely was there a woman. They lived in rooms that had no cooking facilities. It was either that or eating in restaurants. This was eating in a home and she was a good cook."[2] Added to the traffic in and out of houses in order to procure food was the traffic generated by people who were coming for meals.

Utilities are the most obvious connection of a house to the city, and vice versa. Before piped water and gas, deliverymen brought water, coal, and kerosene to the house. Before water closets handled sewage, scavengers employed by the city emptied "night soil" from privy boxes. Washington's extensive alley system facilitated this; privies were located in the rear of the yard, providing easy access to the scavengers, and were maximum distance from the house. Similarly, icemen delivered their product through the alley to the back door of the house, or even through an outside door directly into the icebox. Coal deliveries were often to the front of the house, through a temporary chute into the basement. In addition to deliverymen, servants came and went from houses. While live-in servants were not common in speculative, middle-class row houses, employees who worked by the day, or even once a week, would have undertaken many of the household tasks in the nineteenth century, and their comings and goings would have part of the rhythm of the street.

The neighborhoods were not as uniformly residential as many are today, providing opportunities for shopping and employment. Row houses were frequently the site of small businesses, providing homes for the proprietors on the upper floors. Storefront windows and at-grade entrances today, especially on corner buildings, denote some of these shops; many have been converted to single-family homes. Frank Taylor, quoted above, attended Peabody School at Fifth Street and Stanton Square. More than half a century later he recalled of the five-block walk from his home, "When I walked to school I passed about 20 of the small businesses so characteristic of the neighborhood. I loitered at such interesting places as a barley candy factory or a tin shop." He remembered his neighborhood as full of shops: "A large variety of such businesses were scattered through the predominantly residential neighborhood. In every block small businesses intermingled with the homes, churches, and schools. I have recalled more than 40 businesses within a radius of five city blocks around my home all providing services and employment." Similarly, Betty Sizer, who grew up at 131 Tenth Street NE in the 1930s, remembered five businesses within a one-block radius of her home. At the intersection of Tenth and Constitution, there was a District Grocery on the southeast corner and Katz's grocery on the northeast. One block away, at Eleventh and Constitution, were Kaufman's dry goods, which "carried anything from school supplies, dishes and such, yard goods, thread and small gift items," on the northwest corner; Read's Drugs, which "had a pharmacy and soda fountain, magazines, and things like that," on the northeast corner; and a Sanitary Grocery, which later became Safeway, on the southwest corner. The Katz, Kaufman, and Read families all lived over their stores.[3] The conversion of these and many other small commercial buildings to residential uses created neighborhoods that are far more homogeneous and static than they once were.

The constant motion of people connected row houses to the larger city, as housewives, servants, and children came and went through the day; people shopped for food and other items in buildings that may have also housed the shopkeeper and his family; deliverymen and peddlers plied their wares through the streets. Houses viewed historically may seem frozen and inert, but in fact they were well connected to the city through the people who came and went. The row house was linked by its party walls to its neighbors, but the network of streets and alleys facilitated the house's connection to the neighborhood.

The row houses linked neighborhoods as well, as the city took on a uniform appearance of attached houses with fenced front yards, a generous placement of trees, wide streets and even wider avenues leading to public buildings, to downtown, and to other row-house neighborhoods. The row houses differed in size and appearance depending on when they were built, how much they cost, and to whom they were marketed, but the overall appearance of the city was one of densely packed small houses, suggesting both individuality and community—families in their own houses, connected inexorably to their neighbors and to the city.

The Washington row house is also connected, more intangibly, to the history of the city as an illustration of its growth, both in population and in real estate, as well as its governance, through the regulations it issued and the urban renewal it undertook, all at the behest of the federal government. And the row house attaches as well to larger trends in the country, whether public health, racial exclusion, technological change, or economies of scale in construction. This small building, often just 16 or 17 feet wide with a total 1,000 square feet of living space on two floors, adapted to the circumstances of many occupants over time. Its plan changed over time, and the nature of its owners and occupants changed as well. Through two centuries of changes, the row house proved to be practical, efficient, and home-like, and it characterizes Washington, DC, as a place where people live.

APPENDIX

Building Regulations, 1791

George Washington issued regulations for the new capital city on October 17, 1791:

1st. That the outer and party walls of all houses within the said city, shall be built of brick or stone.

2d. That all buildings on the street shall be parallel thereto, and may be advanced to the line of the streets, or withdrawn therefrom, at the pleasure of the improver; but where any such building is about to be erected, neither the foundation or the party wall shall be begun without first applying to the person or persons appointed by the commissioners to superintend the buildings within the city, who will ascertain the lines of the walls to correspond with these regulations.

3d. The wall of no house to be higher than forty feet to the roof, in any part of the City; nor shall any be lower than thirty-five feet on any of the avenues.

4th. That the person or persons appointed by the commissioners to superintend the buildings, may enter on the land of any person to set out the foundation and regulate the walls to be built between party and party, as to the breadth and thickness thereof; which foundation shall be laid equally upon the lands of the persons between whom such party walls are to be built, and shall be of the breadth and thickness determined by such person proper; and the first builder shall be reimbursed one moiety of the charge of such party wall, or so much thereof as the next builder shall have occasion to make use of, before such next builder shall any ways use or break into the wall. The charge of value thereof, to be set by the person or persons so appointed by the Commissioners.

5th. As temporary conveniences will be proper, for lodging workmen, and securing materials for building, it is to be understood that such may be erected, with the approbation of the commissioners; but they may be removed or discontinued by the special order of the commissioners.

6th. The way into the squares, being designed, in a special manner, for the common use and convenience of the occupiers of the respective squares, the property in the same is reserved to the public, so that there may be an immediate interference on any abuse of the use thereof by any individual, to the nuisance or obstruction of others. The proprietors of the lots adjoining the entrance into the squares, on arching over the entrance and fixing gates in the manner the commissioners shall approve, shall be entitled to divide the space over the arching, and build it up with the range of that line of the square.

7th. No vaults shall be permitted under the streets, nor any encroachments on the footway above, by steps, stoops, porches, cellar doors, windows, ditches, or leaning walls, nor shall there by any projection over the street, other than the eaves of the house without the consent of the commissioners.

8th. These regulations are the terms and conditions under and upon which conveyances are to be made, according to the deeds in trust of the land within the city.

Source: Appleton P. Clark Jr., "Origin of the Building Regulations," *RCHS* 4 (1901): 166–67.

NOTE ON SOURCES

A few sources cited in the endnotes require a bit more explanation. One of the best sources for research on buildings in Washington, DC, is the building permits, available on microfilm through the National Archives (NARA RG#351) and accessible also at the People's Archive (formerly the Washingtoniana Collection) of the DC Public Library. The microfilmed permits date from 1877 to 1949. The information given by the permits (and especially on the application form for the permit) is extremely valuable to architectural historians: date, owner, architect, builder, size, materials, and so forth. I have cited them frequently in this book.

Under the sponsorship of the DC Historic Preservation Office, this raw material has been compiled into the DC Historical Building Permits Database (publicly accessible and available through Microsoft Access). Brian Kraft, who undertook this work, also generously responded to my queries, issuing reports from that database on specific issues. This enabled me to identify trends in row-house construction, as well as significant builders and architects responsible for row houses. I have cited these reports as "Permits Database Reports."

The database of building permits is also available in graphic form at HistoryQuest DC, a mapping application produced by the DC Historic Preservation Office and available through the DC Office of Planning website (planning.dc.gov/node/1203082). The interactive GIS mapping application allows users to pinpoint specific buildings and call up the information from the database and other sources.

Another important website is Mapping Segregation in Washington, DC (mappingsegregationdc.org), which includes maps of areas that had racially restrictive covenants. Mara Cherkasky and Sarah Jane Shoenfeld, who produced this website, also include a number of primary documents regarding racial discrimination in the city. Their work has broken new ground in understanding and explicating institutional racism in Washington.

Information on Washington's builders and architects is available through two other important sources, available online, "DC Builders and Developers Directory" and "DC Architects Directory," both sponsored by the DC Historic Preservation Office. "DC Builders and Developers Directory" (2012) compiles information on twenty-five builders and developers, and the "DC Architects Directory" (2011) has information on one hundred architects. Both are available through this address: planning.dc.gov/page/dc-history.

All three of these projects received funding, at least in part, from the National Park Service, U.S. Department of the Interior, through the DC Historic Preservation Office, DC Office of Planning. I am very grateful for this expenditure of public funds and for the work involved in these projects, which not only has benefited me but also will benefit historians for years to come.

NOTES

Abbreviations

ES	*Evening Star* (Washington, DC)
HABS	Historic American Buildings Survey
JSAH	*Journal of the Society of Architectural Historians*
LC	Library of Congress
NYT	*New York Times*
RCHS	*Records of the Columbia Historical Society*
SS	*Sunday Star* (Washington, DC)
WH	*Washington History*
WP	*Washington Post*
WPTH	*Washington Post-Times Herald*

Introduction

1. Although christened Pierre, L'Enfant adopted the name Peter when he moved to the United States. Increasingly, historians are using that name, as in the recent work by Kenneth R. Bowling, *Peter Charles L'Enfant: Vision, Honor, and Male Friendship in the Early Republic* (Washington, DC: Friends of the George Washington University Library, 2002).
2. For a more thorough discussion of *vernacular architecture,* see Thomas Carter and Elizabeth Collins Cromley, *Invitation to Vernacular Architecture: A Guide to the Study of Ordinary Buildings and Landscapes* (Knoxville: University of Tennessee Press, 2005), 7–13. Carol Willis, *Form Follows Finance: Skyscrapers and Skylines in New York and Chicago* (Princeton: Princeton Architectural Press, 1995), 7, 32, similarly argued that skyscrapers' forms resulted from local conditions.
3. Row houses range farther than the Eastern Seaboard; Chicago and St. Louis have them too. Because row houses are so important to the fabric of various urban areas, architectural historians have provided city-specific studies of their row houses. See Bainbridge Bunting, *Houses of Boston's Back Bay: An Architectural History, 1840–1917* (Cambridge, Mass.: Harvard University Press, 1967); Charles Lockwood, *Bricks and Brownstone: The New York Row House, 1783–1929* (2nd ed., New York: Rizzoli, 2003; orig. pub., New York: Abbeville Press, 1972); Jeffrey Alan Cohen, "The Queen Anne and the Late Victorian Townhouse in Philadelphia, 1878–1895"

(Ph.D. diss., University of Pennsylvania, 1991); Stefan Muthesius, *The English Terraced House* (New Haven: Yale University Press, 1992); Mary Ellen Hayward and Charles Belfoure, *The Baltimore Rowhouse* (New York: Princeton Architectural Press, 2001); and Charles Duff, *The North Atlantic Cities* (Liverpool: Bluecoat, 2019).

The published literature on Washington's nonfederal buildings is limited in scope but includes, on housing, especially, Kathryn Schneider Smith, ed., *Washington at Home: An Illustrated History of Neighborhoods in the Nation's Capital* (2nd ed., Baltimore: Johns Hopkins University Press, 2010); Richard Longstreth, ed., *Housing Washington: Two Centuries of Residential Development and Planning in the National Capital Area* (Chicago: Center for American Places, 2010); James M. Goode, *Capital Losses: A Cultural History of Washington's Destroyed Buildings* (Washington, DC: Smithsonian Institution Press, 1979); and James M. Goode, *Best Addresses: A Century of Washington's Distinguished Apartment Houses* (Washington, DC: Smithsonian Institution Press, 1988).

In Washington in 1934, the totals were 51,562 row houses, 26,751 detached and semi-detached dwellings, 8,136 flats, 1,653 hotels and rooming houses, and 1,522 apartment houses. S. G. Lindholm, Zoning Commission of the District of Columbia, "Experiences with Zoning in Washington, D.C., 1920–1934" (1935), 34.

4. Washington has benefited from several recent histories, including the comprehensive Chris Myers Asch and George Derek Musgrove, *Chocolate City: A History of Race and Democracy in the Nation's Capital* (Chapel Hill: University of North Carolina Press, 2017).
5. See Thomas C. Hubka, *How the Working-Class Home Became Modern, 1900–1940* (Minneapolis: University of Minnesota Press, 2020).
6. Marcia McAdoo Greenlee, "A Methodology for the Study, Identification and Evaluation of Afro-American Historic Places" (Ph.D. diss., George Washington University, 1982), 197.
7. Ad for houses on M Street NE, between 4th and 5th, *ES* April 25, 1889, p. 3. E. C. Gardner, "Washington and Its Architecture," *ES* December 24, 1886, p. 4, and February 5, 1887, p. 3. By the 1920s, houses on the ends were referred to as "semi-detached." Houses on the ends of rows receive only passing attention in this book, because their plans often differed drastically from their neighbors. Semi-detached houses or row-house flats, while often modest housing, also have different constraints on their plans, so they are not considered here.
8. Carl Lounsbury makes this point about row houses in sixteenth- and seventeenth-century London. Carl R. Lounsbury, *Essays in Early American Architectural History: A View from the Chesapeake* (Charlottesville: University of Virginia Press, 2011), 77.
9. Emily Badger and Quoctrung Bui, "Housing Scarce, Cities Erase Single-Family Lots," *NYT* June 19, 2019, pp. A-1, A-13. An example of a Park View rehab is 432 Manor Place, which was sold for redevelopment in 2019. Cameron Logan, in his history of historic preservation in Washington, *Historic Capital: Preservation, Race, and Real Estate in Washington, D.C.* (Minneapolis: University of Minnesota Press, 2017), xxiii, also notes that the "ideal of the row house neighborhood, revived by sweat equity and community spirit, has now withered."

1. Six Plans

1. Ad, *ES* July 28, 1966, p. 30.
2. "Two Buildings Get Age Honors in D.C.," *ES* March 1, 1926, p. 37. The nearby Law House was the other possibility.
3. Thomas C. Hubka, *How the Working-Class Home Became Modern, 1900–1940* (Minneapolis: University of Minnesota Press, 2020), 62–63. One example of a detached kitchen, documented by HABS but since demolished, was at 2411 Pennsylvania Avenue NW.
4. Alley dwellings are discussed further in chapters 3, 5, and 6.
5. Beyer Blinder Belle, "Carter G. Woodson Home: Historic Structure Report," National Park Service, 2008. James A. Jacobs, "Carter G. Woodson House," HABS, 2013. Ad, *WP* July 11, 1889, p. 3. U.S. Manuscript Census, 1880. City directories, 1887, 1890. "General S. S. Henkle Dead," *ES* May 21, 1895, p. 3.
6. Permit #1632, June 23, 1880; see Note on Sources.
7. Permit #928, October 24, 1891. Deed Book 191, p. 44, October 3, 1919, Nancy D. Robb to John H. Thomas and wife. City directories. U.S. Manuscript Census. Tax assessment books. Articles in the *Evening Star,* including "Mrs. Spranger Dead," June 21, 1895; "Mrs. Darling Dead," January 6, 1910; "Appeals to Court," April 18, 1902; "Musical and Dramatic," March 18, 1882; "Mrs. Darling's Charges," April 19, 1895; "Darling's Dying Statement," May 13, 1895.
8. On the building permit, King left the line for "architect" blank. Permit #928, October 24, 1891. In city directories, though, such as the ones for 1887 and 1890, he described himself as a "builder and architect." "Developing the City," *Washington Sunday Herald,* March 23, 1890, p. 14. "The Builders' Exchange," *Sunday Herald,* March 29, 1891, p. 20. "Thomas J. King, Elk Incorporator, Dies," *ES* September 28, 1933, p. A-9. The later addition is found in Permit #23417, October 8, 1940.
9. Permits Database Report; see Note on Sources. The totals are 1,641 houses less than 16 feet wide, 1,469 at 16 feet or more in the 1880s; in the 1890s, 1,462 less than 16 feet, 3,105 at 16 feet or more. The permits database does not track bay windows, but in her dissertation, based on a statistical sample of building permits from the 1880s and 1890s, Melissa McLoud found that about half of the houses did not have bay windows. Melissa McLoud, "Craftsmen and Entrepreneurs: Buildings in Late Nineteenth-Century Washington, D.C." (Ph.D. diss., George Washington University, 1988), 212. It was, of course, possible to put a bay window on a house as narrow as 13 feet, such as 905–11 C Street SE or 622–30 C Street SE; both rows were built in 1886. W. B. Tuthill, *The City Residence: Its Design and Construction* (New York: Wm. T. Comstock, 1890), 16.
10. An example of a short lot and basement kitchen is the row house at 420 Tenth Street SE, at the obtuse corner of Pennsylvania Avenue. Designed in 1893 in conjunction with its neighbor on the corner, this bay-fronted house with a side-hall plan was two rooms deep, with the kitchen in the basement. "420 Tenth Street, Southeast (House), Washington, District of Columbia," HABS drawings, LC. James A. Gannon Sr., "Washington at the Turn of the Century," *RCHS* (1963–65), 316. The house, a bay-windowed L-plan, was at 1113 Massachusetts Avenue NW. Mary Church Terrell, *A Colored Woman in a White World* (New York: Humanity Books, 2005; orig. pub., 1940), 154.
11. Ads, *ES* June 29, 1894, p. 10.

12. U.S. Manuscript Censuses. City directories. Trust for Bernice G. Ruff, June 27, 1941, Document No. 1941021427; the deed included a racial covenant. The story does not end with the Ruffs, of course. Gertrude sold the house in 1951, just a few years after the courts had struck down racial covenants. Deed, Ruff and Crump to Darden, October 5, 1951, Document No. 1951042888. The new owner, Crettie Darden, was Black. Gertrude moved to Hyattsville, Maryland, and died the next year. Racial covenants and shifts in population are discussed in chapters 5 and 6.
13. 2200–28 First Street NW: Permit #113, July 17, 1899. Ad, *ES* April 21, 1900, pt. 2, p. 1. Middaugh used Simmons's plan with the V-shaped indentation, without crediting any architect on the building permit, for houses at 1835–45 N. Capitol Street.
14. Roman brick is shorter and wider than regular brick, measuring roughly 2 by 12 by 4 inches, compared to the usual 2¼ by 8 by 4 inches. 2300 block of First Street, west side: Permit #1311, March 13, 1902. 2300 block of First Street, east side: Permit #2170, June 22, 1902. Ad, *WP* October 26, 1902, p. 29. "Real Estate Market," *WP* August 17, 1902, p. 26. Ad, *WP* October 26, 1902, p. 29. No record of this copyright could be found in the U.S. Copyright Office, Library of Congress. Allan B. Slauson, ed., *A History of the City of Washington: Its Men and Institutions* (Washington DC: Washington Post, 1903), 232. On First Street, Simmons's row houses sold for $6,850 while Bohn's were advertised at $5,590.
15. Mary F. Rainey to Snowdon Ashford, Inspector of Buildings, September 5, 1903, filed with Permit #1311, March 14, 1902, courtesy of Bronwyn Irwin.
16. Permit #1644, February 25, 1905.
17. "Popularity of Residence due to Social Conditions," *ES* November 22, 1913, pt. 2, p. 2. "An English 'At Home,'" *ES* November 8, 1879, p. 7. Sarah Bradford Landau, in writing of New York row houses, called this an American basement plan: "The entrance to the house, often centered, was either at ground level or a few steps above. . . . The dining room, formerly at the front of the basement story, was now officially removed to the first floor, leaving a reception hall in its place." She also noted that "today the American basement house is usually mislabeled as 'English' basement," although it appears to be a contemporary term in Washington, at least. Landau, "The Row Houses of New York's West Side," *JSAH* 34 (March 1975): 28.
18. Waggaman's two brothers, Henry and Thomas, were also in the real estate business, although they usually operated separately. In 1887 the three of them bought the tract known as Woodley. That year John advertised himself as a "real estate expert." 1887 city directory, p. 839. When Waggaman built his row houses, he left the three corners of the square empty, building his houses on inner lots. He then sold off the corners: "For Sale—To Builders and Investors—exceptional opportunity to buy some valuable corner ground in square 735, four squares from Capitol and new National Library." *ES* September 12, 1892, p. 3. Diane Shaw Wasch, "Models of Beauty and Predictability: The Creation of Wesley Heights and Spring Valley," *WH* 1, no. 2 (Fall 1989): 59–60.
19. Permit #2600, June 4, 1892. There was no builder listed on the permit, which was signed by the architect. Burden, the son of a builder, designed his first house in 1888, when he was twenty-four. He seems to have had a thriving practice in designing houses, including four other projects for John F. Waggaman. His last commission was in July 1894. He obtained a job working for the building inspector, then was hired on by the War Department. In 1908 his wife sued for divorce, alleging cruelty and drunkenness. She received alimony of a little more than half his salary.

"District Government," *ES* February 12, 1895, p. 2. "Clerical Changes," *ES* March 21, 1905, p. 10. "Sues for Legal Separation," *ES* January 16, 1908, p. 13. "Mrs. Burden Gets Alimony," *ES* February 5, 1908, p. 13.

20. Ad, *ES* September 18, 1893. Waggaman seems to have suffered reversals in the 1890s and after. He retired to his house near Annapolis in 1909 at the age of fifty-six, putting his real estate in a trust to benefit his family. According to a legal decision, when the trustee "took charge of the estate it was practically insolvent" but was restored to a sound condition by 1926. *Waggaman v. Helvering,* U.S. Court of Appeals for the District of Columbia Circuit, 78 F. 2d 721 (DC Cir. 1935) May 13, 1935. In his retirement, a nurse lived with Waggaman and his wife, indicating that he may have had health problems. He had experienced some financial success, though; as his obituary noted, "His estate on the South River is one of the show places in Maryland, and is replete with interesting mementoes of his European trips." *WP* May 21, 1918, p. 16. Assessment books. City directories.
21. "Popularity of Residence." Other examples on Capitol Hill include 917–23 North Carolina Avenue SE, built in 1891, 249–55 Twelfth Street SE, built in 1892, and 632–38 C Street NE, built in 1892.
22. Permit #893, April 18, 1924.
23. "Say Old Houses, Made New, Find Ready Purchasers," *ES* January 22, 1916, pt. 2, p. 2.
24. "Washington Architecture," *ES* February 5, 1887, p. 3. "Popularity of Residence."
25. Trust 192301130153, January 13, 1923. "Marriage Licenses," *ES* October 7, 1918, p. 8. City directories. Permit for garage: Permit #178, July 11, 1924. "Deaths," *ES* May 21, 1925. "Marriage Licenses," *ES* February 20, 1929, p. 9. "Rockville," *ES* February 11, 1930, p. 11.
26. Permit #6676, March 28, 1922.
27. The totals for 1924: 16 feet wide, 303; 17 feet, 287; 18 feet, 465; 19 feet, 75; and 20 feet, 283. Permits Database Reports; see Note on Sources.
28. "Sleeping Porches Wanted by Those Who Buy Homes," *ES* January 22, 1910, pt. 2 p. 2. "Closed Porches Backed," *ES* January 26, 1928, p. 26.
29. Ad, *ES,* April 26, 1909, p. 3. "Gruver Addresses 'Y' Realty Class," *ES* November 28, 1925, p. 25. Louis Justement, "Fine Taste Shown in Row Designing," *ES* June 26, 1926, p. 35.
30. Justement, "Fine Taste," 35.
31. One of the few scholarly treatments of this type is Evelyn Montgomery, "Beyond the American Foursquare: The Square House in Period Perspective," *Buildings and Landscapes* 25, no. 2 (Fall 2018): 48–65. Montgomery calls it "the workhorse of middle-class domesticity" (48). It receives some attention in Thomas C. Hubka, *Houses without Names: Architectural Nomenclature and the Classification of America's Common Houses* (Knoxville: University of Tennessee Press, 2013), 57, where he calls it "one of the most uniform and well-known pre–WWII floor plans in America." Gustav Stickley, best known for his promotion of the bungalow, published a plan of this type in 1909, reproduced in Elizabeth Collins Cromley, *The Food Axis: Cooking, Eating, and the Architecture of American Houses* (Charlottesville: University of Virginia Press, 2010), 136. It was even popular abroad; in his study *The English Terraced House* (New Haven: Yale University Press, 1992), 99, Stefan Muthesius calls it "a type of crucial importance, as it has remained largely unchanged to this day, the standard speculative suburban type of house," and pictures it on p. 90.

Image from E. Mary Ellen Hayward and Charles Belfoure, *The Baltimore Rowhouse* (New York: Princeton Architectural Press, 2001), 138. W. Edward Orser, "The Making of a Baltimore Rowhouse Community: The Edmonson Avenue Area, 1915–1945," *Maryland Historical Magazine* 80, no. 3 (Fall 1985): 207. For an example of the use of the name "colonial," see "Twelve Homes Completed," *ES* April 3, 1920, pt. 2, p. 2. "Petworth Homes Ready for the Fall Market," *ES,* September 11, 1915, pt. 2, p. 2.

32. Cromley, *The Food Axis,* 138–43. Gwendolyn Wright, *Building the Dream: A Social History of Housing in America* (Cambridge, Mass.: MIT Press, 1981), 168–72. Clifford Edward Clark Jr., *The American Family Home, 1800–1960* (Chapel Hill: University of North Carolina Press, 1986), 163–68. Hubka, *How the Working-Class Home,* 85–133.
33. Linda Binsted, "Complexity without Contradiction: Chloethiel Woodard Smith and Daniel Urban Kiley's Capitol Park, Washington, DC" (M.A. thesis, University of Virginia, 2018), 46. Cromley, *Food Axis,* 190, notes the disappearance of the dining room in mid-twentieth-century houses more generally.
34. "Patio Townhouses," *House and Home* 20 (July 1961): 146–47, 152–55. "Patio Row Houses Set for Southwest," *WP* June 18, 1960, p. B13.
35. The newspaper noticed this placement of the kitchen in the front of renovated houses in Georgetown and Alexandria as early as 1934. George L. Williams, "What $100 Can Do for a Town House," *ES* September 29, 1934, B-2. Drawings in Drayer collection, LC, Plan 1201.
36. Kate Wagner, "The Case for Rooms," *Citylab* (www.citylab.com), August 6, 2018. Beth Broome, "A Modern Classic," *Architectural Record,* September 2018, 83. The effect of the COVID pandemic in 2020–21 has yet to be determined, but with more people working at home the disadvantages of the open plan became apparent.

2. Constraints

1. Kim Prothro Williams, *Lost Farms and Estates of Washington, D.C.* (Charleston: History Press, 2018), 27. Chris Myers Asch and George Derek Musgrove, *Chocolate City: A History of Race and Democracy in the Nation's Capital* (Chapel Hill: University of North Carolina Press, 2017), 5.
2. Agreement signed in Georgetown, March 31, 1791, quoted in John W. Reps, *Washington on View: The Nation's Capital since 1790* (Chapel Hill: University of North Carolina Press, 1991), 14.
3. Pamela Scott, "'This Vast Empire': The Iconography of the Mall, 1791–1848," in *The Mall in Washington, 1791–1991,* ed. Richard Longstreth (Hanover, N.H.: University Press of New England, 1991), 37–46.
4. Charles Duff, *The North Atlantic Cities* (Liverpool: Bluecoat, 2019), 10, points out that these row-house cities were all in the North Atlantic. Carl R. Lounsbury, *Essays in Early American Architectural History: A View from the Chesapeake* (Charlottesville: University of Virginia Press, 2011), 77. Andrew Scott Dolkart, *The Row House Reborn: Architecture and Neighborhoods in New York City, 1908–1929* (Baltimore: Johns Hopkins University Press, 2009), 9. William John Murtagh, "The Philadelphia Row House," *JSAH* 16, no. 4 (December 1957): 8. William Francis Smith and T. Michael Miller, *A Seaport Saga: Portrait of Old Alexandria, Virginia* (Norfolk, Va.: Donning, 1989), 32–33. "A Shared Heritage," 46–48. Al Cox, Historic Preservation Manager and Architect, City of Alexandria, telephone interview by author,

May 25, 2018. Daniel D. Reiff, *Washington Architecture, 1791–1861: Problems in Development* (Washington, DC: U.S. Commission of Fine Arts, 1971), 54.

5. P. C. L'Enfant to the president of the United States, August 19, 1791, reproduced in "L'Enfant's Reports to President Washington, Bearing Dates of March 26, June 22, and August 19, 1791," *RCHS* 2 (1899): 44.
6. Appleton P. Clark Jr., "Origin of the Building Regulations," *RCHS* 4 (1901): 170. In addition, Boston had a regulation providing for party walls as early as 1683. "American Notes: Boston Building Ordinances, 1631–1714," *JSAH* 20, no. 2 (May 1961): 91.
7. Clark, "Origin," 168–69. It is uncertain how much of Jefferson's response was his own, or his influence on the commissioners, or the commissioners' own opinion. Samuel Burch, comp., *A Digest of the Laws of the Corporation of the City of Washington* (Washington, DC: James Wilson, 1823), 48.
8. J. L. Sibley Jennings Jr., "Artistry as Design: L'Enfant's Extraordinary Plan," *Quarterly Journal of the Library of Congress* 36, no. 3 (Summer 1979): 248–49.
9. Clark, "Origins," 169. Jennings, "Artistry," 249.
10. George Washington's regulation of June 25, 1796, Office of the Superintendent of the City of Washington, *Regulations of Buildings, etc.* (no publisher, 1815), 10.
11. Jennings, "Artistry," 248, attributed the prohibition of projections to L'Enfant's desire to plant street trees and the fear that construction under the right-of-way would interfere with that. Jennings also pointed to a Parisian regulation that may have been a model for this one. The revised regulation allowed "areas or ditches to be made, walled on the street side with good stone walls at least eighteen inches thick, of the height, and palisaded with iron, as aforesaid, to the centre of the wall, leaving seven feet between the line of the street and the palisading." Wheat Row has a good example of these areaways; see fig. 4. According to the 1845 regulation, steps could project 5 or 7 feet, depending on the width of the footway. Colonnades and open porches were also permitted but could project no farther than stairs could. William Quereau Force, comp., *The Builder's Guide, Containing Lists of Prices and Rules of Measurement, etc.* (Washington, DC: Robert A. Waters, 1851), 87, 94–95. This was the only building regulation issued between the 1820s and 1871, suggesting either that the regulations worked, provoking no need for change, or that they were widely ignored. William B. Webb. *The Laws of the Corporation of the City of Washington* (Washington, DC: R. A. Waters, 1868), 64–66.
12. Reps, *Washington on View,* 22.
13. Jennings, "Artistry," 240.
14. Adam Costanzo, *George Washington's Washington: Visions for the National Capital in the Early American Republic* (Athens: University of Georgia Pres, 2018), 27. L'Enfant himself bought one of the lots: Lot 30 in Square 127, which is bound by Seventeenth, Eighteenth, H, and I Streets NW. Lot 30 has a 40-foot frontage on Seventeenth Street and extends 118 feet at its deepest, but only 85 feet on one side, with the rear lot line abutting the diagonal alley. James Dudley Morgan, "Maj. Pierre Charles L'Enfant, the Unhonored and Unrewarded Engineer," *RCHS* 2 (1899): 157. King to President, September 25, 1803, quoted in Burch, *Digest,* 355.
15. Ralph E. Ehrenberg, "Mapping the Nation's Capital: The Surveyor's Office, 1791–1818," *Quarterly Journal of the Library of Congress* 36, no. 3 (Summer 1979): 288. John Stewart, "Early Maps and Surveyors of the City of Washington, DC," *RCHS* 2 (1899): 59. The number of squares fluctuated, as areas previously thought unbuildable, such as at the intersection of avenues, were platted. The number 1,236 ap-

peared in a 1794 description. Reps, *Washington on View,* 46. The number of squares with alleys is from Katherine Grandine and Kimberly Prothro, "Blagden Alley/Naylor Court Historic District Registration Form" (National Register of Historic Places, National Park Service, 1990), sec. 8, p. 7.

The survey of Square 127, as recorded in the DC Office of the Surveyor's Record Book 1, p. 127, is instructive. The square is divided into 33 lots with diagonal alleys. The accompanying legend notes which lots were to be held by the original proprietor and which to be sold by the government, as agreed on October 10, 1791. Another legend notes that the dimensions (written in red) correcting the original dimensions were made by McDermott, recorded on July 16, 1793. Clearly, the lots were laid out previous to McDermott's involvement.

16. Kenneth R. Bowling, *Creating the Federal City, 1774–1800: Potomac Fever* (Washington, DC: AIA Press, 1988), 104. Reps, *Washington on View,* 31–32.
17. In June 1795 the agreement was amended to permit Greenleaf to build houses of any description as long as they had the same square footage and two stories, but they were built of brick. *Washington Gazette,* September 28, 1796, quoted in Allen C. Clark, *Greenleaf and Law in the Federal City* (Washington, DC: W. P. Roberts, 1901), 129. They were on Square 651.
18. "1911 Pennsylvania Avenue NW, Application Form" (Joint Committee on Landmarks of the National Capital, 1984). James M. Goode, *Capital Losses: A Cultural History of Washington's Destroyed Buildings* (Washington, DC: Smithsonian Institution Press, 1979), 169. A remnant of the Seven Buildings survives in the form of the facades of two of them, surrounded by new construction.
19. Reps, *Washington on View,* 32. Isaac Weld, quote in Reps, *Washington on View,* 48. As Costanzo, *George Washington's Washington,* 152, pointed out, the completeness of the city plan meant that all areas of it were open to settlement, so the new residents spread themselves out.
20. Washington County was governed by a Levy Court appointed by Congress. William M. Maury, *Alexander "Boss" Shepherd and the Board of Public Works* (Washington, DC: George Washington University, 1975), 2. The city's 1822 regulations changed this first regulation slightly, dropping the square-footage restriction and effectively permitting two-story frame row houses by providing that frame houses not exceed 20 feet from the sill to the top ridge of the roof. An act "modifying the preceding act" specified that frame buildings could not be built within 24 feet of a brick or stone building. Force, *Builder's Guide,* 89–90.
21. Quoted in Reps, *Washington on View,* 94. Constance McLaughlin Green, *Washington: A History of the Capital, 1800–1950* (Princeton: Princeton University Press, 1962), 1:21.
22. Green, *Washington,* 2:89. Reps, *Washington on View,* 152, quote on 164.
23. Quoted in Reps, *Washington on View,* 177.
24. 16 Stat. L. 82, "An Act authorizing the corporation of the City of Washington to set apart Portions of Streets and Avenues as Parks for Trees and Walks," April 6, 1870, quoted in William Tindall, "The Origin of the Parking System of This City," *RCHS* 4 (1901): 78. Bowen had also advocated for this in his annual mayoral addresses. *Message of the Mayor to the Boards of Aldermen and Common Council of the City of Washington, D.C.* (Washington, DC: Chronicle Printers, 1868), 9. *Message of the Mayor of the City of Washington Transmitted to the Two Boards of the City Council* (Washington, DC: Chronicle Printers, 1869), 22.

25. *Laws of the Corporation of the City of Washington Passed by the 68th Council* (Washington, DC: McGill and Witherow, 1871), chap. 15.

26. Maury, *Alexander "Boss" Shepherd,* 4. Moderate Republicans, including Shepherd, backed Matthew Emery, who became mayor after Bowen, less than a year before the mayoral system of government was replaced.

27. Maury, *Alexander "Boss" Shepherd,* 51.

28. "A Comprehensive Plan of Improvements," *ES* June 20, 1871, p. 1. Quoted in Reps, *Washington on View,* 177.

29. *Report of the Joint Select Committee of Congress Appointed to Inquire into the Affairs of the Government of the District of Columbia* (Washington, DC: GPO, 1874), 2049. Cluss biographer Tanya Beauchamp confirms his ubiquity: "Between 1862 and 1876 his office designed and superintended the construction of virtually all the public buildings erected by the Washington city government." Tanya Edwards Beauchamp, "Adolph Cluss: An Architect in Washington during Civil War and Reconstruction," *RCHS* 71/72 (1971–72): 339. Many aspects of Cluss's life and career are explored in Alan Lessoff and Christof Mauch, eds., *Adolf Cluss, Architect: From Germany to America* (privately printed by the Historical Society of Washington and Stadtarchiv Heilbronn, 2005).

30. Adolf Cluss, "Report of Inspector of Buildings," *Report of the Board of Public Works of the District of Columbia* (Washington, DC: GPO, 1872), 91.

31. *Building Regulations of the District of Columbia* (Washington, DC: Republican Job Office Print, 1872), 10, 20.

32. "Building Regulations of the District of Columbia," *Fourth Annual Report of the Commissioners of the District of Columbia* (Washington, DC: GPO, 1877). The regulations also required that builders pay a fee to obtain a permit.

33. The 1882 regulations specified that wooden bay windows of any height were permitted when attached to wooden buildings. *Building Regulations of the District of Columbia* (Washington, DC: Judd and Detweiler, 1882), 17.

    The 1885 regulations were the first to regulate buildings on alleys, ordering that permits not be granted until arrangements were made for "proper drainage" of the alley. *Building Regulations of the District of Columbia* (Washington, DC: Judd and Detweiler, 1885), 10. They also restricted the width of bay windows for the first time, depending on the width of the building. Bay windows were limited to 14 feet wide, and only one bay window was permitted on fronts less than 35 feet wide. For wider buildings, the projections could not occupy more than 50 percent of the front or 40 percent of the side, if exposed. *Building Regulations* (1885), 24.

    The 1887 regulations required a certain amount of the front to be left uncovered by bay windows. If the building was less than 15 feet wide, 2 feet 6 inches of the building line had to be left open; if the building was less than 20 feet wide, 3 feet 6 inches of it had to be left at the building line; and buildings between 20 and 35 feet wide had to leave 4 feet 10 inches at the building line. *Building Regulations of the District of Columbia* (Philadelphia: Dunlap and Clarke, 1887), 8, 18, 22, 23, 24.

    The form of bay windows, not just their size, was affected by provisions issued subsequent to the 1891 regulations, which indirectly promoted chamfered corners. They also laid out an intricate calculation for bay windows that seemed to encourage chamfering: "No such projection shall extend beyond the space included between two lines drawn from the intersection of the building line and party lines in front of the lots to be built upon, and making an angle of 45 degrees with said building line." *Regulations Governing the Erection, Removal, Repair, and Maintenance of Buildings* (Washington, DC: Judd and Detweiler, 1902), 87.

34. Alteration Permit #468, September 7, 1888. Cole's plans provided for 5-foot-deep bay windows on Massachusetts Avenue that were 26 feet 6 inches wide and 16 feet 6 inches wide, while the bay windows on M Street were 29 and 16 feet wide.

35. *ES* December 23,1889, p. 5, and December 27, 1889, p. 2. "Opposed to Advancing the Case," *ES* December 29, 1890, p. 1. "Building Regulations of the District of Columbia," *The Washington Architects, Contractors, and Builders Directory, 1892–93* (Baltimore: Monumental, 1892), 171–72. The streets of Washington were technically owned by the federal government, and the U.S. Army Corps of Engineers, under supervision of the secretary of war, took responsibility for them. In 1933, the National Park Service of the Department of the Interior took over this responsibility. Elizabeth Barthold, "L'Enfant-McMillan Plan of Washington, DC" (HABS, LC, 1993), pp. 21, 47, 51. *Building Regulations* (1902), insert after p. 86. Adopted October 23, 1891. The federal oversight lasted until 1906, when the secretary of war conceded that he need review only those projections of buildings on land adjoining public reservations. By then, bay windows and towers had fallen out of favor. "War to Congress," *ES* February 3, 1906, p. 9.

36. *Regulations Governing the Erection, Removal, Repair and Electric Wiring of Buildings in the District of Columbia* (n.p., 1897). "New Building Laws," *ES* June 29, 1897, p. 1.

37. Henry H. Glassie, "Victorian Homes in Washington," *RCHS* (1963–65), 361. Green, *Washington,* 2:89.

38. Joseph West Moore, *Picturesque Washington* (Providence: J. A. and R. A. Reid, 1887), 52.

39. Frederick Gutheim, *Worthy of the Nation: The History of Planning for the National Capital* (Washington, DC: Smithsonian Institution Press, 1977), 110.

40. Alison K. Hoagland, "Nineteenth-Century Building Regulations in Washington, D.C.," *RCHS* 52 (1989): 68.

41. Steven J. Diner, Jerome S. Paige, Margaret M. Reuss, and Irving Richter, *Housing Washington's People: Public Policy in Retrospect* (Washington, DC: University of the District of Columbia, 1983), 14–17, 20–22.

42. "More Air," *ES* July 15, 1905, p. 4.

43. "Approves Changes," *ES* October 14, 1905, p. 9. Lot coverage was restricted to 75 percent unless it faced on two streets, and interior or "inclosed" courts had to have a minimum of 12 feet in each dimension. The law stipulated: "For each increase in height of five feet in height of building over twenty feet there shall be an increase of six inches in width" of the court. *Report of the Commissioners of the District of Columbia for the Year Ended June 30, 1906* (Washington, DC: GPO, 1906), 54. The building inspector's original proposal had been to require enclosed courts to be 7 feet wide. Subsequent regulations continued to modify this requirement somewhat. The 1909 regulations, while limiting lot occupancy to 90 percent, called for courts to be a minimum of 4 feet 6 inches wide, increasing if the building was more than 25 feet high or if the ell was more than 25 feet long. *Regulations Governing the Erection, Removal, Repair and Maintenance of Buildings . . . in the District of Columbia* (Washington: Carnahan Press, 1909), 55. The 1920 zoning regulations for the row-house district expanded the minimum width for open courts slightly to

5 feet. S. G. Lindholm, Zoning Commission of the District of Columbia, "Experiences with Zoning in Washington, D.C., 1920–1934," 10.

44. "Real Estate Gossip," *ES* April 28, 1906, pt. 2, p. 2.

45. "Bungalow Type Houses in Increasing Demand," *ES* June 17, 1916, part 2, p. 2.

46. As described in *Building Regulations* (1902), 89, "porches with open balustrade not more than five feet high above parking or pavement, open from handrail to roof, will not be limited in width except as to the nine inches from party line extended on each side." This prevented connected rows of porches on connected rows of houses.

47. *Building Regulations* (1909), 61.

48. "Changes of Fashion in Building Modes," *ES,* November 11, 1911, pt. 2, p. 4.

49. "New Area Chosen for Houses in Rows," *ES* April 20, 1912, pt. 2, p. 2. "Citizens Oppose Row House Building," *ES* October 22, 1925, p. 2. "Citizens Move to Bar Row Houses in Section," *ES* December 13, 1925, p. 10. "Trend from Row House Seen in Suburban Developments," *ES* May 6, 1922, 14.

50. "Points Out Some Advantages of Row-House Construction," *ES* January 9, 1926, p. 24. "Architects' Drawings of the Nine Model Homes in the Star's Demonstration," *ES* June 26, 1926, p. 9. Also, one was a three-unit "community house."

51. "Zone Regulation Bans Row Houses," *WP* July 27, 1920, p. 12. Lindholm, "Experiences with Zoning," 9. Gutheim, *Worthy of the Nation,* 164. The commission soon realized that apartment houses should have been excluded from the Area A as well, so in 1923 it created an A-Restricted area that prohibited them, followed by restrictions on semi-detached houses. The boundaries of the row-house area included Georgetown, then ran up to Piney Branch, Spring, and Rock Creek Church roads to North Capitol, south to Florida and Benning, and along the Anacostia and Potomac rivers, excluding downtown. With the adoption of the zoning code, the building regulations no longer governed the size of courts or coverage of the lots; these became zoning functions.

52. Zoning Commission of the District of Columbia, "Zoning Regulations" (1920), 2, 12. Lindholm, "Experiences with Zoning," 9. "Ball Club Seeks to Add to Stands," *ES* January 15, 1924, p. 4. "Zoning Body Cuts Building Height," *ES* March 21, 1924, p. 1. "Protests Widening Pine Branch Road," *ES* February 12, 1924, p. 24. "Attached Houses in Suburbs Scored," *ES* March 17, 1924, p. 19. "Leaders Join Fight for Zones Having Apartments Ban," *WP* March 16, 1924, p. 2. "Delegation Defends Fraternity Houses at Zoning Hearing," *WP* June 20, 1924, p. 2. "To Grant Hearing in Zoning Angle," *ES* December 20, 1924, p. 2.

53. "Wardman in Tilt over Zone Rules," *ES* August 25, 1926, p. 2.

54. "Claim Zoning Hits Home Ownership," *ES* August 15, 1925, p. 6. "Few Row-Type Houses Being Built in District Area," *ES* October 30, 1948, p. 23.

55. Kenneth T. Jackson, "Federal Subsidy and the Suburban Dream: The First Quarter-Century of Government Intervention in the Housing Market," *RCHS* 50 (1980): 421–51. There are several excellent accounts of federal involvement in urban planning in Washington in the postwar period, especially Howard Gillette, *Between Justice and Beauty: Race, Planning, and the Failure of Urban Policy in Washington, D.C.* (Baltimore: Johns Hopkins University Press, 1995), 151–69. See also Gutheim, *Worthy of the Nation,* 229–82. Paul Valentine, "Blacks Total 77 Per Cent of District's Population," *WP* January 24, 1976, p. B1.

56. Urban renewal in Southwest has also been well treated by several sources, in

addition to Gillette and Gutheim cited above. See Richard Longstreth, "Brave New World: Southwest Washington and the Promise of Urban Renewal," in *Housing Washington: Two Centuries of Residential Development and Planning in the National Capital,* ed. Richard Longstreth (Chicago: Center for American Places, 2010), 255–80. Francesca Russello Ammon, "Commemoration amid Criticism: The Mixed Legacy of Urban Renewal in Southwest Washington, D.C.," *Journal of Planning History* 8, no. 3 (August 2009): 175–220. Francesca Russello Ammon, "Southwest Washington, D.C., Urban Renewal Area," HABS, LC, 2004. Keith Melder: "Southwest Washington: Where History Stopped," in *Washington at Home: An Illustrated History of Neighborhoods in the Nation's Capital,* ed. Kathryn Schneider Smith (Baltimore: Johns Hopkins University Press, 2010), 88–104. My account relies on these sources.

57. Quoted in Ammon, "Commemoration," 183. Gutheim, *Worthy of the Nation,* 259. Longstreth, "Brave New World," 255. The authority and funding for this vast remaking of a neighborhood began with federal legislation, the District of Columbia Redevelopment Act of 1945, which created the Redevelopment Land Agency to acquire slum areas and redistribute the land. The Housing Act of 1949 provided the funding, and this was one of the first major projects under the act. Subsequently, the Housing Act of 1954 supported selective rather than wholesale demolition, but by that time Southwest's plans were set and demolitions had begun.

58. Ammon, "Southwest," 11, 13, 15. Paul S. Green, "Old Southwest Remembered: The Photographs of Joseph Owen Curtis," *WH* 1, no. 2 (Fall 1989): 42–57. *Southwest Remembered: A Story of Urban Renewal,* film prod. and dir. by Dolores Smith, 1990. Ammon, "Commemoration," 188. Longstreth, "Brave New World," 268.

59. Longstreth, "Brave New World," 257.

60. Smith's innovative plan clashed with requirements for density, but she was able to aggregate the town houses with the apartment building and achieve the desired density. Jane Jacobs, "Washington—20th-Century Capital?," *Architectural Forum* 104 (January 1956): 100. Clustering the town houses was also problematic. In an effort to stem the construction of alley dwellings, the zoning code had, several decades earlier, adopted a provision requiring each house to face the street on its own lot. To circumvent this, Smith argued that each cluster of adjoining houses, which were all rentals, constituted a building. Longstreth, "Brave New World," 165, 263.

61. "Descriptive Data," 1964 Homes for Better Living Program, sponsored by the American Institute of Architects, Smith collection, Carton 211, Folder 36, LC. "The Capitol Park Town Houses" brochure, Smith Collection, Carton 213, Folder 12, LC.

62. Ami Stewart, "Georgetown Architects' Dream for 'New Town in the City,'" *The Georgetowner,* March 26, 1959, p. 1.

63. "Georgetown Flavor for Southwest," *WP* February 16 1963, p. D4.

64. John B. Willmann, "Town House Comes Back Strong," *WP* February 19, 1966, p. D1. Wolf Von Eckardt, "The Row House Revival Is Going to Town—Not to Mention Country," *WP* July 24, 1966, p. G7.

65. Longstreth, "Brave New World," 276. Ammon, "Commemoration," 198, 207, 206.

66. Ammon, "Commemoration," 185.

67. Asch and Musgrove, *Chocolate City,* 402. Dennis E. Gale, *Washington, D.C.: Inner-City Revitalization and Minority Suburbanization* (Philadelphia: Temple University Press, 1987), 114. Governmental interventions other than Southwest's urban renewal brought whites back to the city. In the early 1970s the Maryland and

Virginia counties abutting Washington instituted moratoriums on new construction because of the incapacity of the region's shared sewer system. As a result, Washington was one of the few places in the region where new housing could be built, accounting for some of the influx of the white population. Valentine, "Blacks Total," B1. Sharon Conway, "Prince George's Lifts Sewer Moratorium," *WP*, October 18, 1977, p. C1. Donald P. Baker, "Sewer Moratorium in Maryland to Be Eased within a Few Months," *WP* October 3,1975, p. A9.

68. Cameron Logan, *Historic Capital: Preservation, Race, and Real Estate in Washington, D.C.* (Minneapolis: University of Minnesota Press, 2017), 6–24. Kathleen Menzie Lesko, Valerie Babb, and Carroll R. Gibbs, *Black Georgetown Remembered: A History of Its Black Community from the Founding of "The Town of George" in 1751 to the Present Day* (Washington, DC: Georgetown University Press, 2016), 95–97.
69. Logan, *Historic Capital,* 116–22. *2020: District of Columbia Historic Preservation Plan: Preserving for Progress* (DC Historic Preservation Office, 2018), 46.

3. Facades

1. For much of the 1880s, about a third of the building permits for speculative row houses did not indicate an architect, and in the early 1890s it was about a quarter. This changed in the early twentieth century, though. Beginning about 1906, when construction picked up again after some slow times, less than 5 percent of permits for speculative row houses left the architect line blank, and that continued, with some exceptions, into the 1920s until, by 1926, none did. Thus by the time that near-identical row houses were being produced by the hundreds, architects had the greatest role, and when row houses were at their most individual, architects were consulted less frequently. Permits Database Reports; see Note on Sources. This usage of architects correlates somewhat with requirements for drawings being submitted with the building permit. In 1887, the building regulations first required that the building inspector examine the drawings, but by 1902, the requirements insisted that drawings be submitted with the permit application. *Building Regulations* (1887), 10–11, and (1902), 21.
2. *The Brickbuilder* 15, no. 11 (November 1906): 234. My thanks to Emily Eig for this reference. See Jeffrey Alan Cohen, "The Queen Anne and the Late Victorian Townhouse in Philadelphia, 1878–1895" (Ph.D. diss., University of Pennsylvania, 1991), for an analysis of the influence of larger architectural trends on architects who were designing upscale row houses in Philadelphia in the late nineteenth century.
3. On the importance of consumers, see Alan Gowans, *The Comfortable House: North American Suburban Architecture, 1890–1930* (Cambridge, Mass.: MIT Press, 1986), xiv, and Barbara Miller Lane, *Houses for a New World: Builders and Buyers in American Suburbs* (Princeton: Princeton University Press, 2015), 43–44. Margaret Supplee Smith and John C. Moorhouse, "Architecture and the Housing Market: Nineteenth Century Row Housing in Boston's South End," *JSAH* 52, no. 2 (June 1993): 177. Marcia McAdoo Greenlee, "A Methodology for the Identification, Study and Evaluation of Afro-American Places" (Ph.D. diss., George Washington University, 1982), 208–9. Greenlee drew on interviews of ten residents of two blocks of Eleventh Street NW; she had conducted six of the interviews in 1980–81, and Letitia W. Brown had conducted the remainder in 1973–74.
4. Thomas C. Hubka, *Houses without Names: Architectural Nomenclature and the*

Classification of America's Common Houses (Knoxville: University of Tennessee Press, 2013), 37. In her study of builders in late-nineteenth-century Washington, Melissa McLoud, "Craftsmen and Entrepreneurs: Builders in Late Nineteenth-Century Washington, D.C." (Ph.D. diss., George Washington University, 1988), 170, likewise identified the origin of the design of a row house in the constants, followed by the application of ornament. Zachary J. Violette, *The Decorated Tenement: How Immigrant Builders and Architects Transformed the Slum in the Gilded Age* (Minneapolis: University of Minnesota Press, 2019), 23, illuminated the application of ornament, in defiance of reformers' examples, by immigrant builders. Charlotte V. Brown, "The Advance in Industrial Enterprise: Building with the New Technology, 1865–1900," in *Architects and Builders in North Carolina: A History of the Practice of Building,* by Catherine W. Bishir, Charlotte V. Brown, Carl R. Lounsbury, and Ernest H. Wood III (Chapel Hill: University of North Carolina Press, 1990), 265, also noted the importance of the contractor to the design process, calling him "an arbiter of taste."

5. Robert H. Harkness, "The Old Glass-House," *RCHS* 18 (1915): 218. Constance McLaughlin Green, *Washington: A History of the Capital, 1800–1950* (Princeton: Princeton University Press, 1962), 1:192. Stilson Hutchins and Joseph West Moore, *The Nation's Capital: Past and Present* (Washington, DC: Post, 1885), 311. City Directory (1887). "Building Construction," *WP* June 12, 1912, p. 76. "See Fall Activity," *ES* August 17, 1910, p. 10. "Building Construction," *WP* June 12, 1912, p. 76.
6. Henry Glassie, *Folk Housing in Middle Virginia: A Structural Analysis of Historic Artifacts* (Knoxville: University of Tennessee Press, 1975), 91.
7. A. J. Downing, *The Architecture of Country Houses* (New York: Dover, 1969; orig. pub., 1850). "New Washington," *Harper's New Monthly Magazine* 50, no. 297 (February 1875): 320.
8. James M. Goode, *Capital Losses: A Cultural History of Washington's Destroyed Buildings* (Washington, DC: Smithsonian Institution Press, 1979), 183–85. Julie Nicoletta, "1318 Vermont Avenue, NW (Mary McLeod Bethune House)," HABS, LC, 1993.
9. The approximate totals: in 1885, 1,300 row houses constructed; 1886, 1,000; 1887, 900; 1888, 850; 1889, 1,050; 1890, 1,300; 1891, 1,290; and 1892, 2,000. The annual total did not reach 1,000 again until 1908. Permits Database Reports.
10. *Building Regulations* (1882), 17, stated that wooden bays could be only one story. Hutchins and Moore, *Nation's Capital,* 311. "A Glimpse of Some Washington Homes," *Harper's New Monthly Magazine* 70 (March 1885): 520.
11. *Building Regulations* (1877), 30.
12. E. C. Gardner, "Washington Architecture: The Congressman and the Architect Continue the Discussion, IV," *ES* January 15, 1887, p. 2.
13. Ads, *ES* January 1, 1910, p. 17, and January 3, 1910, p. 15.
14. Federal Writers' Project, Works Progress Administration, *Washington: City and Capital* (Washington, DC: GPO, 1937), 110.
15. Deed 192402140228, February 14, 1924, Wardman and Bones to Arthur L. and Jessie M. Buckman, Lot 16, Square 2098.
16. "Home to Typify English Village," *ES* January 28, 1922, p. 12. Wardman also traveled to England once a year. Sally Lichtenstein Berk, "The Richest Crop: The Row Houses of Harry Wardman (1869–1938), Washington, D.C. Developer" (M.A. thesis, George Washington University, 1988), chap. 1, p. 14.

17. Berk, "The Richest Crop," chap. 7, p. 8. Email communication with Caroline Mesrobian Hickman, March 25, 2020. "Homes to Typify English Village," *ES* January 28, 1922, p. 12. "6 New Tracy Place Residences Ready," *WP* September 10, 1922, p. 43. Ads, *ES* November 4, 1924, p. 16, and June 4, 1924, p. 3.
18. Wall Reports Book 68, p. 90, June 16, 1922, DC Surveyors Office. The lots were 190 feet deep with garages on the alley. On the north side of Klingle, which had shorter lots in places and a favorable topography, garages were placed in basements with access off the alley.
19. Boss and Phelps, "Foxhall Village: A Village in the City," brochure, 1927. "Quick Development of Foxhall Village Attracts Comment," *WP* June 26, 1927, p. R2.
20. Eve L. Barsoum, "Glover-Archbold Park: Registration Form" (National Register of Historic Places, 2006). Goode, *Capital Losses,* 10–11, 119–21.
21. Richard Conn, "Foxhall Community at Half Century: A Fond Look Backwards" (Foxhall Community Citizens Association brochure, 1979), 3. Elizabeth Breiseth, Laura Trieschmann, Ellen Jenkins, and Janet Flynn, "Foxhall Village Historic District: Registration Form" (National Register of Historic Places, 2007), sec. 8, p. 20. DC Architects Directory; see Note on Sources. James M. Goode, *Best Addresses: A Century of Washington's Distinguished Apartment Houses* (Washington, DC: Smithsonian Institution Press, 1988), 290–92.
22. "Greenwich Parkway OK'd," *ES* March 12, 1926, p. 9. "Homes in Foxhall Village Embody Many Features of Unusual Architecture," *ES* September 3, 1927, p. 13.
23. "Homes in Foxhall Village Embody Many Features," p. 13. Breiseth et al., "Foxhall Village," sec. 8, p. 28.
24. Conn, "Foxhall Community," 17, 19. In 1932 Boss and Phelps began developing land north of Reservoir Road, where they built detached houses in a Colonial Revival style and named it Colony Village.
25. Conn, "Foxhall Community," 7, 13. Ad, *ES* December 19, 1925, p. 7, described the Reservoir Road houses as "priced $9,100 and up." Permit #10172, May 7, 1925, for 30 houses at 4450–78 Reservoir Road and 4451–79 Dent Place; the Dent Place houses were not built on this permit (see Permit #2328 September 1, 1925). The estimated cost of construction of the Reservoir Road houses was $6,000 each. "Columns of Steel in Foxhall Homes," *WP* July 7, 1929, p. R2. Permit #118815, November 2, 1928, for 5 houses at 1800–04 Forty-Fourth Street and 4401–03 Greenwich Parkway. The estimated cost of construction for these houses was $10,000 each. A third developer, Cooper Lightbrown and Son, built 6 Tudor Revival row houses at Foxhall Road and P Street in 1933. Breiseth et al., "Foxhall Village," sec. 7, p. 2.
26. Boss and Phelps, "Foxhall Village."
27. "Foxhall Village Group Homes Are Distinctive," *ES* September 28, 1929, p. 13. "Foxhall Village Homes Opened by Boss and Phelps," *WP* October 4, 1925, p. R5. Elizabeth Meacham Robertson, "Foxhall, Beautiful Village, Is Built on Historic Farm," *WP* April 28, 1929, p. R1. Portions of this article were repeated in a Boss and Phelps brochure, "A Thing of Beauty Is a Joy Forever," ca. 1930, in MLK vertical files. In recent decades "group house" has taken on another meaning, that of unrelated adults living together.
28. Ad, *WP* October 17, 1926, p. R8; brochure, 1930; and ad in National Theatre program, 1931, all posted on website gloverparkhistory.com, accessed April 2, 2020. Ads, *ES* December 31, 1924, p. 28, and *ES* January 27, 1925, p. 32.
29. One exception is the Art Deco row at 1331–37 Huidekoper Place NW, built in 1937.

30. "Shop Talk," *ES* November 2, 1940, p. 24. "Modern Row Houses," *Architectural Forum* 75, no. 1 (July 1941): 68–69. 4116–36 Arkansas Avenue NW: Permit #229400, 1940, reel 624. DC Architects Directory. Many of the front porches have been enclosed.
31. "5,000 Visit Model Home in First Month," *WP* November 24, 1940, p. R4. 4100–14 Arkansas Avenue: Permit #241104, 1941, reel 642; 4020 Arkansas: Permit #244971, reel 648. Ads, *ES* November 30, 1940, p. 21; June 23, 1941, p. 45; November 9, 1940, p. 23; November 24, 1940, p. R5; October 26, 1940, p. 21. "Modern Row Houses," 68.
32. Permit #261642, 1943, reel 694. Shapiro, Inc., is the same development firm that the U.S. Senate accused of price gouging in the 1920s, as described in chapter 5. Here, when Shapiro was prevented by the Rent Control Administration from charging $100 a month rent, Shapiro demanded the entire year's rent payment in advance. The Rent Control Administration disallowed this. "31 New Houses Made Available on Basis of Year Advance Rent," *WP* February 22, 1944, p. 4. "D.C. Landlords Warned on Excess Advance Rents," *ES* April 4, 1944, p. 14. Joseph H. Abel and Fred N. Severud, *Apartment Houses* (New York: Reinhold, 1947), 77. Another example of a modernist group is the "community houses" (i.e., a row of three) at 3626–30 Jenifer Street NW, built in 1952.
33. Cameron Logan, *Historic Capital: Preservation, Race, and Real Estate in Washington, D.C.* (Minneapolis: University of Minnesota Press, 2017), 42–48, also discusses the relationship of colonial architecture to preservation, particularly in Georgetown.
34. Eve L. Barsoum, "Colonial Georgetown: The Power of Myth," *Re-creating the American Past: Essays on the Colonial Revival,* ed. Richard Guy Wilson, Shaun Eyring, and Kenny Marotta (Charlottesville: University of Virginia Press, 2006), 183–95. Fiske Kimball's "restoration" of Dumbarton House was particularly aggressive. Harold Donaldson Eberlein and Cortlandt van Dyke Hubbard, *Historic Houses of George-Town and Washington City* (Richmond: Dietz Press, 1958), 164, described Evermay's late-nineteenth-century alterations as a "misguided 'transmogrification'" of the house and applauded its rescue from its "ignominious, nightmare plight."
35. A 1993 survey found that only 5 percent of Georgetown's buildings were constructed before 1830. Most, 39 percent, were built between 1870 and 1900, and another third between 1900 and 1950. Barsoum, "Colonial Georgetown," 181. Although it could be argued that the percentages may have been wildly different in the 1920s, the establishment of a historic district in 1950 would have slowed down, if not completely impeded, demolitions of the older building stock. Christine Sadler, "Georgetown 'Discovered' in World War Days," *WP* October 30, 1939, p. 15. Robert J. Lewis, "Washington's Restoration Areas: IV, Georgetown," *ES* December 31, 1960, pp. 13–14. Johanna Bockman, "Restoration That Is Neither Historical nor Preserving: The Case of Capitol Hill in the 1940s and 1950s," paper presented at the D.C. Historical Studies Conference, November 13, 2020, suggests that "restoration" actually referred to the restoration of the Southern Confederacy. She tracked residents of a block on Capitol Hill with ties to a "Tidewater aristocracy." She also posits that this meaning of "restoration" accounted for the name of the Capitol Hill Restoration Society.
36. William A. Millen, "Condemned Slums in Georgetown Alley Goes High Hat as Pomander Walk," *ES* September 14, 1951, p. 38. Kathleen Menzie Lesko, Valerie Babb, and Carroll R. Gibbs, *Black Georgetown Remembered: A History of the Black*

Community in the Founding of "The Town of George" in 1751 to the Present Day (Washington, DC: Georgetown University Press, 2016), 82–89. See Rebecca Summer, "The Urban Alley: A Hidden Landscape of Social Change in Washington, D.C." (Ph.D. diss., University of Wisconsin–Madison, 2019). Federal Writers' Project, *Washington,* 714. Lewis, "Georgetown," 13.

37. Robert J. Lewis, "Washington's Restoration Areas: III, Capitol Hill," *ES* November 19, 1960, pp. 25.

38. Robert J. Lewis, "Movement to Reclaim Older Dwellings on Capitol Hill Is Gathering Momentum," *ES* September 17, 1949, p. 26. Lewis, "Capitol Hill," 35. Logan, *Historic Capital,* 51–63, discusses house tours as an indication of preservation interest; Capitol Hill's first house tour was in 1951. Dennis Earl Gale, "Restoration in Georgetown, Washington, D.C." (Ph.D. diss., George Washington University, 1982), 128. Robert J. Lewis, "The Neat and Orderly Colonial Façade," *ES* April 23, 1960, p. D1. The shutters on all three houses have since been removed.

39. Eileen Summers, "'Do It Yourself' Owners Show Homes," *WPTH,* May 21, 1956, p. 24.

40. Isabelle Shelton, "Foggy Bottom Area Gets Face-Lifting," *SS* November 8, 1953, p. 91. "Private Owners Reclaiming Neighborhood Once Known as Capitol Hill 'Slum,'" *ES* August 23, 1947, p. 14. "Owners Who Reclaimed Blighted Area Seek Street Status for Neighborhood," *ES* October 29, 1949, p. 22. Beth Purcell, "Terrace Court, NE, Outdoor Mini Tour," handout, Capitol Hill Restoration Society House and Garden Tour, 2017.

41. "Report of the Chronicler for 1953," *RCHS* 55/56 (1953–56): 398. Kim Prothro Williams, *The DC Historic Alley Buildings Survey* (DC Office of Planning, 2014), 9, 27. "Group Fights City Threat to Close Up Alley Homes," *WP* September 16, 1953, p. 25.

42. Henry H. Glassie, "Victorian Homes in Washington," *RCHS* 63–65 (1963–65): 320–65. Henry Glassie was a lawyer with an interest in Victorian houses and Washington art; his son, with the same name, is a renowned folklorist. Logan, *Historic Capital,* 62. John B. Willmann, "A Brooklynite Gets His Kicks in Old Houses," *WP* October 19, 1974, p. E1.

43. "New Town Houses on Capitol Hill," *ES* November 5, 1965, p. D2. "9 in a Row Built, Sold, on 'Hill,'" *WPTH,* November 6, 1965, p. E13. Also building new Colonial row houses on Capitol Hill in the early 1960s were the Robitschers, who had begun rehabbing houses in Foggy Bottom in the early 1950s. "New Town Houses on Capitol Hill," *WPTH* April 18, 1964, p. E5.

44. J. B. Willmann, "Linde Builds Them New on the 'Hill,'" *WPTH* September 30, 1967, p. C1. The respective addresses are 1700 block Corcoran Street; Macarthur Boulevard and Arizona Avenue; 3900 block Watson Place; and Sixteenth and Irving Streets. Willmann, "Brooklynite Gets His Kicks," p. E1. J. B. Willmann, "Young Couples Take to the 'Hill,'" *WPTH* April 25, 1970, p. D1.

45. Stephanie Cavanaugh, "Barrett Linde, Still Ahead of a Trend," *WP* March 30, 2002, p. H5. Sarah Booth Conroy, "The Fake Federals," *WP* October 3, 1972, p. E2.

46. Vernon Loeb, "Drawing Out the Soul of a Community," *WP* May 30, 1996, p. DC1.

47. Occasionally the facade is misleading. A case in point is the row houses at 144–48 North Carolina Avenue SE, built in 1910 by H. R. Howenstein. The facade is "colonial," leading one to assume a quadrant plan, but the plan is a side hall with a back building. Permit #713, August 9, 1910.

4. Health and Comfort

1. See Melanie A. Kiechle, *Smell Detectives: An Olfactory History of Nineteenth-Century Urban America* (Seattle: University of Washington Press, 2017), for an overview of health threats carried by air and signified by odors.
2. "Latest Intelligence," *New York Daily Times,* March 20, 1857, p. 1, cited in Ruth D. Reichard, "A 'National Distemper': The National Hotel Sickness of 1857, Public Health and Sanitation, and the Limits of Rationality," *Journal of Planning History* 15, no. 3 (2016): 176.
3. Herbert Winslow Hill, *The New Public Health* (New York: Macmillan, 1920; orig. pub., 1916), 9.
4. Brian D. Crane, "Filth, Garbage, and Rubbish: Refuse Disposal, Sanitary Reform, and Nineteenth-Century Yard Deposits in Washington, D.C.," *Historical Archaeology* 34, no. 1 (2000): 21–22. "Report of the Health Officer," *Annual Report of the Commissioners for the District of Columbia* (Washington, DC: GPO, 1878), 87. Annmarie Adams, *Architecture in the Family Way: Doctors, Houses, and Women, 1870–1890* (Montreal: McGill-Queen's University Press, 1996), 30. Kiechle, *Smell Detectives,* 78–81.

   In 1866 an article in *Harper's New Monthly Magazine* held that exhalations consisted of carbonic acid (i.e., carbon dioxide), which, if "taken undiluted into the lungs . . . is a fatal poison, causing death." "The American People Starved and Poisoned," *Harper's New Monthly Magazine* 32 (May 1866): 762. Nearly thirty years later, noted sanitarian Dr. John S. Billings argued that defective ventilation caused fatalities by forcing people to breathe "air contaminated with organic products thrown off by the lungs and skin." Not only was exhalation bad, in terms of producing carbon dioxide, but it could transmit disease, especially pulmonary tuberculosis. John S. Billings, *Ventilation and Heating* (New York: Engineering Record, 1893), 19–20.

   Not every room in a house got a window. The 1872 building regulations required windows on the front and back of a row house, which would have provided adequate light and air to houses that were two rooms deep. *Building Regulations* (1872), 20. The requirement was repeated in the 1877 regulations but then dropped for the next twenty years. In 1897 the building inspector attempted to ensure adequate ventilation for row houses that were three rooms deep by specifying the size of the opening between un-windowed rooms and those with windows. For an interior room, the opening into an adjacent room, which had to have either a window or a ventilating skylight, had to be at least one-tenth of the square footage of the windowless room. "New Building Laws," *ES* June 20, 1897, p. 1.
5. Robert R. Hershman, "Gas in Washington," *RCHS* 50 (1948/1950): 148, 153. Sarah Pressey Noreen, *Public Street Illumination in Washington, D.C.: An Illustrated History* (Washington, DC: George Washington University, 1975), 11. "Light for the City," *WP* February 13, 1896, p. 4. William O. Beck, *100 Years of Matchless Service: Potomac Electric Power Company, 1896–1996* (privately printed, 1996), 35. James A. Gannon Sr., "Washington at the Turn of the Century," *RCHS* 1963–65: 315. Initially the light produced by gas lamps was quite dim, but the adoption of the Welsbach mantle in the late 1880s increased the candlepower from 7 to 250. Electric lights available in the 1920s had a candlepower of 1,500. David E. Nye, *Electrifying America: Social Meanings of a New Technology, 1880–1940* (Cambridge,

Mass.: MIT Press, 1990), 17. Or, as stated by Robert J. Gordon, *The Rise and Fall of American Growth: The U.S. Standard of Living since the Civil War* (Princeton: Princeton University Press, 2016), 118: "The initial electric lamps were about three times brighter than the brightest kerosene lamps, but by 1920, improvements in the metal filaments made them ten times brighter than kerosene." As a contemporary expert, Dr. B. W. Richardson, wrote, "Lamps, candles, and gaslights, rob the air of a part of its vital constituent, and supply in return products which are really injurious to life. Gaslight is in this respect the most hurtful." B. W. Richardson, "Health at Home," *Appleton's Journal: A Magazine of General Literature,* no. 48 (April 1880): 313.

6. "American People Starved and Poisoned," 762. In Britain, stoves were widely rejected in favor of open fires, due to their ventilating capability. Stephen Mosley, "Fresh Air and Foul: The Role of the Open Fireplace in Ventilating the British Home, 1837–1910," *Planning Perspectives* 18 (2003): 19. Billings claimed that while Americans preferred a room temperature of 68 to 70 degrees F., the British accepted a room temperature of 60 degrees F., so that "open fireplaces and grates can therefore be used there more extensively than here." Billings, *Heating and Ventilation,* 23. Although the dangers of the closed stove were widely publicized, no stove could be truly "closed," since it needed to draw oxygen to feed the fire. Advice givers recommended additional registers and flues in the room to assure the free flow of air. "American People Starved and Poisoned," 771.
7. Thirty-eight springs existed in the District. In 1865 there were 1,400 public wells. Julie D. Abell and Peter D. Glumac, "Beneath the MCI Center: Insights into Washington's Historic Water Supply," *WH* 9, no. 1 (Spring/Summer 1997): 26, 29. This article traces the persistent use of private wells and cisterns even after the introduction of a public water supply. Harry C. Ways, *The Washington Aqueduct, 1852–1992* (privately printed, 1996[?]), 5, 29. Major J. D. Arthur, "Water Supply System," in *Planning and Building the City of Washington,* ed. Frederick Haynes Newell (Washington Society of Engineers, privately printed, 1952), 131.
8. Thomas W. Symons, "Report of the Engineer," *Annual Report of the Board of Commissioners for the District of Columbia* (Washington, DC: GPO, 1887), 502, 491. Arthur, "Water Supply System," 131. When the reservoir was temporarily drained and water was piped directly from the river into people's homes, the engineer noted that "the water was much more than usually turbid, a condition which gave rise to considerable complaint." "Report of the Engineer," *Annual Report of the Board of Commissioners for the District of Columbia* (Washington, DC: GPO, 1890), 416. Gannon, "Washington at the Turn of the Century," 314.
9. "Report of the Water-Registrar," *Annual Report of the Board of Commissioners for the District of Columbia* (Washington, DC: GPO, 1876), 85–86. "Report of the Engineer," *Annual Report of the Board of Commissioners for the District of Columbia* (Washington, DC: GPO, 1886), 473. "Report of the Engineer" (1887), 483.
10. *Annual Report of the Commissioners of the District of Columbia* (Washington: GPO, 1879), 6. Timothy Lubey, "Report of the Water-Registrar," *Annual Report of the Commissioners of the District of Columbia* (1875), 264, 267. The next year Lubey blamed a particular design of toilet, the Hopper Water Closet, in which "the water is turned on in general by turning a crank, whereupon the water runs until turned off." There were 16,137 of this style of water closet in people's homes. "Report of the Water-Registrar" (1876), 84. But seven years later Samuel A. Robinson, the inspec-

tor of plumbing, thought Hopper water closets were far preferable to valve closets. Robinson, "Report of the Inspector of Plumbing," *Annual Report of the Board of Commissioners for the District of Columbia* (Washington, DC: GPO, 1883), 308. "To Buy Water Meters," *WP* July 15, 1906, p. 16. U.S. Department of the Interior, Census Office, *Report on the Social Statistics of Cities in the United States at the Eleventh Census: 1890,* ed. John S. Billings (Washington, DC: GPO, 1895), 33, 29. Average consumption of water in cities across the country was 90 gallons per person per day (24).

11. J. P. Noyes, "Our Water Question," *WP* August 10, 1903, p. 9. "The District Water Supply," *ES* November 28, 1890, p. 1. The death rate per 100,000 people before filtration was 79, dropping to 48 after filtration, and to 7 after chlorination. Arthur, "Water Supply System," 136. John Gaub, "Some Relations between the Water Supply and Typhoid Fever in Washington, D.C.," *Journal of the American Water Works Association* 1, no. 4 (December 1914): 728, cites the deaths per 100,000 as 74.0 in 1900 and 33.1 in 1907. He attributed the drop to 16.2 in 1913 to "the fly campaign" (733). See also Alexandra M. Lord, "Dangerous Waters: On the Trail of Typhoid in Washington, D.C.," *WH* 30, no. 2 (Fall 2018): 57–65.
12. George Preston Brown, *Sewer-Gas and Its Dangers* (Chicago: Jansen, McClurg, 1881), 17. This is not to be confused with sewer gas that accumulates in unventilated pipes and has the potential to explode. Philip A. McCombs, "Sewer Gas Danger Found in Suburbs," *WP* September 13, 1972, p. B1.
13. Wm. Paul Gerhard, *House-Drainage and Sanitary Plumbing* (New York: D. Van Nostrand, 1882), 123. Brown, *Sewer-Gas,* 220–21.
14. E. C. Gardner, *The House That Jill Built, after Jack's Had Proved a Failure* (Springfield, Mass.: W. F. Adams, 1896; orig. pub., 1882), 177. Gerhard, *House-Drainage,* 121.
15. *Building Regulations* (1872), 14. The 1872 regulations also permitted a ventilating flue instead of a window, but this provision was omitted from the 1877 and subsequent regulations.
16. Smith Townsend, "Report of the Health Officer," *Annual Report of the Commissioners for the District of Columbia* (Washington, DC: GPO, 1879), 160. *Building Regulations* (1877), 28. *Building Regulations* (1902), 91.
17. Appropriations for culverts and arches in the streets, beginning in 1810, indicated efforts to channel stormwater through intersections; these constructions were eventually consolidated into closed conduits, which fed into the canal and other waterways. J. B. Gordon, "Drainage and Sewerage," in Newell, *Planning and Building,* 141. Household sewage was expressly forbidden from using this system. Green, *Washington,* 1:212, 255. It is not clear when this policy changed.
18. William M. Maury, *Alexander "Boss" Shepherd and the Board of Public Works* (Washington, DC: George Washington University, 1975), 31. Howard Gillette Jr., *Between Justice and Beauty: Race, Planning, and the Failure of Urban Policy in Washington, D.C.* (Baltimore: Johns Hopkins University Press, 1995), 73. *New York Times,* December 4, 1872, p. 2, cited in John W. Reps, *Washington on View: The Nation's Capital since 1790* (Chapel Hill: University of North Carolina Press, 1991), 190. By the end of the 1870s, sewers in Georgetown and Northwest Washington emptied into Rock Creek, eastern and southern Washington into James Creek and then into the Eastern Branch, and the central city into the "B Street Main," which

was the intercepting sewer adjacent to the former canal. Green, *Washington,* 2: 43, 45. Much of the latter flowed west into the Potomac River, where it was deposited on tidal flats. "Official Supervision of Plumbing in Washington," *Sanitary Engineer* 7, no. 1 (December 7, 1882): Supplement 1. "Official Supervision of Plumbing," 1. New York and Brooklyn adopted plumbing regulations a few months after Washington. In 1890 Congress authorized a review of the city's sewer system, calling on three eminent sanitarians. The report recommended construction of intercepting sewers and trunk lines, whose implementation was slowed by erratic congressional appropriations, and disposition of the sewage farther downstream. In 1907 the city opened a pumping station at the foot of New Jersey Avenue near the Navy Yard to pump sewage across the Eastern Branch and south three miles to deep water in the Potomac across from Alexandria, which was, the 1890 report asserted, "so far from the city that it can not return on the flood tide." "The Sewerage of the City," *ES* July 18, 1890, p. 2. The city finally began construction of a sewage treatment plant in 1935.

19. Ad, *ES,* April 26, 1909, p. 3. Jonathan K. Allen, *Sanitation in the Modern Home* (Chicago: Domestic Engineering, 1907), 61. F. F. Westbrook, "Some of the Effects of Sunlight on Tetanus Cultures," *Journal of Pathology and Bacteriology* 3 (1896): 70. H. L. Seymour, "Sunlight Engineering in Relation to Housing and Town Planning," *Journal of the Royal Astronomical Society of Canada* 14, no. 4 (May 1920): 130.
20. "Building Operations," *ES* August 14, 1905, p. 2. "Ventilation Discussed," *ES* August 14, 1905, p. 2. "More Air," *ES* July 15, 1905, p. 4.
21. The real estate agent predicted in 1906 that "these attic-effect houses will become a decided feature of Washington before long." "In Past and Future," *SS* April 8, 1906, pt. 7, p. 4. C. M. D'Enville, "Sleeping Outdoors for Health," *Country Life in America* 16 (May 1909): 43.
22. Ad, *ES* December 17, 1910, pt. 2 p. 1. Similarly, Middaugh and Shannon advertised "Homes of Sunlight and Ventilation" *ES* November 6, 1911, p. 3.
23. The fixed bathtub relied on piped hot water, which saw its own advances in the early twentieth century. Coal-fired cookstoves often included chambers in which to heat water, which was stored in an adjacent boiler. The arrival of gas in the home meant that it could heat water directly, and hot water in the bathtub no longer relied on a fire going in the kitchen cookstove. Alison K. Hoagland, *The Bathroom: A Social History of Cleanliness and the Body* (Santa Barbara, Calif.: Greenwood Press, 2018), 36–37. "Bathtubs in New Houses," *WP* June 13, 1907, p. E1. "More and Larger Bathrooms," *ES* May 23, 1909, p. 26. Baltimore had required bathtubs in new houses twenty years earlier. "Bathing in the Falls," *Baltimore Sun,* July 25, 1888, p. 4.
24. *Building Regulations* (1909), 61. Shannon and Luchs, "The Home of Fulfillment" (brochure, 1909).
25. Irwin Hood (Ike) Hoover, *Forty-Two Years in the White House* (Boston: Houghton Mifflin, 1934), 7, recalls President Benjamin Harrison's family's reluctance in 1889 to use the electricity that had been newly installed in the White House. "Rose by Magic's Wand," *WP* December 7, 1890, p. 5. Beck, *100 Years of Matchless Service,* 3. John DeFerrari, *Capital Streetcars: Early Mass Transit in Washington, D.C.* (Charleston, S.C.: History Press, 2015), 84–93. John DeFerrari, "Electricity, Streetcars, and the Transformation of Washington, D.C., 1880–1900," presentation given at 42nd Annual Conference on D. C. Historical Studies, November 12–15, 2015.

26. Green, *Washington,* 2:50.

27. "Regulations for Electric Wiring," *ES* June 21, 1897, p. 2. Jordan Wankoff, "Potomac Electric Power Company," *International Directory of Company Histories,* ed. Paula Kepos (Detroit: St. James Press, 1992) 6: 552. "Where the Company and Its Customers Meet," *Enlightened Homes* [publication of the Potomac Electric Power Company] 1, no. 3 (November 1929): inside front cover. The growth from 1910 to 1930 is consistent with national trends. Nye, *Electrifying America,* 23, 239. In 1915 Potomac Electric reduced rates substantially from 10 cents per kwh for the first 120 kwh per month, then 5 cents per kwh, to 10 cents per kwh for the first 10 kwh, then 3 cents per kwh. "Lower Rates for Electricity," *WP* December 5, 1915, p. E9. Mara Cherkasky and Phylicia Fauntleroy Bowman, *The First 100 Years: Protecting the Public Interest, 1913–2013: The Public Service Commission of the District of Columbia* (privately printed, 2016), 99. By 1940, 96 percent of Washington dwellings had electric lighting and 78 percent had a refrigerator, although only 3 percent had electric ranges. Bureau of the Census, *Housing,* 457, 458. "For a New Year of Convenience," *Enlightened Homes* 2, no. 1 (January 1930): 12–13. Potomac Electric Company ad, *WP* October 21, 1916, p. 5.

28. "Arthur F. Carroll," *WP* June 12, 1912, p. L82. Ad, *WP* October 21, 1916, p. 5. Ad, *ES,* February 12, 1924, p. 17.

29. Gannon, "Washington at the Turn of the Century," 316, describes the hot-air system: "A coal pile in the corner [of the basement] supplied the furnace which sent heat to the open hot air ventilators throughout the house." Ruth Schwartz Cowan, *More Work for Mother: The Ironies of Household Technology from the Open Hearth to the Microwave* (New York: Basic Books, 1983), 96. By 1940 nearly 88 percent of Washington's dwellings had some form of central heat. Bureau of the Census, *Housing,* 458.

30. Ellen H. Richards, *The Cost of Shelter* (New York: J. Wiley and Sons, 1905), 96. Thomas C. Hubka, *How the Working-Class Home Became Modern, 1900–1940* (Minneapolis: University of Minnesota Press, 2020), 179, discusses the house size reduction theory. 2613–31 Sherman Avenue, 2603–11 Sherman Avenue, 915–19 Euclid Street, and 776–80 Fairmont Avenue NW, Permits #167, July 10, 1911, and #1009, August 22, 1911. "Buy on Sherman Ave.," *WP* October 20, 1918, p. RE2.

31. Permit #868, October 16, 1891. Ad, *ES* September 7, 1892, p. 2. Ad, *WP* December 1, 1914, p. 13. Permit #1608, September 23, 1912. Real Estate Trust Co. built eight houses with central heating and electric lighting at a cost of less than $2,200 each. The "low-down tank" on the toilet was a recent innovation, contrasting with the raised water tank with pull chain.

32. Ad, *ES* June 26, 1926, Model Homes Section, 33. U.S. Manuscript Census, 1900. U.S. Department of the Interior, Census Office, *Report on the Social Statistics of Cities,* comp. George E. Waring Jr. (Washington, DC: GPO, 1887), 52. In 1880 there were 299 servants per 1,000 families in Washington, falling to 152 in 1920. David M. Katzman, *Seven Days a Week: Women and Domestic Service in Industrializing America* (New York: Oxford University Press, 1978), 61. See the classic work on the subject of domestic labor, Ruth Schwartz Cowan, *More Work for Mother,* cited in note 29 above. Hubka, *How the Working-Class Home,* 191–94, questions Schwartz Cowan's thesis, arguing that working-class residents never had servants and the housewife performed all the domestic chores, so the introduction of electricity and other amenities was truly transformational for her. Mary Z. Gray, *301 East*

Capitol: Tales from the Heart of the Hill (privately printed, 2013), 79, who grew up on Capitol Hill in the 1920s, recalled a washerwoman who transported the laundry on a squeaky baby carriage: "The carriage was piled high with sun-bleached sweet-smelling white linens, ironed and nearly folded. She dropped them off at Granny's, and picked up the soiled batch to take away."

33. Nye, *Electrifying America,* 240, 253.
34. "More Windowless Bathrooms Permitted without Hearing," *ES* February 6, 1952. Before this action, regulations permitted windowless bathrooms with mechanical ventilation in buildings greater than five stories tall. Windowless bathrooms were permitted in apartment buildings in 1946. "D.C. Refuses to Amend Code to Reduce Size of Kitchens," *ES* May 28, 1946, p. 22. "'Windowless' Baths Allowed," *WPTH* December 12, 1954, reported a "recent" FHA ruling. "Ruling Eases Bathroom Curbs," *WP* July 19, 1957, p. A18. If a bathroom had no window, it had to have "an electrical tie-in to the light switch that automatically turns on the ventilation when the room is in use." "Changes Approved in Plumbing Code," *ES* July 19, 1957, p. 21.
35. "Housewives Oppose Windowless Kitchens," *WP* January 29, 1952, p. B1. "Windowless Kitchens," *WP* February 3, 1952, p. B4. The primary concern of the Health Department was that the windowless kitchen not be repurposed as a habitable room, so the regulations restricted its size. "Kitchens without Windows Approved after Four Additions to Building Code," *WP* October 24, 1956, p. A1.
36. "D.C. Refuses to Amend Code to Reduce Size of Kitchens," *ES* May 28, 1946, p. 22. Joseph H. Abel and Fred N. Severud, *Apartment Houses* (New York: Reinhold, 1947), 37, 38. "Windowless Kitchens," *WPTH,* October 1, 1956, p. 24.
37. Tilton: Permits #496, October 24, 1881, and #729, January 21, 1882. Price: Permit #452, September 16, 1893. Walker: Permit #1811, March 3, 1879. "Believes High Fences Should Be Eliminated," *ES* March 20, 1915, pt. 2, p. 2.
38. Raymond Arsenault, "The End of the Long Hot Summer: The Air Conditioner and Southern Culture," *Journal of Southern History* 50, no. 4 (November 1984): 611, 610.
39. Martha Hamilton, "D.C. without A.C.? Life Here Would Be Positively B.C.," *WP* June 16, 1994, p. A10. Nicola Twilley, "Home Smog," *New Yorker,* April 8, 2019, p. 34. The COVID pandemic also drew attention to the benefits of ventilation. An expert advised, "Increase fresh air exchange whatever way you can. . . . If it's feasible, open the windows, even for a short amount of time." Elisabeth Kwak-Hefferan, *NYT* November 29, 2020, p. D9.

5. Building and Selling

1. Melissa McLoud, "Craftsmen and Entrepreneurs: Builders in Late Nineteenth-Century Washington, D.C." (Ph.D. diss., George Washington University, 1988), 40.
2. John Hitz, "Homes for the People in the City of Washington," *Journal of Social Science* 15 (1882): 137. Constance McLaughlin Green, *Washington: A History of the Capital, 1800–1950* (Princeton: Princeton University Press, 1962), 2:27, based on census of manufactures.
3. McLoud, "Craftsmen and Entrepreneurs," xii.
4. McLoud, "Craftsmen and Entrepreneurs," 127–30, 259–63. "Wants," *ES* April 27, 1864, p. 2. Permits Database Report; see Note on Sources. In the 1880s, Gessford built only five buildings that were not dwellings: a church, a warehouse, and three

stables (as well as some combination stores and dwellings). Of the single (non-speculative) houses he built, 7 were for clients and 12 were for himself. Some of these were quite grand, such as the $7,000 house at 638 E. Capitol Street for Isaac Childs in 1889, or the Appleton P. Clark Jr.–designed house for George P. Zurhorst at 203 Third Street SE in 1890. In neighborhoods other than Capitol Hill, in the 1880s Gessford built 10 projects: 5 sets of row houses and 5 single houses. His success enabled him to invest in other ventures, including a bank and a grate, mantel, and tile business. "The Capital Trust Co.," *ES* March 14, 1891, p. 1. "A Dissolution of Partnership Wanted," *ES* September 18, 1893, p. 7. Gessford died in 1894 at the age of sixty-three. "Died," *ES* February 2, 1894, p. 5.

5. Permit #1337, 1889, reel 123. Permit #42, 1893, reel 178. For information on Brent, see Betty Bird, "Interim Report: Thematic Study of African American Architects and Builders in Washington, DC," Phase II (1994), vol. 2. McLoud, "Craftsmen and Entrepreneurs," 133–38, discusses other African American builders of row houses.
6. McLoud, "Craftsmen and Entrepreneurs," 62, xiv, 90. Permits Database Report.
7. DC Commissioners began regulating wall thickness in 1795. Cellar walls had to be 18 inches thick, and upper-story walls 9 inches thick, but thicker if the building was more than one story tall. Washington, D.C., Office of the Superintendent of the City of Washington, *Regulations of Building, Etc.* (1815), 7–8, Regulation no. 3, July 20, 1795. Regulations also required wrought iron straps to anchor the beams and joists into the brick walls. *Building Regulations* (1872), 9–10. Harry Wardman ad for row houses with "steel-girded reinforced construction," ES May 23, 1908, pt. 2, p. 1. Harry Kite ad for row houses with "high-grade reinforced steel construction," ES November 22, 1913, pt. 2, p. 1. My thanks to David Haresign and his colleagues at Bonstra Haresign Architects for clarifying some of these issues for me.
8. John Clagett Proctor, ed., *Washington, Past and Present: A History* (New York: Lewis Historical, 1930), 2: 869. Quotation from Walter Galenson, *The United Brotherhood of Carpenters: The First Hundred Years* (Cambridge, Mass.: Harvard University Press, 1983), 18. Organization of the United Brotherhood of Carpenters resulted in the daily wage growing from $1.50 to $2.00 before unionization in 1881, to $2.50 afterward, to $3.00 by 1891. "For Sale," *ES* August 20, 1889, p. 3.
9. Adam Constanzo, *George Washington's Washington: Visions for the National Capital in the Early American Republic* (Athens: University of Georgia Press, 2018), 56. The experience of a Black brick contractor is mentioned in "The Center Market Investigation," *ES* July 21, 1871, p. 4, and discussed in Helen Tangires, "Adolf Cluss and Public Market Reform," in *Adolf Cluss, Architect: From Germany to America*, ed. Allen Lessoff and Christopher Mauch (privately printed by the Historical Society of Washington and Stadtarchiv Heilbronn, 2005), 161. Bird, "Interim Report," 31–32. Andrew T. Hilyer, comp. and ed., *The Twentieth Century Union League Directory: A Compilation of the Efforts of the Colored People of Washington for Social Betterment* (privately printed, 1901), directory, pp. 13–101, 157.
10. "Others May Strike," *ES* March 6, 1906, p. 12. "Fight to a Finish," *ES* March 5, 1906, p. 2. "Helpers on Strike," *ES* March 8, 1906, p. 10.
11. "Decide upon Lockout," *ES* June 6, 1907, p. 1. "Real Estate Gossip," *ES* May 18, 1907, p. 14.
12. "Building Construction," *WP* June 12, 1912, p. 74–75. "Combat 'Open Shop,'" *ES* March 7, 1907, p. 15. "Building Construction," *WP* June 12, 1912, p. 76. H. R. Howen-

stein built one set of three row houses at 144–48 North Carolina Avenue SE, in just a little more than two months. He applied for his building permit on August 9, 1910, and the assistant inspector of buildings, who visited the site frequently, deemed the work 99 percent complete on October 19. Permit #713, August 9, 1910.

13. "Real Estate Gossip," *Evening Star,* September 22, 1906, p. 14. Permits Database Report.

14. Allan B. Slauson, ed., *A History of the City of Washington: Its Men and Institutions* (Washington, DC: Washington Post, 1903), 232. 51 R Street NW: Permit #1505, January 30, 1893. Edward Kern went on to serve as an inspector of buildings for the city from 1897 to 1923, which may have also been a useful contact for Middaugh. "Edward Kern Dies; Rites Tomorrow," *ES* July 11, 1935, p. A-11.

15. One permit on which Middaugh is listed as architect is for 50–54 S Street, Permit #963, 1899. "A Residence Section," *ES* May 19, 1906, p. 18. Building permits show Middaugh and Shannon built 412 row houses in Bloomingdale. Middaugh built a house for his family in the heart of Bloomingdale, at the corner of First and Bryant NW, but in a center-hall Colonial Revival form, not a row house. Permit #62, July 10, 1904. Ad, *ES* October 6, 1906, p. 25. "Mr. Bohn Is Buried," *ES* June 20, 1910, p. 15.

16. 130–34 Adams Street, Permit #1330, November 16, 1905, for 3 buildings; 135–51 Adams Street, Permit #1519, November 26, 1905, for 9 buildings; 136–42 Adams Street, November 26, 1905, for 4 buildings; 2219–25 Flagler Place, Permit #1521, November 26, 1905, for 4 buildings. "Real Estate Gossip," *ES* April 16, 1906, pt. 2, p. 2.

17. 447–57 Park Road, Permit #2133, February 18, 1906; 446–56 Park Road, Permit #110, July 11, 1906; 435–45 Park Road, Permit #1571, November 6, 1906; 436–44 Park Road and 3416 Park Place, Permit #1989, December 11, 1906. Each permit was for 3 buildings or 6 units. They announced the houses a few months earlier: "'Whitney Close' to Be Improved with Houses," *WP* December 17, 1905, Real Estate section p. 3. "Real Estate Operations Show a Slight Falling Off," *WP* February 25, 1906, p. E2. "Investment Goes On despite Dullness in the Market," *ES* December 17, 1910, pt. 2, p. 2.

18. Ad, *ES* October 20, 1906, pt. 2, p. 1. 3530–40 Warder Street, Permit #0017, July 3, 1906; 436–44 Manor Place, Permit #804, September 9, 1906; 3523–33 Warder Street, Permit #805, September 10, 1906; 426–34 Manor Place, Permit #1723, November 16, 1906; 423–35 Manor Place, Permit #1722, November 16, 1906. At the end of 1906, they started on a set of 18 identical row houses on Luray Place; in early 1907 they built 15 more on Luray Place and 7 on Newton Place. 435–69 Luray Place, Permit #1990, December 11, 1906; 414–22 Luray Place, Permit #2632, March 1, 1907; 424–42 Luray Place, Permit #3992, June 11, 1907; 422–34 Newton Place, Permit #2687, March 6, 1907. Ad, *ES* November 24, 1906, pt. 2, p. 1.

19. On the Washington Sanitary Improvement Company, see Elizabeth Hannold, "The Influence of Sanitary Houses Can Not Be Over Estimated" in *Housing Washington: Two Centuries of Residential Development and Planning in the National Capital Area,* ed. Richard Longstreth (Chicago: Center for American Places, 2010), 133–57. Sally Lichtenstein Berk, "The Richest Crop: The Row Houses of Harry Wardman (1869–1938), Washington, D.C. Developer" (M.A. thesis, George Washington University, 1988), chap. 1, p. 6, chap. 3, p. 6, and appendix 2. DC Builders and Developers Directory; see Note on Sources. 2203–33 First Street NE, Permit #1258,

December 2, 1904; 2235 First Street, Permit #1258, December 2, 1904; 83 W Street, Permit #1330, December 13, 1904. "Homes Sell Fast in Bloomingdale," *WP* December 17, 1905, p. RE3. Permits Database Report.

20. 1822–24 Biltmore Street NW, Permit #1427, November 15, 1905. 132–48 Quincy Place NE, Permit #1593, November 8, 1906; 1628–34 Eckington Place, Permit #1592, November 8, 1906; 115–45 Quincy Place, Permit #2137, January 2, 1907. Ad, *ES* May 23, 1908, pt. 2, p. 1.
21. Shannon and Luchs, "Home of Fulfillment," unpaginated. The houses were 4600–04 Fourteenth Street and 1403–27 Buchanan Street NW, Permit #1587, September 6, 1909.
22. "Much Civic Expansion due to Work of Operative Builders," *ES* October 1, 1910, pt. 2, p. 2. "Big Total Reached," *ES* March 1, 1913, pt. 2, p. 1. Building permits for speculative row houses were closer to 650 in 1910–12, but Wardman was probably including double and freestanding houses in his total. "Wardman Sales Grow," *WP* April 27, 1913, p. R1. 1407–19 Perry Place NW, Permit #2656, November 20, 1912; 1408–16 Perry Place, Permit #2763, November 28, 1912; 1501–27 Buchanan Street NW, Permit #2858, December 5, 1912.
23. Ad *ES,* February 18, 1928, p. RE20.
24. DC Builders and Developers Directory. Of these, Santmyers designed 221–35 Tennessee and 222–44 Warren. Ad, *ES* November 22, 1913, pt. 2, p. 1. Ad, *ES* March 20, 1915, pt. 2, p. 2.
25. "Plumbing Experts," *WP* February 24, 1907, p. 30. Ad, *ES* October 2, 1926, p. 22. "Completes New Residence," *WP* July 23, 1916, RE2. "Of English Basement Type," *WP* September 16, 1915, p. 18. "D. J. Dunigan Dead at White Oaks Home," *WP* September 25, 1928, p. 4.
26. "Vision and Courage Lead to Success for Morris Cafritz," *WP* June 20, 1926, p. M20. "Man of Vision Chosen to Construct Life Model House in Nearby Maryland," *WP* February 26, 1939, p. L4. DC Builders and Developers Directory.
27. "W. C. Miller Cites Housing Needs," *ES* December 5, 1931, p. B-2.
28. "Building History Outlined to Class," *ES* December 1, 1928, p. 20. "Points Out Some Advantages of Row-House Construction," *ES* January 9, 1926, p. 24. "W. C. Miller Cites Housing Needs," *ES* December 5, 1931, p. B-2.
29. "The Building Season," *ES* March 16, 1887, p. 2. Leroy O. King, *100 Years of Capital Traction: The Story of Streetcars in the Nation's Capital* (privately printed, 1976; orig. printed, 1972), 17, 129. "Trend of Investors," *SS* April 8, 1906, pt. 7, p. 6.
30. "Claim Zoning Hits House Ownership," *ES,* August 15, 1925, p. 7.
31. S. G. Lindholm, Zoning Commission of the District of Columbia, "Experiences with Zoning in Washington, D.C., 1920–1934," 18.
32. McLoud, "Craftsmen and Entrepreneurs," 140–50.
33. Donna J. Rilling, *Making Houses, Crafting Capitalism: Builders in Philadelphia* (Philadelphia: University of Pennsylvania Press, 2001), 52. Mary Ellen Hayward and Charles Belfoure, *The Baltimore Rowhouse* (New York: Princeton Architectural Press, 2001). 114–16. Sherry H. Olson, *Baltimore: The Building of an American City* (Baltimore: Johns Hopkins University Press, 1980), 117, 219–20. W. Edward Orser, "The Making of a Baltimore Rowhouse Community: The Edmonson Avenue Area, 1915–1945," *Maryland Historical Magazine* 80, no. 3 (Fall 1985): 211 and 224n25. "Ground-Rent Plan Is Still In Use," *ES* April 19, 1930, B-9.

    In cities with a population of more than 100,000, those with the greatest homeownership rates in 1920 were Omaha, Baltimore (46.3 percent), Minneapolis, St. Paul, and Philadelphia (39.5 percent). Washington's rate was 30.3 percent, and the average among the twenty-six largest cities was 26.9 percent. U.S. Department of Commerce, Bureau of the Census, *Mortgages on Homes* (Washington, DC: GPO, 1923), 59.

34. "Building Loan of D.C. Dates Back to 1866," *Washington Herald,* October 9, 1932, from vertical files, Martin Luther King Jr. Memorial Library. "Building Associations," *ES* March 12, 1887, p. 2. Hitz, "Homes for the People," 136.
35. "Per Capita Investment in Building and Loan Associations," *ES* January 6, 1923, p. 15. "Building Associations Popular with Masses," *ES,* December 31, 1910, p. 4. "Business More Active," *WP* May 10, 1891, p. 10.
36. Marc A. Weiss, *The Rise of the Community Builders: The American Real Estate Industry and Urban Land Planning* (New York: Columbia University Press, 1987), 32. "Survey of Housing and Rental Conditions in the District of Columbia," Senate Report no. 530, 68th Cong., 1st Sess. (1924), pp. 11, 7.
37. Joseph West Moore, *Picturesque Washington* (Providence: J. A. and R. A. Reid, 1887), 244. "Real Estate Market," *WP* November 26, 1899, p. 14. Ad, *ES* May 29, 1907, p. 17. "In Past and Future," *ES,* April 8, 1906, pt. 7, p. 4.
38. "Real Estate Market," *WP* October 10, 1897, p. 14. Ad for 537 and 541 Kenyon Street NW, *ES* November 11, 1911, pt. 2, p. 4. Ad *ES* March 21, 1925, p. R17.
39. Ads, *WP* October 26, 1902, p. 29. Ad, *ES* October 30, 1920, pt. 2, p. 3. Ad, *ES* March 1, 1913, pt. 2, p. 1. Ad, *WP,* May 25, 1924, p. R5.
40. Carroll D. Wright, "The Economic Development of the District of Columbia," *Proceedings of the Washington Academy of Sciences* 1 (1899): 180. Ad, *ES* April 21, 1900, p. 17. "Real Estate Operations Show Slight Falling Off," *WP* February 25, 1906, p. E2. "Wardman Sales Grow," *WP* April 27, 1913, p. R1. DC Builders and Developers Directory.
41. Ads, *ES* February 18, 1928, RE20. Ad, *ES* May 30, 1925, p. 19.
42. U.S. Congress, House, District of Columbia Rent Commission, *Hearings before the Subcommittee of the Committee on the District of Columbia, House of Representatives,* 68th Cong., 1st Sess. (Washington, DC: GPO, 1924), p. 387, 390–91.
43. "32 Houses Completed in Woodley Place Block," *WP* March 2, 1924, p. R2.
44. U.S. Congress, Senate, *Survey of Housing and Rental Conditions in the District of Columbia,* Senate Report no. 530, 68th Cong., 1st Sess. (1924), p. 11. Ad, *WP* May 25, 1924, p. R5. "$2,000,000 Sales of Houses Reported by Shapiro Company," *WP* July 6, 1924, p. ES15. 2701–19 Woodley Place and 2511–15 Woodley Road, Permit #9387, May 5, 1924, for 12 buildings. 2721–67 Woodley Place, Permit #10885, June 11, 1924, for 24 buildings. The building permit for 2700–62 Woodley Place is missing from the National Archives, having been used as an exhibit for the congressional report.

    The active partner in Joseph Shapiro, Inc., at this time was Jacob B. (always referred to as J. B.), Joseph Shapiro's son, who signed the building permits. J. B. had been born in Russia in 1900 and immigrated to the U.S. as a child. J. B. started in the business at age nineteen when he graduated from college, and by 1927 he had made $2 million, although the housing market began a severe downturn that year. J. B. was also indicted for fraudulent intent and for mail fraud stemming from his senate testimony. "Shapiro, on Stand, Says He Amassed $2,000,000 in 7 Years," *ES* June 18, 1931, p. 17. The firm built the modern row houses on the 1700 block of Harvard Street NW, discussed in chapter 3. The firm also ran into other legal troubles, including flouting the War Production Board's orders. "District Attorney Waits for Data on Apartment Priority Violations," *ES* October 11, 1944, p. 5. In 1927 J. B.'s brother, Maurice, joined the firm, which was renamed Shapiro, Inc., after the death of Joseph in 1941.

45. Ad, *ES* November 22, 1924, p. 23. "Capital Builders Combine to Block Pay Increases," *SS* March 8, 1925, p. 1. "The Bull by the Horns," *ES* August 17, 1907, p. 10. "View of Building Trades," *ES* May 12, 1907, p. 5.
46. For example, "Help Wanted: Architect—Excellent opportunity for competent young architect to connect with large, progressive operative builder. State salary and experience." *ES* December 20, 1924, p. 22. Berk, "'The Richest Crop,'" appendix III, pp. 1–7.
47. George Santmyers obituary, *WP-TH* December 27, 1960, p. B3. Santmyers obituary, *ES* December 27, 1960, p. B-4. "The D.C. permits database credits Santmyers with designing 15,689 buildings by 1949, while only a handful of other architects designed more than 1,000 buildings and no other listed in the database designed more than 1,600." DC Architects Directory; see Note on Sources. One ad that did note the architect was a Stone and Fairfax ad for row houses at the corner of 13th and Lamont NW, which mentioned that they were "Designed by Albert H. Beers, architect for many of the most attractive residences in the northwest," but neglected to mention Wardman, the developer. Ad, *ES* April 26, 1909, p. 3.
48. Letitia Woods Brown, *Free Negroes in the District of Columbia, 1790–1846* (New York: Oxford University Press, 1972), 11, 151–65. William Henry Jones, *The Housing of Negroes in Washington, D.C.: A Study in Human Ecology* (Washington, DC: Howard University Press, 1929), 28. Letitia W. Brown, "Residence Patterns of Negroes in the District of Columbia, 1800–1860," *RCHS* 69/70 (1969–70): 69, 77.
49. Brown, "Residence Patterns," 72–73. John Michael Vlach, "Evidence of Slave Housing in Washington," *WH* 5, no. 2 (Fall/Winter 1993/94): 66. Vlach, "From Slavery to Tenancy: African-American Housing in Washington, D.C., 1790–1890," *Housing Washington,* 10.
50. James Borchert, *Alley Life in Washington: Family, Community, Religion, and Folklife in the City, 1850–1970* (Urbana: University of Illinois Press, 1980), 18. Borchert posits that the first alley dwellings were built in the 1850s. Kim Prothro Williams, *The DC Historic Alley Buildings Survey* (DC Office of Planning, 2013), 13.
51. Borchert, *Alley Life,* 40. *Building Regulations* (1877), 28. *Building Regulations* (1887), 18. *Building Regulations* (1872), 20.
52. Act reproduced in *Building Regulations* (1902), 90.
53. James Borchert, "Builders and Owners of Alley Dwellings in Washington, D.C., 1877–1792," *RCHS* 50 (1980): 346. Sporadic attempts to give condemnation power to the local government resulted in the demolition of 300 alley dwellings between 1873 and 1877, more in the 1890s, and 375 between 1906 and 1911. Borchert, *Alley Life,* 45, 47. Philanthropic institutions attempted to provide new lodging for alley residents. The Washington Sanitary Improvement Company, established in 1887, which offered a 5 percent return to investors, was succeeded by the Sanitary Housing Company in 1904, offering 4 percent. Because the housing they built was primarily two-family flats, it is outside the scope of this study. See Hannold, "'The Influence of Sanitary Houses,'" 133–57. One plea for delay described in "Alley Law May Be Suspended," *ES* December 15, 1917, pt. 2, p 2. "Private Owners Reclaiming

Neighborhood Once Known as Capitol Hill 'Slum,'" *ES* August 23, 1947, p. 14. The movement to preserve alley dwellings is discussed in chapter 3.

54. Edith Elmer Wood, "Four Washington Alleys," *Survey* 31 (December 6, 1913): 251. Ben Bradlee, "Life in an Alley within Shadow of Capitol Dome," *WP* December 19, 1948, p. M21. Lisa Goff, *Shantytown, USA: Forgotten Landscapes of the Working Poor* (Cambridge, Mass.: Harvard University Press, 2014), 142, discusses the perceived "picturesqueness" of dilapidated housing. Saidiya Hartman, *Wayward Lives, Beautiful Experiments: Intimate Histories of Riotous Black Girls, Troublesome Women, and Queer Radicals* (New York: Norton, 2019), 5–6, notes the reformers' inadequate understanding of alley dwellers' lives.

55. Borchert, *Alley Life,* 32–36. U.S. Senate, Committee on the District of Columbia, *Persons Owning or Renting Houses or Rooms in the So-Called "Inhabited Alleys" in the District of Columbia,* 63rd Cong., 1st Sess., Senate Doc. no. 120 (1913). 601–07 Browns Court, Permit #1504, February 24, 1890. Ad, *ES,* August 20, 1889, p. 3. Ad, *ES* October 14, 1892, p 3. Wood, "Four Washington Alleys," 251.

56. The total of alley dwellers is just within the old city. Borchert, *Alley Life,* 42. Jones, *Housing of Negroes,* 31. *Report of the Commissioners* (1897), p. 199, 202. The Snows Court square is Square 28, explored more fully in next chapter.

57. This is square 965, bound by Massachusetts, Tenth, Constitution, and Eleventh Streets NE, which is discussed in more detail in the next chapter. Similarly, Borchert, *Alley Life,* 10–11, mapped Black households in a twelve-block area in Northwest. On the streets, Blacks and foreign-born whites occupied about half of the wood-frame dwellings, while the brick ones were overwhelmingly white-occupied.

58. Willard B. Gatewood, *Aristocrats of Color: The Black Elite, 1880–1920* (Bloomington: Indiana University Press, 1990), 39. Robert L. Boyd, "Southern Black Metropolis: Position, Place, and Population below the Mason-Dixon Line," *Journal of African American Studies* 23, no. 3 (September 2019): 270. "Washington's Colored People," *ES* December 19, 1883, p. 2. For more on the Woodson House, see chapter 1. Unrelated to this history, in 2020 the mayor ordered part of Sixteenth Street painted "BLACK LIVES MATTER." See also John DeFerrari, "Black Lives on 16th Street," *WH* 32, no. 1/2 (Fall 2020): 14–16. Eric S. Yellin, "'It Was Still No South to Us': African American Civil Servants at the Fin de Siècle," *WH* 21 (2009): 36, 34, 40. Betty Bird, "Building Community: Housing for Middle-Class African Americans in Washington, D.C., and Prince George's County, Maryland, 1900–1955," *Housing Washington,* 63. Jones, *Housing of Negroes,* 57.

59. Deed 192509170320, recorded September 17, 1925, for Square 3122, Lot 18, 2214 First Street.

60. Deed 19310616289 recorded June 3, 1931, for Square 3123 Lot 29, 2209 First Street. Property Holder's Agreement, September 1, 1925, Doc. no. 192510060083. $2,000 was about a third of the cost of the house, but it was not clear to whom one would pay such a fine, as the deed restrictions were not a governmental effort. "Restriction Favored," *ES* March 16, 1927, p. 28.

61. "Work to Start at Once on 16 Small Houses," *ES* May 29, 1920, pt. 2, p. 1. "Homes for the Colored Reported in Big Demand," *ES* February 3, 1923, p. 16.

62. Jones surveyed whites and identified other motivations, of which "fear of public opinion" was the most common. Others included "Negroes lower tone of community," "Negroes too gregarious," and "Negroes' social habits objectionable." Jones, *Housing of Negroes,* 77. Deed 192509170320, recorded September 17, 1925, for Square 3122, Lot 18, 2214 First Street.

63. Deed for 4920 Upton Street NW, and brochure for Columbia Heights posted on Mapping Segregation website, mappingsegregationdc.org; see Note on Sources. 1947 ad, reproduced in Diane Shaw, "Wesley Heights and Spring Valley: Persistency in Consistency," in *Washington at Home: An Illustrated History of Neighborhoods in the Nation's Capital,* ed. Kathryn Schneider Smith (2nd ed., Baltimore: Johns Hopkins University Press, 2010), 427. See also her discussion on 425.
64. Permit #5451, May 26, 1911. Mara Cherkasky, "'For Sale to Colored': Racial Change on S Street, NW," *WH* 8, no. 2 (1996/97): 48–49.
65. Ad, *SS* May 30, 1926, pt. 1, p. 3. "Property Trusteeships Seen as Racial Covenant Substitutes," *ES* May 4, 1948, p. A-4.
66. Sarah Jane Shoenfeld and Mara Cherkasky, "'A Strictly White Residential Section': The Rise and Demise of Racially Restrictive Covenants in Bloomingdale," *WH* 29, no. 1 (2017): 37.
67. Cherkasky, "'For Sale to Colored,'" 49, and Ad, *ES* January 28, 1923, reproduced on p. 48. Mara Cherkasky and Sarah Jane Shoenfeld, "Bloomingdale Historic District Registration Form," National Register of Historic Places (2017), Sec. 8, pp. 54, 59.
68. Mary Church Terrell, *A Colored Woman in a White World* (New York: Humanity Books, 2005; orig. pub., 1940), 149–55.
69. Ernest Eiland quoted in Cherkasky, "'For Sale to Colored,'" 50. Code of Ethics quoted in Cherkasky, "'For Sale to Colored,'" 51, and on the Mapping Segregation in DC website. The code of ethics clause remained until 1966, although apparently it was ignored beginning in the mid-1950s. See also Herbert U. Nelson, "The Real Estate Code of Ethics," *Journal of Land and Public Utility Economics* 1, no. 3 (July 1925): 270–75. "Citizens Plan Race Segregation in City," *ES* April 11, 1912, p. 24. My thanks to Sarah Shoenfeld and Mara Cherkasky for these sources.
70. Ad, *ES* April 2, 1910, pt. 2, p. 6. For a Wardman ad, see *WP* September 9, 1923, p. 44, in which he lists four properties, one of them denoted "For Colored." "Work to start at once on 16 small houses . . . for colored occupants," *ES* May 29, 1920, pt. 2, p. 1, described houses to be built by Harry Kite at Irving and Georgia Streets. These appear to be the following: 711–19 Irving, Permit #3344, November 27, 1919; 721–29 Irving, Permit #4178, February 8, 1920; 731–39 Irving, Permit #5107, March 24, 1920. Ad, *ES,* August 11, 1920, p. 24.
71. Jones, *Housing for Negroes,* 93, 92, 91, 128. Civil rights attorney Charles Houston confirmed the difference in prices in 1941, when he assembled a list of properties on the 100 block of Adams Street NW. The houses available to Black purchasers sold for nearly twice the amount of those protected by covenant. Mapping Segregation website. Terrell, *A Colored Woman,* 135.
72. M. Sammye Miller, "An Early Venture in Black Capitalism: The Capital Savings Bank in the District of Columbia, 1888–1902," *RCHS* 50 (1980): 366. Marcia M. Greenlee, "Shaw: Heart of Black Washington," in *Washington at Home: An Illustrated History of Neighborhoods in the Nation's Capital,* ed. Kathryn Schneider Smith (Northridge, Calif.: Windsor, 1988), 123. My thanks to Phylicia Bowman for compiling statics on Black homeownership rates from the U.S. Census, American Community Survey. Jones, *Housing for Negroes,* 128. *Mortgages on Homes,* 59.

73. Kenneth T. Jackson, "Federal Subsidy and the American Dream: The First Quarter-Century of Government Intervention in the Housing Market," *RCHS* 50 (1980): 430–32. FHA, "Map of the Metropolitan Area of Washington, D.C., Showing Division of Metropolitan Area into Residential Sub-Areas according to Type or Grade," 1937, reproduced on Mapping Segregation website.
74. Sandra R. Heard, "Making Slums and Suburbia in Black Washington during the Great Depression," *American Studies* 57, no. 4 (2019): 6. *The Washington Afro American Report* (Washington Afro American, 1946), 22. Jones, *Housing for Negroes,* 61–62. For an example of a detached-house suburb populated by African Americans, see Ruth Ann Overbeck and Kia Chatmon, "Deanwood: Self Reliance at the Eastern Front," *Washington at Home,* 265.
75. Statistics compiled by Phylicia Bowman. Nationally, for most of the twentieth century Black homeownership rates lagged behind whites by about 20 percentage points. William J. Collins and Robert A. Margo, "Race and Homeownership, 1900–1990" (National Bureau of Economic Research Working Paper 7277, 1999), 37–38, www.nber.org/papers/w7277. In 2010 the national figures, per Wikipedia, were 73.8 percent of the homes occupied by whites were owned by them, while 46.2 percent of those occupied by Blacks were owned by them.

6. Owning and Renting

1. Joseph West Moore, *Picturesque Washington* (Providence: J. A. and R. A. Reid, 1887), 244. Carroll D. Wright, "The Economic Development of the District of Columbia," *Proceedings of the Washington Academy of Sciences* 1 (1899): 180.
2. U.S. Department of Commerce, Bureau of the Census, *Mortgages on Homes* (Washington, DC: GPO, 1923), 24–25, 59. By 1940, 49 percent of Washington's row houses were owner-occupied.
3. U.S. Department of the Interior, Census Office, *Report on the Social Statistics of Cities,* comp. George E. Waring Jr. (Washington, DC: GPO, 1887), pt. 2, p. 52.
4. Most of the information in this chapter relies on a few primary sources, which are not cited repeatedly. The manuscript censuses of 1880, 1900, 1910, 1920, 1930, and 1940 furnished important information that is denoted by those years in the text. (The 1890 manuscript census does not survive; manuscript censuses after 1940 are not yet open to the public.) City directories are another source, providing the primary resident's name, occupation, and address. Both the censuses and the city directories were consulted through HeritageQuest. General Assessment tax books, consulted at the National Archives and Historical Society of Washington, provided ownership information. All other sources are cited individually. After 1940, only block-level, as opposed to household-level, statistics are available. Three of the case study squares had apartment buildings, and those populations are not differentiated, so the block-level statistics are less meaningful to row houses.
5. "Leasehold Property at Auction," *ES* March 9, 1866, p. 3.
6. "Horse's Kick Proves Fatal," *WP* January 3, 1898, p. 2. Owner Alice Drury filed a permit for repairs in 1892 (Permit #1598, March 3, 1892), but by 1893 Noah Price was the owner, when he received a permit to build a 12-by-20-foot fuel shed on the rear of the lot. Permit #452, September 16, 1893.
7. Leonard's frame building on the corner of 25th and I Streets appears on the 1919

Baist map, but the 1928 Baist map shows this lot as vacant. A raze permit (#234321, July 8, 1940) was probably for the outbuilding on the rear of the lot. Permit to raze Price's house, 928 Twenty-Fourth Street, #A-53643, April 21, 1954.

8. Measuring 448 by 550 feet in its longest dimensions, it is a large square.
9. Suzanne Berry Sherwood, *Foggy Bottom, 1800–1975: A Study in the Uses of an Urban Neighborhood* (Washington, DC: George Washington University, 1978), 11–12.
10. Edward Casey built 2433–35 I Street, and in 1881 added the house at 2431. Because regulations then required buildings to be constructed of masonry, the new row house was brick, with a flat roof and a one-story bay window. Permit #1017, April 6, 1881. 2429 I: Permit #1849, May 26, 1885.
11. 2413–19 I Street: Permit #1671, May 6, 1885. Duvall and Marr sold all of them to Thomson H. Alexander, who subsequently sold them to noted architect T. Franklin Schneider in the late 1890s. In 1900 the four houses on the street were rented to African American families, including Ralph Hunter, a day laborer; Muskey Bunday, a carpenter; Mary White, whose daughter Lillie was a saleswoman; and Robert Lewis, a butler. By 1913 the house at 2417 had apparently been upgraded, because it was advertised as "two-story six-room and bath brick dwelling in good condition." "Auction," *ES* June 19, 1913, p. 21. Although these row houses have been altered and rebuilt over the years, the house at 2419 appears to be in the most original condition.

    2421–27 I Street: Permit #267, June 14, 1889. In 1900 the renters included John Ganley, a day laborer; Fred Newyahr, a clerk in a clothing store; John Harrison, a bricklayer; and Mary O'Connell, a widow, who lived there with her four grown sons—two molders, an electrician, and a printer. The Tayloe family continued to hold onto two of these houses until 1950, when a Tayloe descendant sold 2421 and 2423 I Street to Phyllis Stockman. Deed 19500201174. He had apparently lost the other two for unpaid taxes in 1940. Deed 1940021462.

    2407–11 I Street: Permit #4493, May 18, 1909. The renters of these 1,400-square-foot houses in 1920 were all African American: Charles Harper, a rigger for a granite company; William J. Davis, a messenger for the War Department; William T. Nolan, a serviceman at an auto supply store; and Jesse White, a cook in a lunch room. All of them had other members of the household who worked as well—children, lodgers, a sister-in-law.
12. Permit #1589, May 8, 1884.
13. The residential appearance of K Street was compromised by construction of the Washington Circle underpass in 1960–62, and the once-generous front yards, originally 35 feet deep, were reduced to the minimum. Matthew B. Gilmore and Joshua Olsen, *Foggy Bottom and the West End* (Charleston, S.C.: History Press, 2010), 153.

    During the Civil War Lowry served as a founder and director of the Bank of the Metropolis and the Mutual Protection Fire Insurance Company, as well as an assistant commissioner of the First Ward. By 1867 Lowry had sold his business, and he may have rebuilt or enlarged his house at that time. *ES* July 9, 1864, p. 2; January 13, 1865, p. 3; July 13, 1863, p. 1, "Affairs in Georgetown," May 20, 1867, p. 2. He was also apparently a target for burglars, two gold watches having been stolen from his house in 1864. "Burglary," April 9, 1864, p. 2. When he died in 1880 at the age of eighty-three, still living in this house, he left $10,000 to the Washington City Orphan Asylum, $10,000 to his brother, $25,000 to his sister, and the remainder to his widow. His estate auctioned off his "nearly new family carriage, stylish pair of black horses, [and] double set gold-mounted harness." The stable was around the corner on Twenty-Fourth Street, where Lowry had owned an additional lot. "Georgetown," November 24, 1880, p. 8; "Condensed Locals," December 4, 1880, p. 8; "Auction Sales," January 19, 1881, p. 3. Four years after his death in 1880, a new organization called the Association for Works of Mercy acquired Lowry's house to serve as a "refuge for outcast women." "The Relief of Fallen Women," *ES* April 21, 1884, p. 4. In 1892 they received a permit for a large 28-by-18-foot addition with a bay window, although this does not appear on fire insurance maps. Permit #186, July 22, 1892. In 1900 twenty-eight white women, ranging in age from five to fifty-three, were living here. For a description of this institution from another point of view, see Patricia Miller, *Bringing Down the Colonel: A Sex Scandal of the Gilded Age and the "Powerless" Woman Who Took On Washington* (New York: Picador, 2018), 133–48. In 1911 the association moved to larger quarters and sold this house to the Catholic Church, which in 1923 built a parochial school, St. Stephen's, on the corner lot. The nuns who served that school lived in this house. St. Stephen's school building transferred to Immaculate Conception Academy, a girls' school, in 1954. The school and house were demolished in 1985 to build a new apartment building. St. Stephen the Martyr, the Catholic church associated with the parochial school, was founded in 1866 at the corner of Twenty-Fifth and Pennsylvania, just a block away, and still survives there, though in a later building.

By 1870 Brown was "retired from business" at fifty years old. When the house was auctioned in 1881, it was described as a "desirable three-story Dwelling House." "Sale of Desirable Residence," *ES* May 26, 1881, p. 3. By 1886 the house was owned and occupied by Horace Jarboe, a cooper and carriage maker. In the early twentieth century a series of renters occupied the house until the Visayan Club bought it in 1937 to serve as an outpost of Filipino expatriates who lived in DC. The 1940 census showed seven male lodgers there, all Filipino. The house gained fame as the residence of Bienvenido N. Santos, a prominent Filipino novelist, who served in Washington as a public information officer for the Philippine government in the 1940s and wrote about this house as a gathering place for the Filipino community. The house is now owned by St. Paul's Episcopal Church, which built a new church building at 2430 K Street in 1947, after it was displaced by the construction of George Washington University Hospital.

At 2424–26 K Street, Louise Veerhoff arranged for two 18-foot-wide two-story row houses to be built in 1885. Permit #2035, June 22, 1885. The estimated cost of construction was $1,300 each. Also in 1885, Veerhoff commissioned three dwellings on the alley behind her K Street houses. Just two years later, Veerhoff sold all five buildings to Jonathan B. Diamond for $10,000. "Sale of Real Estate," *ES* August 12, 1887, p. 3. In 1890 J. H. Grant built two three-story brick buildings at 2418–20 K Street. Nicholas R. Grimm was the architect for these buildings, which were 15 feet 6 inches wide with three-story bay windows, and cost $3,500 apiece, or about three times more than the small dwellings on I Street. Permit #2387, June 9, 1890.

14. 947 Twenty-Fifth Street: Permit #2346, May 21, 1879. The building permit also included a provision for a one-story wood and coal shed, set in the rear of the yard, that measured 12 by 20 feet. The small building next door was apparently extant in 1878 when C. H. Wood sold it to E. Hughes for $469.60. "Deeds in Fee Have Been Filed," *ES* February 11, 1879, p. 4. In 1880, sixty-five-year-old John S. Webb, a cooper, lived there with his wife. The greenhouse appeared on E. F. M. Faehtz and Fred W. Pratt, *Map of the City of Washington* (1873).

15. 951 I Street: Permit #910, December 12, 1883. 949 I Street: Permit #2317, June 3, 1890.
16. Permit #1000, August 4, 1909.
17. 915–19 Twenty-Fifth Street: Permit #4276, May 11, 1909. 955–63 Twenty-Fifth Street: Permit #2028, October 18, 1911.
18. The Snow's Court name, which first appears in the 1860 city directory, is shrouded in mystery. Borchert, *Alley Life,* 25, cites Daniel D. Swinney, "Alley Dwellings and Housing Reform in the District of Columbia" (M.A. thesis, University of Chicago, 1938), who attributes the name to C. A. Snow, publisher of the *National Intelligencer,* who owned property in this square. Quoting Swinney, Borchert says that Snow "constructed a greenhouse and four frame houses in the interior of the block, and it was called Snow's Alley." But no Snow is shown as owning property in this square in the 1859 or 1864 tax books. Chester A. Snow, a patent attorney and real estate developer, owned, first in trust and then directly by him, three alley dwellings, which stood on land that had been platted off from a lot on Twenty-Fourth Street in 1872, where Thomas Martin built four small frame dwellings. Snow acquired them by 1886; the houses were removed by 1903, although Snow, and then his successor company, continued to hold onto the property until 1959. Deed Doc. No. 1959008451. Chauncey H. Snow, of Snow, Coyle and Company, owned the *National Intelligencer* from 1865 to 1869.

    The 1857 Boschke map shows about a dozen buildings on the alley, but these were not necessarily dwellings, as alleys accommodated a number of other functions. Noah Price's stable is just one example; as late as 1914, Wilbur F. Nash built a 25-by-96-foot three-story brick stable, still extant, in the southwestern portion of the alley. Permit #85, July 2, 1914.

    The one exception to all-Black alley residents was recorded in the 1910 census, when a family of Russian immigrants operated a grocery store in the alley. Samuel Live, his four children, and a Polish servant lived in the same building as their store. Reformer Frederick Weller had noted their presence in 1905, calling them a "family of persecuted Russian Jews." Charles Frederick Weller, *Neglected Neighbors: Stories of Life in the Alleys, Tenements, and Shanties of the National Capital* (Philadelphia: John C. Winston, 1909), 99.

    Landlords, although they generally maintained ownership of multiple alley dwellings, subdivided their lots so that each house was on its own lot. This may have been to avoid having them categorized as "tenements," or multifamily buildings, which required plan review per *Building Regulations* (1872), 20.
19. *Report of the Commissioners of the District of Columbia* (Washington, DC: GPO, 1897), 1: 199. Police survey numbers from Weller, *Neglected Neighbors,* 11. Wilbur Vincent Mallalieu, "A Washington Alley," *Survey* 29 (October 19, 1912): 69. "In Dark Snow's Alley," *WP* November 1, 1891, p. 14. Although the census appears to be an undercount, it does link named people to specific houses and is used here to shed light on the row houses in Snow's Court.
20. Permit #1597, May 9, 1884. Originally 2440–46 Snow's Court, now 8–20.
21. In 1885 Duvall and Marr built 5 alley dwellings on lots separated from, but directly behind, the 4 houses they had built at 2413–19 I Street. Permit #1672, May 6, 1885. On the adjacent lot, also subdivided, the Tayloe family built 4 alley dwellings in 1890. Permit #1161, November 12, 1890. Behind her lots on K Street, Louise A. Veerhoff built 3 alley dwellings. Permit #1909, June 4, 1885. In 1890, behind 2418–

20 K Street, James H. Grant built 2 alley dwellings. Permit #2388, June 9, 1890. Veerhoff's and Grant's alley dwellings no longer stand. Norment's alley dwellings: Permit #365, August 14, 1890. Originally these houses were numbered 2435–47; they are now 1–7 Snow's Court.

22. Permit #1502, March 7, 1888. Weller, *Neglected Neighbors,* 98. Originally numbered 2406, -08, -10; current numbers 21, 22, 23 Snow's Court.

23. Daniel D. Swinney, "Washington: A City of Beauty and a City of Slums" (summary of a thesis, "Alley Dwellings and Housing Reform in the District of Columbia," University of Chicago, 1938), 9. Weller, *Neglected Neighbors,* 95. In 1938 Swinney, "Washington," 11, reported a number of lodgers who were "an economic asset to the families with whom they live," paying a few dollars a week. Saidiya Hartman, *Wayward Lives, Beautiful Experiments: Intimate Histories of Riotous Black Girls, Troublesome Women, and Queer Radicals* (New York: Norton, 2019), 90–91, discusses the complex households in the Black ghetto as a survival strategy.

24. Weller, *Neglected Neighbors,* 95. Mallalieu, "Washington Alley," 70. Swinney, "Washington," 8–9.

25. Thomas Jesse Jones, "The Alley Homes of Washington," *Survey* 28 (October 19, 1912): 67. Mallalieu, "Washington Alley," 70. Weller, *Neglected Neighbors,* 94.

26. Mallalieu, "Washington Alley," 70. Borchert, *Alley Life in Washington,* 185. Swinney, "Washington," 24. Swinney contrasts the 114 arrests in Snow's Court with the 22 arrests on the block surrounding Snow's Court. Hartman, *Wayward Lives,* 70, gives a different view of crime, positioning it as a reasonable response to impossible conditions.

27. Elizabeth Clark-Lewis, *Living In, Living Out: African American Domestics in Washington, D.C., 1910–1940* (Washington, DC: Smithsonian Books, 2010; orig. pub., 1994), 74.

28. Borchert, *Alley Life in Washington,* 138, citing Forestall, "Trends in Housing," 32. Swinney, "Washington," 11.

29. D.C. Board of Commissioners, *Persons Owning or Renting Houses or Rooms in the So-Called "Inhabited Alleys" in the District of Columbia* (Washington, DC: GPO, 1913). Omitted from this list, inexplicably, was Samuel Norment, who owned 7 dwellings in Snow's Court. Other alleys were not as plagued by absentee ownership. Schott's Alley on square 725 (bound by First, Second, B, and C Streets NE) listed 23 owners of 37 lots. Fourteen of the owners had Italian surnames, including 7 who lived in their alley dwellings. But across the city, most owners of alley dwellings were absentee. "Auction Sales," *ES* October 17, 1888, p. 6. Ad, *ES* November 1, 1887, p. 3. Swinney, "Washington," 26, 25.

30. The statistics on homeownership: In 1900, 11 owner-occupied houses out of 66 on the streets. In 1910, 10 out of 67. In 1920, 12 out of 73. In 1940, 16 out of 80. Homeownership was not recorded in the 1880 census. Swinney, "Washington," 10, found in 1938 that 17 of 39 heads of household had lived on Snow's Court more than ten years, although not always in the same house.

31. The office component of Potomac Plaza, although planned, was never built. Pamela Scott and Antoinette J. Lee, *Buildings of the District of Columbia* (New York: Oxford University Press, 1993), 212. James M. Goode, *Best Addresses: A Century of Washington's Distinguished Apartment Houses* (Washington, DC: Smithsonian Institution Press, 1988), 413–17. 911–13 Twenty-Fifth: Permit #B9182, March 23, 1956. The previous buildings on the site of the Twenty-Fifth Street apartment build-

ing were demolished in 1957. For 941, Permit #B27266; for 943, Permit #B27265; for 945, Permit #B27267, all on August 26, 1957. The first multifamily building had been built in 1940. Developers Edwin Shelton and K. J. Hardy took three of the lots at the corner of Twenty-Fifth and I Streets, including the site of John Leonard's original home, and built a 75-foot-wide building to accommodate "Negro Flats," denoting their probable tenants. Permit #234618, July 16, 1940. Eileen Summers, "'Do It Yourself' Owners Show Homes," *WPTH,* May 21, 1956, p. 24.

32. "Private Funds Have Rehabilitated Snow's Court," *ES* May 14, 1955, p. 30. Dennis Earl Gale, "Restoration in Georgetown, Washington, D.C., 1915–65" (Ph.D. diss., George Washington University, 1982), 213–14. Isabelle Shelton, "Foggy Bottom Area Gets Face-Lifting," *SS* November 8, 1953, p. D-14.
33. Summers, "'Do It Yourself' Owners Show Homes," p. 24. William W. Nash, *Residential Rehabilitation: Private Profits and Public Purposes* (New York: McGraw-Hill, 1959), 16–17. A decade later, the Robitschers had moved to Bryn Mawr, Pennsylvania, but were building neo-Colonial row houses on Capitol Hill. "New Town Houses on Capitol Hill," *WPTH* April 18, 1964, p. E5. "Private Funds Have Rehabilitated Snow's Court," *ES* May 14, 1955, p. 30.
34. This and following quotations from Betty Sizer Junge, "Growing up at 131 10th Street, NE," typescript, n.d., courtesy of Mark Edwards.
35. "Rooms Furn." *SS* July 9, 1933, p. 60. "Rooms—Furn. and Unfurn." *SS* July 9, 1933, p. 60. "Rooms Furnished," *SS* June 21, 1942, p. 64. Abbreviations spelled out for clarity. "Light housekeeping" meant minimal cooking facilities, such as a hot plate. Paul Groth, *Living Downtown: The History of Residential Hotels in the United States* (Berkeley: University of California Press, 1994), 124.
36. Deed 1932006415, March 16, 1932. Two lodgers lived in the house in 1930, even before Charles Sizer's death.
37. Square 965 is about a mile east of the Capitol and a little more than a mile north of the Navy Yard in what is now a leafy, quiet neighborhood. At 232 by 456 feet in its longest dimensions, the square is about half the size of Square 28. The block was slow to develop, and only two buildings have been demolished, so what stands today are mostly the first buildings on the site. Susan Meyers documented the middle-class nature of Capitol Hill in "Capitol Hill, 1870–1890: The People and Their Homes," *RCHS* 49 (1973–74): 285–86.
38. On Tenth Street, three nineteenth-century row houses were built individually: 113 Tenth (Permit #827, September 27, 1886); 111 Tenth (Permit #892, October 4, 1886); and 109 Tenth (Permit #1529, February 6, 1891). The first of the quadrant-plan row houses, akin to 1002 Massachusetts Avenue, was built at 107 Tenth (Permit #4002, April 4, 1914). On Eleventh Street, there were two individually built houses. At 150, R. A. Ragan built a two-story brick bay-front in 1886 (Permit #517, August 23, 1886). Down the street at 126, the lot remained empty until filled with a two-story house, now two flats, sometime after 1967. 134–48 Eleventh Street NE: Permit #1565, March 11, 1886. "Thomas E. Smithson Dies at Home in City," *ES* December 17, 1918, p. 7.
39. 115–19 Tenth Street NE: Permit #262, August 22, 1882; 121–25 Tenth Street NE: Permit #1571, March 26, 1889; 127–31 Tenth Street: Permit #2094, June 30, 1885; 112–16 Eleventh Street NE: Permit #494, March 18, 1889.
40. 156 Eleventh Street NE: Permit #1679, June 28, 1883. 154 Eleventh Street NE: Permit #1995, June 15, 1885. 152 Eleventh Street NE: Permit #1766, April 1, 1890.

1013 Constitution Avenue NE: Permit #448, August 25, 1890. Similarly, but on a smaller scale, James L. Suman, who had grown up a block away at 228 Tenth Street NE, built a bay-front house at 1009 Constitution in 1882. Suman, who lived there for only a year or two, was a plumber and the son of a minister turned treasury clerk. In 1885 his widowed mother built a bay-front house next door at 1007 Constitution, which she used for rental income. Both houses were designed by architect Nicholas T. Haller. 1009 Constitution: Permit #522, October 13, 1882. 1007 Constitution: Permit # 169, July 23, 1885.

41. At the corner of Tenth and Constitution, the 18-by-30-foot two-story brick building was estimated to cost only $800 and was designed to house a dairy and dwelling. 133 Tenth Street NE: Permit #878, February 22, 1883. Twelve years later, a new owner made a considerable addition along Constitution Avenue—a 17-by-22-foot building with a bay window. Permit #47, July 10, 1895. 1024 Massachusetts Avenue NE: Permit #1062, September 27, 1906. The only row houses on Massachusetts that were speculatively built are the pair at 1004–06, constructed in 1890 for Wright and Stockett, designed by the architect Julius Germuiller. Permit #1291, December 2, 1890.
42. Brent's house was gone by the time of the 1909 Baist map. Twenty years later William P. O'Brien, proprietor of an ice plant, built a new house with a balustered porch that stretched across the Massachusetts Avenue front and wrapped around the corner. Permit #128800, November 8, 1929.
43. 108 and 110 Alley: Permit #862, October 5, 1887.
44. "Marriage License Applications," *ES* May 12, 1951, p. 29. The source for most of the following: Betty Sizer Junge, "Growing Up at 131 10th." "Houses for Sale—NE," *ES* March 24, 1951, p. 16. "Apts. Furn.," *ES* April 21, 1952, p. 35. "Rooms Furnished—NE," *SS* May 18, 1952, p. 89. "Rooms Furnished—NE," *ES* June 9, 1942, p. 39. Abbreviations spelled out for clarity. The Kushners owned this house and the one next door at 129 until 1969. Deed Doc. No. 1969019901.
45. 1615 C Street: Permit #3961, 1913. 1728 Corcoran Street: Permit #2053, April 30, 1890.
46. "Closing Exercises," *ES* June 17, 1905, p. 7. "Mrs. Josephine Carrick, 76, D. C. Teacher for 49 Years," *ES* April 27, 1969, p. 56. Josephine seems to have shaved some years off of her age; the 1900 census listed her birth year as 1886, and she graduated from high school in 1905. At her death in 1969, she must have been closer to eighty-three years old. The schools at which she taught: Payne, Smothers, Deanwood, Lovejoy, Logan, Cleveland, and Mott. "Miss [Florence] Patterson, D. C. Teacher for 44 Years," *ES* September 1, 1965, p. 33. Their father had died in 1937. Obituary, *ES* May 24, 1937, p. 13.
47. Deed 1935011609, May 11, 1935, Commissioners of DC to T. J. Rout. Deed 1936001678, January 20, 1936, T. J. Rout and wife to Josephine and Florence Patterson. By the time they moved, their mother had died as well. Ida Patterson memorial: *ES* September 16, 1950, p. 31. She had died one year earlier. 301 Madison Street: Permit #138785, 1930. Lawrence Carrick obituary: *ES* November 22, 1958, p. 6. 6314 Sixteenth Street: Permit #10483, 1924. "Mrs. Josephine Carrick." "Miss Patterson."
48. Mapping Segregation in DC website; see Note on Sources.
49. Originally, Square 155 had a conventional arrangement, with an I-shaped alley slightly twisted at one end to accommodate the angle created by New Hampshire

Avenue. But in 1883 investors John B. Alley and William Sharon, who owned the entire square, subdivided it differently, running 45-foot-wide Corcoran Street east–west through the middle, with two parallel alleys. Liber 12, Folio 7, February 2, 1883, DC Surveyor's Office. The southern half of a square is still extensive, stretching 805 feet on Q Street and 210 feet on Seventeenth.

50. Liber 16, Folio 80, January 24, 1889. Schneider also reoriented some lots so that they faced Seventeenth Street. 1701–59 Q Street and 1602–08 Seventeenth Street (34 buildings), BP #1315, February 7, 1889. The houses at 1745–57 Q have been demolished. Lex Rieffel, personal interview by author, 1709 Q Street, November 6, 2018. Serpentine stone is also known as greenstone. See Jane Elizabeth Dorchester, "The Evolution of Serpentine Stone as a Building Material in Southeastern Pennsylvania, 1727–1931" (M.A. thesis, University of Pennsylvania, 2001). Around the corner on Seventeenth Street, Schneider built 4 much plainer brick row houses: three stories with two-story bays, ornamented with patterned brickwork above the round-arched third-story windows and modillioned cornices below checkerboard-patterned parapets.

51. James M. Goode, *Capital Losses: A Cultural History of Washington's Destroyed Buildings* (Washington, DC: Smithsonian Institution Press, 1979), 132–33. DC Architect's Directory; see Note on Sources. *Selections from the Work of T. F. Schneider, Architect* (Washington, DC, 1894). "Real Estate Gossip," *ES,* November 2, 1889, p. 11; December 3, 1889, p. 5; December 18, 1889, p. 6; and "Real Estate Transfers," *WP* June 11, 1889, p. 7. 1710–48 Q Street (20 buildings): Permit #1783, March 22, 1891. 1536–40 Seventeenth Street and 1700–08 Q Street (8 buildings): Permit #814, October 9, 1891. "In Real Estate Circles," *WP* June 30, 1889, p. 6; "A Row of New Houses," *WP* August 23, 1889, p. 7; "A Scaffold Falls Down," *WP* July 10, 1889, p. 8. Schneider retired in 1915 at the age of fifty-six.

52. Liber 15, Folio 153, March 8, 1888, D.C. Surveyors Office. 1740–56 Corcoran Street (9 buildings): Permit #1520, March 10, 1888. "Real Estate Gossip," *ES* November 2, 1889, p. 11. 1730–38 Corcoran Street NW: Permit #2137, May 29, 1889. 1732 Corcoran Street has been demolished and replaced. 1762–64 Corcoran Street NW: Permit #1573, March 7, 1890. 1726–28 Corcoran Street NW: Permit #2053, April 30, 1890. 1722–24 Corcoran Street NW: Permit #193, July 27, 1891. 1710–14 Corcoran Street NW: Permit #228, July 30, 1891. "Francis Majesky," *WP* December 30, 1913, p. 14. Like Schneider's houses on Corcoran Street, none of these row houses had projections beyond the building line, Corcoran Street being too narrow, at 45 feet, for such a luxury. Instead, the building fronts were set back from the building line, so that stairs and bay windows did not extend past it. The roadway was 24 feet wide, flanked by 10½-foot-wide sidewalks.

53. The two singly built houses were at 1760 Corcoran, where in 1895 Mary Wilcox, a seventy-five-year-old widow, built a row house for herself, hiring eminent architect Glenn Brown to design a three-story dwelling with three-story round bay window (Permit #1085, January 17, 1895), and 1758 Corcoran, where Luther Fristoe, a real estate professional, hired architect George S. Cooper to build a house in 1896 (Permit #1636, May 9, 1896).

The square also had two grand houses on New Hampshire Avenue, the more prestigious address. In 1892, John Dalzell, congressional representative from Pennsylvania, commissioned the house at 1605 New Hampshire Avenue, hiring architect Albert Burnley Bibb. The three-story brick house measured 49 by 70 feet and cost $18,000 to construct; it had a round tower at the acute angle formed by the intersection of the avenue and the alley. (Permit #2269, May 6, 1892). Dalzell, who represented the Pittsburgh area in Congress from 1887 to 1913, lived here with his wife, son, daughter, her army officer husband and their daughter, and an extensive live-in staff. In 1910, Woodbury Blair built an even larger house next door at 1607. Jules H. deSibour was the architect of this Colonial Revival mansion, measuring 44 by 80 feet and taking advantage of the oblique angle of the corner of New Hampshire and Corcoran. Costing $46,000 to construct, this three-story brick house had a balustraded mansard roof, a modillioned and dentiled cornice, flat-arched windows set in recessed arches, and an elaborately decorated pedimented doorway with fluted pilasters. Woodbury Blair was essentially Washington royalty; the son of Montgomery Blair, he grew up in Blair House, across the street from the White House, and according to his obituary, as a child he played with President Lincoln's children. He married Emily Wallach, daughter of Robert Wallach, a former mayor of Washington. Woodbury and Emily had no children but were attended by a staff of seven live-in servants. Blair also owned a summer house in Newport and at his death left an estate worth $1.2 million. Permit #5735, April 15, 1910. "Blair, Lawyer, Clubman, Dies of Pneumonia," *WP* October 15, 1933, p. 14. "$1,233,714 Blair Estate Goes to Wife," *WP* November 7, 1933, p. 15. "Erecting a Model Home," *WP* June 12, 1910, p. R2. The rest of the row houses on this square were not as large or impressive as Schneider's rows. Four brick buildings predated his constructions on this square, three on Q at the corner of Eighteenth, which have been demolished, and one on Seventeenth at the corner of Corcoran, which has been much altered. 1618 Seventeenth Street NW: Permit #1310, March 28, 1885.

54. 166 people in 18 houses on Corcoran Street, 182 people in 28 houses on Q Street, per 1940 census.

55. "Strivers Section Historic District Nomination Form" (National Register of Historic Places, 1984).

56. Another trend visible on this square was the growing preference for apartments, rather than large houses. One early apartment building was built at 1718 Corcoran Street in 1893. Permit #2002, April 11, 1893. Known as the Analoston Flats, the building made the social columns at least once, when Mrs. Eugenia Cuthbert hosted a wedding in her apartment there. "Social and Personal," *WP* July 3, 1896, p. 7. Thirty years later, the next apartment building, the Queensborough, was added to the square—the eight-story building at 1614 Seventeenth Street. Permit #736, July 20, 1922. This one made the news for a raid, during which police found 15 quarts of "alleged champagne" and 34 quarts of "alleged liquor" in an apartment in 1924, during Prohibition. "'Real Stuff' Seized in Raid, Police Say," *WP* May 3, 1924, p. 5. And nearly forty years after that, the final apartment building was constructed at the corner of Q and Eighteenth Streets. Imperial House, developed in 1962 by Nathan Landow and Lawrence Brandt and designed by Donald H. Drayer, offered 109 efficiencies and 57 one-bedroom units. John B. Willmann, "Young Builders on the Move," *WP* October 27, 1962, p. B1. John B. Willmann, "They Come from Here and There," *WP* January 18, 1964, p. E1. For this last one, 6 row houses were demolished: the corner house, 1771–73 Q Street, owned by army officer George Van Wyck (Permit #883, November 7, 1884), while the houses at 1769 (lot 54), and 1761 Q Street (lot 50), predated Schneider's row houses and appeared on the 1887 Hopkins map. The houses at 1763 (Permit #1798, April 20, 1889) and 1765 (Permit

#18, July 2, 1890) were both designed by Schneider for individual owners. The last of the group, 1767, was designed by A. B. Bibb (Permit #2465, May 23, 1892).

57. 1728 Corcoran: Deed 1965008690, March 16, 1965. Drawings of 1730 Corcoran in possession of the homeowner, Peter Wolff. "Old Houses Fill New Demand at Circle," *WP* January 23, 1965, E1. "Block Shows Effect of Work," *WP* September 3, 1966, p. E1.

58. Deed 1966018867, June 3, 1966. Ruth Wagner, "When a Sculptor Turns His Mind to Redoing a House," *WP* November 16, 1969, p. 150. Cavanaugh Foundation, www.cavanaughfoundation.org. Cavanaugh also acquired a studio at 1901 Swann Street, nearby, which he christened Swann's Way. More of his sculpture is displayed on that building.

59. Robert and Susan Meehan interview by author, 1740 Corcoran, November 11, 2019. "'Stab Alley' Goes Middle-Class," *WP* October 3, 1971, p. E1. The architect was William H. Shoemaker. Drawings in the owners' possession.

60. Lex Rieffel, personal interview by author, 1709 Q Street, November 6, 2018. "Old Houses Fill New Demand."

61. This current meaning of "English basement"—a separate living unit in a raised basement—is distinguished from the "English basement" described in chapter 1. Lex Rieffel interview. "Barrett Linde: Enclave Developer," *WP* October 22, 1977, pp. E1, E12. "Apts. Unfurn. D.C." *WP* September 7, 1978, p. F7. Abbreviations removed for clarity.

62. Ella's oldest son was born during her first marriage to Emil's brother. "Weds Brother's Widow," *ES* March 5, 1914, p. 9. Ella died in 1960. Obituary, *ES* February 8, 1960, p. 2. Emil's obituary, *ES* December 1, 1939, p. 4. Deed 192303260155, March 26, 1923. Deed 1941023539, July 15, 1941.

63. Benjamin Ogle Tayloe, the son of John Tayloe III, once reputed to be the wealthiest man in Washington and the owner of the Octagon House, established his country residence on an estate he named Petworth, after the ancestral Tayloe home in England. After his death, Tayloe's daughters sold the 200-acre estate to a syndicate of developers led by Brainard H. Warner and Myron M. Parker in 1888. "Real Estate Gossip," *ES* June 9, 1888, p. 2. The next year, the syndicate combined the property with an adjacent farm to form a 387-acre tract, which they platted. Square 3013 was originally platted as Square 17 of Petworth, with 16 50-by-150-foot lots and no alleys. Subdivisions Book Petworth, Block 17, no date, DC Recorder of Deeds. Sales were slow in Petworth, and for about ten years a portion of the subdivision was used as a golf course by the Columbia Golf Club, which was organized in 1898, with a clubhouse at Seventh and Emerson Streets. In 1911 the club moved to Chevy Chase, Maryland, and became known as the Columbia Country Club. In 1917 the banks that then owned Petworth re-subdivided it. Square 3013 of the Petworth Addition was reorganized into lots with 25-foot fronts, with an H-shaped alley 15 feet wide. This produced 40 lots on the 300-by-400-foot square. The square's new arrangement still did not provide enough lots, because as each developer acquired a portion of the square they re-subdivided the lots for frontages of 20 feet or less, with two exceptions.

64. 801–31 Crittenden Street NW: Permit #4215, November 29, 1921. 4701–09 Ninth Street NW: Permit #7035, March 31, 1922. 802–22 Decatur Street NW: Permit #8430, May 2, 1922.

65. 4702–30 Eighth Street, 800 Decatur, and 801 Crittenden NW: Permit #1026, July 31, 1922. 4731–33 Ninth Street NW: Permit #1888, August 7, 1922.
66. 4719–25 Ninth Street NW: Permit #1060, July 24, 1924. 4711–17 Ninth Street NW: Permit #7706, March 24, 1924.
67. "Work Begun on 53 Petworth Dwellings," *ES* August 26, 1922, p. 13.
68. Ad, *ES,* January 17, 1925, p. 13. Mapping Segregation website, "How Racially Restricted Housing Shaped Ward 4."
69. Minwuyelet Azimeraw, DC Office of Planning, State Data Center, *Monthly Brief: An Historic View of DC's Foreign-Born Population with a Focus on Africa* (November 2015).
70. This process is also known as filtering down. While this process has always been in place, Richard Harris argues it particularly accelerated in the decade or so after World War I, but as this examination has shown, filtering down can happen at different times on different squares within the same city, or even on the same square. Richard Harris, "The Rise of Filtering Down: The American Housing Market Transformed, 1915–1929," *Social Science History* 37, no. 4 (Winter 2013): 539. See also Richard U. Ratcliff, "Filtering Down and the Elimination of Substandard Housing," *Journal of Land and Public Utility Economics* 21, no. 4 (November 1945): 322–30.

Epilogue

1. Frank A. Taylor, "Growing Up on Capitol Hill," *RCHS* 50 (1980): 517–18. Mary Z. Gray, *301 East Capitol: Tales from the Heart of the Hill* (privately printed, 2012), 79–82, recalled a similar variety of peddlers.
2. U.S. Department of the Interior, Census Office, *Report on the Social Statistics of Cities,* comp. George E. Waring Jr. (Washington, DC: GPO, 1887), pt. 2, 52. Helen Au, interviewed by Nancy Metzger, August 20, 2000 (Ruth Ann Overbeck/Capitol Hill History Project, Capitol Hill Restoration Society), 17.
3. Taylor, "Growing Up," 514, 516. Betty Sizer Junge, "Growing up at 131 10th Street, NE," typescript, n.d., courtesy of Mark Edwards. The Sanitary Grocery building had previously been the site of Donohue's grocery store, as noted in chapter 6. Sizer also remembered that there was a People's Drug Store at East Capitol and Eleventh Streets. Gray, *301 East Capitol,* 15, recalled a similar variety of shops with three or four blocks of her home.

INDEX

Italicized page numbers refer to illustrations.